The Ultimate
Rotisserie
Cookbook

The Ultimate
Rotisserie
Cookbook

300 Mouthwatering Recipes
for Making the Most of Your Rotisserie Oven

Diane Phillips

The Harvard Common Press ○ Boston, Massachusetts

To the lunch bunch:

Roberta, Christine, Suzie, Muffie,

Loraine, and Jan.

With all the laughter, it's a wonder

we ever eat anything!

The Harvard Common Press
535 Albany Street
Boston, Massachusetts 02118
www.harvardcommonpress.com

Printed in the United States of America

Printed on acid-free paper

Library of Congress Cataloging-in-Publication Data

Phillips, Diane.
　　The ultimate rotisserie cookbook : 300 mouthwatering recipes for making the most of your rotisserie oven / Diane Phillips.
　　　　p. cm.
　　ISBN 1-55832-232-9 (hc : alk. paper)
　　1. Roasting (Cookery)　I. Title.

TX690 .P49　2002
641.7'1—dc21

2002017282

978-1-55832-233-2

Special bulk-order discounts are available on this and other Harvard Common Press books. Companies and organizations may purchase books for premiums or resale, or may arrange a custom edition, by contacting the Marketing Director at the address above.

20 19 18 17 16 15 14

Jacket design by Night & Day Design
Interior design by Ralph Fowler
Illustrations on pages 3, 4, 11, 36, 73, 85, and 137 by Jackie Aher

Contents

Acknowledgments

Writing this book has been so much fun because of the people who have made it possible for me to pursue my passions—teaching and writing. First, to my husband, Chuck, who has kept the home fires burning, and has offered his support and encouragement (and tasted everything!) with each crazy turn my career has taken. Thank you for being there these 32 years; I could not have done any of this without you. To our daughter, Carrie, and her boyfriend, Eric Mand, thanks for taking the rotisserie and actually using it to give me feedback, and for being crash-test dummies for the recipes! Our son, Ryan, has been a willing participant, eating the food that we produced and not complaining about the lack of homemade chocolate chip cookies in the cookie jar. Thanks, buddy, you know that your comments helped me decide whether a recipe would make it into this book. To the friends who waited patiently for me to finish "just one more chapter" or test recipe and who tasted and tested, thanks for being there, my life is enriched and blessed by each of you.

To my agent and friend, Susan Ginsburg, I am so grateful for your guidance and friendship; without you, none of this is possible. To Annie Leuenberger, her dear assistant, thanks for keeping everything in order, especially during the weeks before deadlines.

My family at Harvard Common Press have become just that, a family. Thanks go to my publisher, Bruce Shaw, for his enthusiasm, support, and love of a good meal; to my wonderful editor, Pam Hoenig, whose good nature and vision have made this book come alive; and to Valerie Cimino,

Christine Alaimo, Skye Stewart, Beatrice Wikander, Sunshine Erickson, Abbey Phalen, Jodi Marchowsky, Virginia Downes, Liza Beth, and Pat Jalbert-Levine, who worked so diligently to promote, design, manage, and market. I am in your debt, and there is more chocolate on the way! Copy editor Deborah Kops was a writer's dream, with her attention to detail and her ability to allow my voice to be heard in the recipes; thanks, Deborah, for making me look so good! To Jed Lyons and all the angels at NBN who represent the book, thank you for taking me to the marketplace, I am deeply grateful to you all.

I have had the luxury of traveling around the country and teaching in cooking schools, and I am indebted to those who have made me feel at home in their kitchens. I would be remiss if I didn't thank the cooking school managers and their students for inviting me in and making me feel welcome, and for letting me have more fun than should legally be possible. A tip of the toque to: Pamela Keith and the staff at Draeger's, Martha Aitken and Doralece Dullaghen and the staffs at Sur La Table, Bob Nemorovski and staff at Ramekins, Cathy Cochran-Lewis and staff at Central Markets, Chan Patterson and staff at Viking Culinary Arts Centers, Larry Oates and staff at KitchenArt, Nancy Pigg and the Fricke family at CooksWares, Mike and Shelley Sackett at Kitchen Affairs, and Sue and Lynn Hoffman and the angels at The Kitchen Shoppe.

You, dear reader, are the only one who can tell me what you like and don't like in the pages that follow, so feel free to visit me on the Web at www.dianephillips.com.

Introduction

Rotisserie cooking is almost as old as time. We're told that cavemen roasted their meats over crude wooden spits. Foods cooked on a spit were commonplace in medieval times, and have been popular throughout culinary history. The Italians are famous for their little windup rotisseries that cook in wood-burning ovens. The French claim that they invented this little number in the 1800s but, of course, we can't get the French and Italians to agree on anything, so we'll just say the Europeans perfected this way of cooking.

When you enter your local grocery store or deli, what's that marvelous smell you inhale? Chances are someone is spinning whole chickens on a rotisserie to entice you into buying one for dinner. Instead of buying one, you can work some culinary magic of your own with this book and a rotisserie—whether it's a small, countertop model or the one that comes with your outdoor barbecue. Recently there has been a resurgence in this type of cooking, with the advent of the macho-man outdoor barbecues and the small electric rotisseries that sit on the counter and spin your dinner. These little wonder machines can twirl a four-pound chicken into a gloriously crispy skinned, moist, and tasty dinner in about one hour. Glistening and golden, this chicken is better than anything you've ever taken home from your local deli.

The countertop rotisseries come with a few recipes and lots of timing charts; the problem is there aren't enough recipes to inspire creativity or imagination. Once you've rotisseried a chicken, where do you go from there? I'll take you on a culinary adventure, and show you how to turn your ho-hum weeknight dinners into flavor-packed barbecues. Whether you are cooking a whole chicken, fish fillets, or beef kabobs, you'll wonder why you've never used a rotisserie before. The advantages of this type of cooking are that the fat melts away and the food self-bastes, so there is no need for constant watching, and it's easy to clean up afterwards. Best of all, this simple method of cooking is comfort food for the soul, perfuming your house with mouthwatering aromas and producing a feast fit for a king.

Rotisserie Basics

Okay, let's start with the basics. If you haven't already bought yourself an electric rotisserie oven, but are thinking seriously about it, here's what you might want to consider as you make your choice.

What Kind of Machine Should I Buy?

When I began testing recipes, I bought a compact, or junior, model rotisserie to see how it worked and to test all the equipment that came with it. This model is great for a family of two, but if you want to be able to prepare more than one chicken at a time, or a large turkey (over ten pounds), several racks of ribs, or larger cuts of beef, pork, and lamb, I would recommend that you get the larger model—the one that isn't called "compact" or "junior" (it doesn't really have a name).

In testing machines, what I looked for was even heating, easy cleanup, and whether the machine did what it promised to do. The two biggest sellers on the market today are the George Foreman Lean Mean Fat Roasting Machine and the Ronco Showtime Rotisserie and BBQ Oven. Each comes in a compact, or junior, size, and a larger size. Both are easy to clean—you can put most of the nonelectric parts in the dishwasher—both heat evenly, and the meat comes out as advertised. You can, literally, "set it and forget it." Salton, Oster, and Sunbeam have also stepped up to the plate; they make compact rotisserie ovens, most of which come with a basket and kabob rods.

DeLonghi makes a convection oven that has a rotisserie built into it, so that you can use the oven for both baking cookies and rotisserie spit cooking. Farberware still makes an open rotisserie—the one many of us remember from childhood. It is used only for spit cooking, and doesn't come with a basket or kabob rods.

When making your purchase, remember that the rotisserie will take up counter space when you are using it; for the most part, it occupies almost as much room as a toaster oven. Do you really need a rotisserie? If you love the taste of grilled food and you don't have a grill that you can use year-round or you don't want to be out in the snow or rain using it, then, yes, I would definitely recommend a rotisserie. For those of you living in apartments or in motor homes or boats, this is a great addition to the kitchen and your culinary repertoire.

Even though I live in California and can grill whenever I please, I love using the rotisserie, because it requires very little attention. If I were grilling outdoors, I'd have to be out there, turning kabobs and meat on the grill; with the rotisserie, I set it and forget it. There are also flare-ups with an outdoor grill, when the fat hits the coals, ignites, and burns parts of the meat. With the rotisserie, there's no fire, no burning.

Your Rotisserie Oven

Most countertop rotisseries come with a spit rod assembly, a rotating basket for smaller items, and kabob skewers. Each one of these tools can help you to make a five-star dinner

The Great Outdoors—The Grill Rotisserie

Although this book deals primarily with the electric tabletop rotisserie, if you have an outdoor rotisserie, all of these recipes will still work. The timing will be a little different, though, given the difference in the heating methods. For that reason, I recommend using an instant-read meat thermometer for testing whether food is cooked through. All the kabobs in the book can be cooked over an outdoor fire as well; if you are using bamboo skewers, make sure you soak them in water for half an hour before using them over an open flame. You will also need to turn the kabobs several times during the cooking period to ensure even cooking.

A grill rotisserie requires an indirect fire; that is, if you are making a charcoal fire, heat the charcoal to the white ash stage, then arrange an aluminum foil drip pan beneath the rotisserie and arrange the coals around that. Many gas grills have a separate burner for the rotisserie attachment, or the manufacturer can give you instructions for attaching the rotisserie and lighting the fire. Check with the manufacturer to see if they recommend attaching a rotisserie to your grill.

in less than one hour. A rotisserie isn't like a slow cooker, where you can put everything for dinner into the pan and it turns into a one-pot meal. Rather, the rotisserie is a great tool for creating a main course or side dishes for your family. You'll have to use your other household appliances to help you prepare the rest of your dinner. Some rotisseries come with special add-ons to help you cook frozen vegetables on the top of the rotisserie (using the radiant heat that it gives off), but I'd suggest you use the rotisserie for what it's designed to do. They all work well; some are enormous and others are just right for a family of four.

I'm going to take you through the parts of the rotisserie so you can understand how to use it and solve any problems you might run into.

The Spit Rod Assembly

Whether you have an outdoor spit barbecue or a countertop electric rotisserie, it will have a spit that is used to hold the food while it is being cooked. On some electric rotisseries, this assembly is also used to hold kabob rods and the rotisserie basket. The electric rotisserie spit rod assembly consists of one gear wheel attached to the spit rods, and another free gear wheel that is attached after the food is loaded onto the rods.

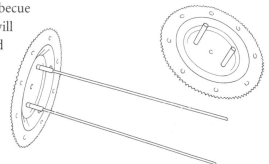

Here are the most important things to keep in mind when using the spit rod assembly:

- Keep food centered and balanced on the spit rod. If the food is not centered or balanced, it might actually fall off the spit or hit the heating elements, causing the machine to stop or stall, or the food to catch fire.
- When placing food on the spit rods, remember that the rods are sharp and can cause injury. So be careful, and keep your hands away from the pointed ends.
- Most electric rotisseries come with some elastic bands for trussing food—you will soon run out of these, so it's a good idea to buy some cotton kitchen string and keep it handy. This will help when you want to truss a chicken or tie a roast. I find it easier to tie the food once it's on the spit. Wetting the string before tying keeps it from burning.
- Groaning from the spit rod assembly can be corrected by taking a Q-tip and lubricating the gear wheel with a drop or two of vegetable oil.

Kabob Rods

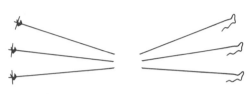

Kabob rods allow you to skewer smaller items and cook them on your rotisserie, and they also serve to position foods like a rack of ribs on the spit rod. The advantage of using a rotisserie to prepare kabobs rather than a grill is that the kabob rod on the rotisserie has a little gear, which helps the kabob to rotate completely. Therefore, every surface of the food will be exposed to the heating element.

Here are some helpful hints for using the kabob rods:

- Thread the kabob rod with food before loading it into the rotisserie.
- Leave a little space between items on the kabob, so that each one will roast, and not steam.
- Load the kabob rod onto the spit rod assembly with the sharp end on the left side; then snap the spring ends into the gear wheel assembly.

Rotisserie Basket

The rotisserie basket is used to roast smaller foods, such as chicken pieces, vegetables, fish steaks, and burgers. The basket is set on the spit rod, then placed in the rotisserie.

These are important tips for achieving success with the basket:

- Make sure that the basket is closed tightly, so that no food can move around while it's cooking.
- If you are cooking a small number of things, crumple a little aluminum foil and stick it into the corners and around the edges of the basket to keep everything tight.
- Make sure the food is not sticking out of the basket, or it will hit the heating element and stop the machine.
- Although some baskets are made of nonstick materials, it is a good idea to coat the basket with a nonstick cooking spray if you are doing burgers, fish steaks, or chicken parts, as they have a tendency to stick because of the pressure of the food against the tightly held basket.
- The George Forman Roasting Oven has an additional large drum type of basket, which can be used for making nonfat French fries and other large grilled items. I recommend that you coat this one with nonstick cooking spray as well.

Cooking in Your Rotisserie

You will need a few pantry staples to help you out on nights when you are in a hurry, but still want to get a great dinner on the table. I recommend that you buy whole chickens and freeze them. Then, when you want one for dinner, defrost it in the microwave, season it, and cook it in the rotisserie. The defrosting will take about 20 minutes, so make sure to take that time into account when planning dinner. Lay in some frozen shrimp, steaks, and roasts, as well. The manufacturers recommend that you bring the meat to room temperature before putting it in the rotisserie, so that it will cook faster. For these recipes, I felt the time I spent marinating or rubbing the meat, or making a sauce was time enough for the food to reach room temperature. If it isn't at room temperature, you will have to add a few extra minutes to the cooking time.

Spices are essential for great rotisserie food. I recommend that you buy a good-quality seasoned salt (either low-sodium or high-octane), or you can use the recipe on page 285 and make one yourself. Dried herbs and spices help to punch up the flavor in rotisserie foods. In addition, make sure to keep plenty of black peppercorns on hand to grind for your dinner. Fresh herbs can be tucked underneath the skin of poultry, flavoring the meat as it cooks, and providing a beautiful pattern on the skin at the same time. Good-quality olive oil to brush on foods before cooking and nonstick cooking spray to coat the rotisseric basket are also essentials.

Cuts of meat that have a great deal of fat on them, such as prime rib, lamb, and duck, will give off quite a bit of fat, which sometimes seeps through the front window of the machine onto the counter. I find that by putting a damp towel underneath the window, I can catch any drips that might occur.

The timers are notoriously inaccurate on these machines (except for those with digital displays). I use a rotisserie timer as the guide, because it is integrated into the machine and turns it off when it has cooked the designated number of minutes.

Some cuts of meat may need a little bit more searing, or a chicken may need a little bit more browning, and if that is the case, there is a feature on some of the machines called "Pause to Sear," which allows you to stop the rotation of the machine without turning off the heat. The meat will brown nicely when it is stopped in front of the heating element.

Cleaning Tips

Follow the manufacturer's instructions for cleaning, and use these tips to help you keep your unit shipshape for a long time.

- After cooking, unplug the unit and allow it to cool completely before you clean it. If necessary, you can remove the spit rod assembly, kabob rods, basket, drip tray and cover, and door and wash them in the dishwasher. Or wash them in hot, sudsy water, using a dishwashing detergent with a grease cutter, such as Dawn.

- To clean the inside of the machine, use a grease-cutting cleaner, such as Orange Clean, or a solution of dishwashing detergent and water. Make sure to remove all traces of the cleaner with water. Never immerse the machine in water.
- If the spit rod assembly becomes blackened from use, clean it with a nontoxic, spray-on oven cleaner; you'll get great results.

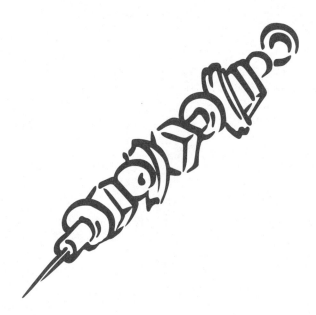

Birds of a Feather

The first recipe I tried when I bought my rotisserie was the whole chicken. It looked so beautiful in the photos, and didn't seem too complicated. But I was afraid it wouldn't stay on the spit, and I would lose it, or it would go flying off somewhere all by itself. Imagine my surprise when, as the ad says, I set it and forgot it, only to come back an hour later to find a gorgeous, golden brown chicken, basting in its own juices, with an aroma that made my mouth water. That chicken was the first of many I have cooked, each with its own unique flavor. In addition to whole chickens, try chunks of chicken spun into every flavor of kabob, as well as delicious burgers, wings, and a whole turkey on the spit. The poultry remains juicy, tender, and moist throughout the cooking time, and the leftovers, if there are any, are terrific.

Birds of a Feather

The recipes in this chapter take a little bit of advance preparation before you turn the bird on the spit. But there are plenty of easy ways to cook poultry that require just one or two pantry ingredients, and these are what I call the no-brainers.

Spicy No-Brainers

Rub the chicken (or turkey) inside and out with any of the following spice blends and roast according to the manufacturer's directions.

- Cavender's Greek seasoning
- Seasoned Salt (page 285)
- Lemon Pepper Rub (page 286)
- Mrs. Dash (any flavor)
- Old Bay seasoning
- Creole Seasoning Rub (page 287)
- Hidden Valley Ranch Salad Dressing mix
- Dry soup mixes, such as Lipton's Onion, Golden Onion, Savory Herb with Garlic, and Fiesta Red Pepper, and Knorr's Leek, Spinach, and Tomato Basil soups
- Gebhardt Chili Powder

Saucy No-Brainers

Prepared sauces are great for rotisserie poultry. If the sauce is high in sugar content, then baste only during the last 10 to 15 minutes of cooking; otherwise, the sauce will burn on the chicken.

- Bottled barbecue sauce or homemade (see Index)
- Hoisin sauce
- Chinese char sui sauce
- Bottled teriyaki sauce or Spicy Teriyaki Sauce (page 314) or Top Secret Teriyaki Sauce (page 315)
- Coarse-grained or Dijon mustard
- Bottled Italian salad dressing
- Bottled Caesar salad dressing
- Green Tabasco sauce
- Mexican-style salsa, puréed in the food processor

The times suggested below are approximate. Always use an instant-read thermometer stuck into the thickest part of the meat to check doneness.

Type of Poultry	Time	Internal Temperature
Whole chicken or duck	15 to 20 minutes per pound	175 degrees
Cornish game hens	15 minutes per pound	175 degrees
Turkey	10 to 12 minutes per pound	175 degrees
Goose	12 minutes per pound	175 degrees
Quail	20 to 25 minutes per pound	165 degrees
Poultry burgers	30 to 35 minutes total	165 degrees
Kabobs	30 to 35 minutes total	175 degrees
Chicken parts	15 minutes per pound	175 degrees

Rotisserie Tips for Birds Roasted Whole

The secret to success with roasting a whole chicken, turkey, or game hen is to truss it and make sure it is balanced evenly on the spit rod assembly, so it doesn't don't flop around. Trussing the bird is not difficult to do. Load it onto the spit rods first; it will be easier to handle. Then tie the ends of the legs together tightly. Working your way up the bird, tie another string around the meaty parts of the legs, and another around the bird's upper body, securing the wings against the bird so they don't flop around while it's on the spit. For turkeys and larger birds, you will also need to tie string around the bird lengthwise three or four times.

Although rotisserie manufacturers do not recommend that you stuff the birds, you can stuff chicken and turkeys. But you mustn't overstuff, or have any stuffing peeking out, as it tends to work itself out with each turn on the spit. Season the bird liberally inside and out before cooking.

Roasting duck and goose in the rotisserie requires a little bit more care. I cut off the wing tips, as they seem to hit the cooking element no matter how tightly you tie them to the bird. Remove any obvious fat, which might cause flare-ups when the bird rotates. Some books instruct you to boil the duck or goose before cooking it on the spit, but when I tried it I found preboiled meat tough and the skin was not crispy enough. On the other hand, duck, goose, and Cornish game hens all benefit from brining before they are roasted (see page 30).

Lemon-Rosemary Rotisserie Chicken

Serves 6   **Tangy lemon and pungent rosemary give this chicken its robust flavor.**

One 4-pound chicken

Lemon-Rosemary Marinade

1/2 cup fresh lemon juice
Grated zest from 1 lemon
5 cloves garlic, minced
1/4 cup fresh rosemary
    leaves
1 teaspoon salt
1 teaspoon freshly ground
    black pepper
1/4 cup olive oil

Wash the chicken inside and out under cold running water and pat it dry. Remove any excess fat from the skin and place the chicken in a 2-gallon zipper-top plastic bag.

In a large mixing bowl, combine marinade ingredients and pour the marinade over the chicken. Seal the bag, and refrigerate, turning frequently, for at least 1 hour and up to 8 hours.

Drain the chicken. Load the chicken onto the spit rod assembly. Truss according to the manufacturer's directions, or tie the legs together and tie another string around the body and wings so the wings don't flop around during cooking (see illustration below) and roast until an instant-read meat thermometer inserted into the thickest part of the thigh registers 175 degrees, about 20 minutes per pound.

Remove the chicken from the spit, cover loosely with aluminum foil, and allow to rest for 10 minutes before carving.

All-American Rotisserie Chicken

Serves 6   No time for fancy sauces? Just massage the chicken with an all-purpose barbecue rub, then cook the chicken—simple, quick, and delicious. Serve this with a fruit or tomato salsa, or All-American Barbecue Sauce (page 324).

One 3 1/2- to 4-pound chicken
1/4 cup All-Purpose Rotisserie Rub (page 288)
1 tablespoon vegetable oil

Wash the chicken inside and out under cold running water and pat dry. Remove any excess fat from the skin.

In a small mixing bowl, combine the rub with the oil until it forms a paste. Rub the chicken on all sides with the rub paste and brush some in the cavity.

Load the chicken onto the spit rod assembly. Truss according to the manufacturer's directions, or tie the legs together and tie another string around the body and wings so the wings don't flop around during cooking. Roast until an instant-read meat thermometer inserted into the thickest part of the thigh registers 175 degrees, about 20 minutes per pound.

Remove the chicken from the spit rod, cover loosely with aluminum foil, and allow to rest for at least 10 minutes before carving.

Ginger-Orange Rotisserie Chicken

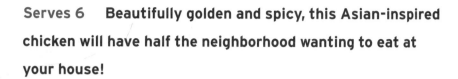

Serves 6   Beautifully golden and spicy, this Asian-inspired chicken will have half the neighborhood wanting to eat at your house!

One 3¹/₂- to 4-pound
 chicken

Ginger-Orange Baste

2 large navel oranges
2 teaspoons peeled and
 grated fresh ginger
¹/₄ cup sugar
2 tablespoons rice vinegar
 or red wine vinegar
2 tablespoons ketchup
2 cloves garlic, minced
2 teaspoons salt
1 teaspoon freshly ground
 black pepper

Wash the chicken inside and out under cold running water and pat it dry. Remove any excess fat from the skin and set the chicken aside.

To make the baste, cut one of the oranges into ¼-inch-thick slices and set aside. In a medium-size mixing bowl, grate the zest from the other orange and juice it into the bowl. Stir in the ginger, sugar, vinegar, ketchup, garlic, 1 teaspoon of the salt, and the pepper. Stir in the orange slices and continue stirring until they are coated.

Sprinkle the cavity of the chicken with the remaining 1 teaspoon of salt. Lift the skin from the back of the chicken and slide some of the orange slices under the skin to make a nice pattern. Baste the outside of the chicken thickly with some of the sauce. Cover the chicken with plastic wrap and marinate in the refrigerator for at least 4, and up to 24 hours in the refrigerator. Boil the remaining sauce and oranges, then cover and refrigerate for use as condiment.

When ready to roast, place the chicken on the spit rod assembly. Truss according to the manufacturer's directions, or tie the legs together and tie another string around the body and wings so the wings don't flop around during cooking. Roast until an instant-read meat thermometer inserted into the thickest part of the thigh registers 175 degrees, about 20 minutes per pound.

Remove the chicken from the spit, cover loosely with aluminum foil, and allow to rest for 10 minutes before carving.

Meanwhile, warm the sauce with the oranges and serve on the side.

Smart Turn

If you would like to do this with chicken pieces, rather than a whole chicken, marinate 2½ pounds chicken parts according to the recipe instructions, reserving the orange slices for a garnish. Load the chicken into the rotisserie basket, attach to the spit rod assembly, and cook for 15 minutes per pound.

Gingery Sesame-Garlic Chicken

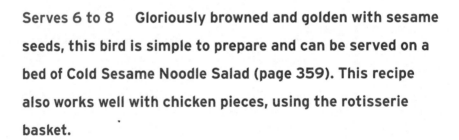

Serves 6 to 8   Gloriously browned and golden with sesame seeds, this bird is simple to prepare and can be served on a bed of Cold Sesame Noodle Salad (page 359). This recipe also works well with chicken pieces, using the rotisserie basket.

One 3½- to 4-pound chicken

Sesame-Garlic Marinade

2 teaspoons toasted sesame oil
1 tablespoon vegetable oil
1 tablespoon rice vinegar
2 teaspoons peeled and grated fresh ginger
3 cloves garlic, chopped

Wash the chicken inside and out under cold running water and pat dry. Trim away any excess fat from the skin. Place the chicken in a 2-gallon zipper-top plastic bag.

In a small mixing bowl, combine marinade ingredients. Pour over the chicken in the bag, seal, turn the chicken to coat, and marinate in the refrigerator for at least 5 hours or overnight.

When ready to roast, remove the chicken from the marinade, pat it dry with paper towels, and place on the spit rod assembly. Truss the chicken according to the manufacturer's directions, or tie the legs together and tie another string

$1^1/_2$ teaspoons Chinese five-spice powder

1 teaspoon salt

1 tablespoon firmly packed brown sugar

2 tablespoons sesame seeds

Garnishes

Sesame seeds

4 green onions, sliced $^1/_2$ inch thick on the diagonal

1 large carrot, cut into 3- to 4-inch-long curls with a swivel peeler

around the body and wings so the wings don't flop around during cooking. Roast until an instant-read meat thermometer inserted into the thickest part of the thigh registers 175 degrees, about 20 minutes per pound.

Remove the chicken from the spit rod, cover loosely with aluminum foil, and allow to rest for at least 10 minutes before carving.

Garnish the chicken with more sesame seeds, the green onions, and carrot curls.

Preparing Your Bird for the Rotisserie

It is imperative that you wash any poultry in lots of cold water. Remove the giblets and neck and save to make stock. Use paper towels to dry the interior of the bird, as well as the outside, and salt the cavity. Make sure that you wash your hands and any utensils such as knives and cutting boards thoroughly in hot, soapy water after handling poultry.

Sun-Dried Tomato Pesto Chicken

Serves 6 to 8   Not only does the pesto flavor this chicken, it also gives it a glorious color.

One 3$\frac{1}{2}$- to 4-pound
  chicken
$\frac{1}{3}$ cup Sun-Dried Tomato
  Pesto (recipe follows)

Wash the chicken inside and out under cold running water and pat dry. Remove any excess fat from the skin. Carefully lifting the skin from the meaty end of the breast, spread some of the pesto under the skin with your fingers. (This won't be pretty, but trust me, it does work.) Work the pesto as far down as you can, trying to get some of it under the skin over the thigh and drumstick without tearing the skin.

Load the chicken onto the spit rod assembly. Truss according to the manufacturer's directions, or tie the legs together and tie another string around the body and wings so the wings don't flop around during cooking, and spread the rest of the pesto evenly over the outside of the chicken. Roast until an instant-read meat thermometer inserted into the thickest part of the thigh registers 175 degrees, about 20 minutes per pound.

Remove the chicken from the spit rod, cover loosely with aluminum foil, and allow to rest for at least 10 minutes before carving.

Sun-Dried Tomato Pesto

Makes about 2½ cups   This simple pesto is great to have on hand when you want to flavor a chicken or lamb roast. It's also terrific tossed into hot pasta for a spicy side dish, or mixed into cooled pasta for a pasta salad.

1½ cups oil-packed sun-dried tomatoes, drained
6 medium-size cloves garlic, peeled
1 cup freshly grated Parmesan cheese
1 cup packed fresh basil leaves
½ cup olive oil
2 tablespoons balsamic vinegar

In a food processor, combine the tomatoes, garlic, Parmesan, and basil. Process for about 1 minute.

With the machine running, gradually add the olive oil and vinegar through the feed tube and process until the mixture is thoroughly incorporated and smooth. Refrigerate until ready to use. This pesto will keep in the refrigerator, covered, for up to 2 weeks or in the freezer for up to 2 months.

Shortcut Sun-Dried Tomato Pesto: Buy prepared basil pesto from the store and process 1½ cups of it with 1½ cups of drained sun-dried tomatoes and 2 tablespoons of balsamic vinegar until smooth.

It Isn't Easy Being Green
Basil Pesto Chicken

○ ● ○

Serves 6 to 8   Serving green chicken to your family may sound like it's part of some alien menu, but this succulent bird is divine hot or cold. It's a great take along for a picnic or a summer supper on the patio. Serve with orzo pasta and sautéed cherry tomatoes.

One 3 1/2- to 4-pound chicken
1/2 cup Basil Pesto (recipe follows) or store-bought pesto

Wash the chicken under cold running water, pat dry, and trim any excess fat from the skin. Carefully lift the skin from the meaty part of the breast and spread some of the pesto under the skin, working it down to the thighs and drumsticks, if you can.

Load the chicken onto the spit rod assembly. Truss according to the manufacturer's directions, or tie the legs together and tie another string around the body and wings so the wings don't flop around during cooking. Spread the remaining pesto evenly over the outside of the chicken. Roast until an instant-read meat thermometer inserted in the thickest part of the thigh registers 175 degrees, about 20 minutes per pound.

Remove the chicken from the spit rod, cover loosely with aluminum foil, and allow to rest for 10 minutes before carving.

Basil Pesto

Makes 3½ cups   This bright green pesto is simple to make and stores well in the refrigerator or freezer. You can use it as a rub on beef, lamb, chicken, and pork.

2 cups packed fresh basil
     leaves
1 cup freshly grated
     Parmesan cheese
3 cloves garlic, peeled
¼ cup pine nuts
½ cup olive oil

In a blender or food processor, process together the basil, Parmesan cheese, garlic, and pine nuts until the garlic and nuts are minced.

With the machine running, gradually add the olive oil through the feed tube and process until smooth.

Pour the mixture into a glass jar and float ½ inch of olive oil on the top. When ready to use, pour off the oil and stir the pesto. It will keep, covered, in the refrigerator for up to 1 week or in the freezer for up to 2 months.

If You Can't Stand the Heat Chicken

Serves 6 to 8   This chicken will scare some away and others will run to the kitchen to make it. After being doused with an entire bottle of Louisiana hot sauce, this chicken comes off the rotisserie a reddish golden color, tender, juicy, and with a kick from the hot sauce. I recommend serving it with lots of cold beer and a cooling potato salad.

One 3^1/$_2$- to 4-pound
  chicken
One 8-ounce bottle
  Louisiana hot sauce
1 teaspoon salt

Wash the chicken inside and out under cold running water and pat dry. Remove any excess fat from the skin and place the chicken in a large mixing bowl. Pour the hot sauce over the chicken, sprinkle with salt, and rub the chicken inside and out with the mixture.

Load the chicken onto the spit rod assembly. Truss according to the manufacturer's directions, or tie the legs together and tie another string around the body and wings so the wings don't flop around during cooking. Roast until an instant-read meat thermometer inserted into the thickest part of the thigh registers 175 degrees, about 20 minutes per pound.

Remove the chicken from the spit rod assembly, cover loosely with aluminum foil, and let rest for 10 minutes before carving.

Chicken Balsamico

Serves 6 to 8   All my favorite flavors in one chicken—life doesn't get much better than this! Flavored with garlic, balsamic vinegar, and pancetta, the crispy skin and succulent meat on this bird are worthy of a five-star restaurant. If you can't get pancetta at your local grocery, substitute 3 strips of bacon.

One 3½- to 4-pound chicken

Garlicky Pancetta-Rosemary Paste

6 cloves garlic, peeled
One ¼-inch-thick slice pancetta, cut into thin strips
¼ cup plus 2 tablespoons balsamic vinegar
3 tablespoons olive oil
1 tablespoon chopped fresh rosemary leaves

Wash the chicken inside and out under cold running water and pat dry. Remove any excess fat from the skin and set aside.

In food processor or minichopper, process the paste ingredients together until it reaches a spreadable consistency.

Carefully lift the skin from the meaty end of the chicken breast and slide some of the paste underneath the skin, working it down to the thighs and drumsticks if you can and being careful not to tear the skin.

Load the chicken onto the spit rod assembly. Truss according to the manufacturer's directions, or tie the legs together and tie another string around the body and wings so the wings don't flop around during cooking, and rub the outside of the chicken with the remaining paste. Roast until an instant-read meat thermometer inserted into the thickest part of the thigh registers 175 degrees, about 20 minutes per pound.

Remove the chicken from the spit rod, cover loosely with aluminum foil, and let rest for 10 minutes before carving.

Moroccan Chicken

Serves 6 to 8   Fragrant with spices from the Casbah, this chicken is beautifully colored, and the aromas will have your family waiting in front of the rotisserie until it's done! Great with a side of couscous and an orange and red onion salad, this dinner is one you'll make often.

One 3$^1/_2$- to 4-pound chicken

Moroccan Spice Paste

4 cloves garlic, peeled
1 teaspoon ground cumin
$^1/_4$ teaspoon ground allspice
1 tablespoon sweet paprika
1$^1/_2$ teaspoons salt
1$^1/_2$ teaspoons turmeric
3 tablespoons vegetable oil

$^1/_2$ cup chopped unsalted pistachios for garnish

Wash the chicken inside and out under cold running water and pat dry. Trim any excess fat from the skin and set the chicken aside.

In a food processor or minichopper, combine the paste ingredients and process until they reach a spreadable consistency. Rub the chicken inside and out with the paste.

Load the chicken onto the spit rod assembly. Truss according to the manufacturer's directions, or tie the legs together and tie another string around the body and wings so the wings don't flop around during cooking. Rub the outside of the chicken with the remaining paste and roast until an instant-read meat thermometer inserted into the thickest part of the thigh registers 175 degrees, about 20 minutes per pound.

Remove the chicken from the spit rod, cover loosely with aluminum foil, and allow to rest for 10 minutes before carving.

Garnish each serving with some of the pistachios.

Marcella's Lemon Chicken

Serves 6 Many years ago, I took a class from master Italian chef Marcella Hazan, and was struck by how simple and delicious the food was. This chicken, inspired by Marcella's, is a great example of unadorned but extraordinary food. Here, crispy skinned chicken is infused with the flavor of fresh lemons.

One 3½- to 4-pound
  chicken
3 lemons
2 teaspoons salt
1 teaspoon freshly ground
  black pepper
¼ cup chopped fresh
  Italian parsley leaves
  for garnish

Wash the chicken inside and out under cold running water and pat dry. Trim any excess fat from the skin and set the chicken aside.

Grate the zest from 1 of the lemons and squeeze it, straining the juice. Combine the zest with the juice, salt, and pepper and rub the chicken inside and out with the mixture. Stuff the chicken with the remaining 2 lemons.

Load the chicken onto the spit rod assembly. Truss according to the manufacturer's directions, or tie the legs together and tie another string around the body and wings so the wings don't flop around during cooking. Roast until an instant-read meat thermometer inserted into the thickest part of the thigh registers 175 degrees, about 20 minutes per pound.

Remove the chicken from the spit rod assembly and, using tongs or heatproof gloves, carefully remove the lemons from the cavity. Allow the chicken to rest, covered loosely with aluminum foil, for 10 minutes before carving.

After carving, you may squeeze the lemons over the chicken, if desired. Garnish with the parsley and serve.

Cilantro-Lime Chicken

Serves 6 Pungent cilantro and the fresh flavors of lime and garlic all permeate this chicken, for a dinner with a little south of the border style. Great to serve cold or hot, it goes well with Refried Bean Bake (page 339) and Southwestern Rice (page 352).

One 3½- to 4-pound
chicken

Cilantro-Lime Marinade

2 tablespoons vegetable oil
¼ cup fresh lime juice
6 cloves garlic, minced
¼ cup chopped red onion
¼ cup chopped fresh
cilantro leaves
1 teaspoon salt
½ teaspoon freshly ground
black pepper
6 shakes Tabasco sauce

¼ cup chopped fresh
cilantro leaves for
garnish

Wash the chicken inside and out under cold running water and pat dry. Remove any excess fat from the skin. Place in a 2-gallon zipper-top plastic bag.

In a small mixing bowl, combine the marinade ingredients, stirring to blend. Pour the marinade over the chicken, seal the bag, and turn it over to coat the chicken. Marinate in the refrigerator for at least 4 and up to 8 hours.

Remove the chicken from the marinade, pat dry, and load onto the spit rod assembly. Truss the chicken according to the manufacturer's directions, or tie the legs together and tie another string around the body and wings so the wings don't flop around during cooking. Roast until an instant-read meat thermometer inserted into the thickest part of the thigh registers 175 degrees, about 20 minutes per pound.

Remove the chicken from the spit rod, cover loosely with aluminum foil, and allow it to rest for 10 minutes before carving.

Garnish each serving with some of the cilantro.

Tandoori Chicken

Serves 6   Spicy, with a gorgeous color, this traditional Indian dish can be done in the rotisserie with no problem at all. The chicken does need to marinate for at least 24 hours before cooking for the proper flavor. Serve with cooling Cucumber-Yogurt Sauce (page 317) and a fresh tropical fruit salad made with mango, pineapple, and papaya.

One 3$^1/_2$- to 4-pound chicken

Tandoori Marinade

1 cup plain yogurt

2 tablespoons fresh lime juice

5 cloves garlic, peeled

2 quarter-size slices peeled fresh ginger

1 teaspoon seeded and finely chopped jalapeño

1$^1/_2$ teaspoons salt

1 teaspoon turmeric

1 teaspoon ground coriander

$^1/_2$ teaspoon ground cumin

$^1/_4$ teaspoon cayenne

2 teaspoons sweet paprika

Wash the chicken inside and out under cold running water and pat dry. Remove any excess fat from the skin and place in a 2-gallon zipper-top plastic bag.

In a food processor, combine the marinade ingredients and process until smooth. Pour the mixture over the chicken, seal the bag, and turn over to coat the chicken. Marinate in the refrigerator for at least 24 hours, turning occasionally.

Remove the chicken from the marinade, pat dry with paper towels, and place on the spit rod assembly. Truss the chicken according to the manufacturer's directions, or tie the legs together and tie another string around the body and wings so the wings don't flop around during cooking. Roast until an instant-read meat thermometer inserted into the thickest part of the thigh registers 175 degrees, about 20 minutes per pound.

Remove the chicken from the spit rod, cover loosely with aluminum foil, and allow to rest for 10 minutes before carving.

Spicy Thai Chicken

—○–●–○—

Serves 6 Fragrant with basil, mint, and cilantro, this easy chicken will become a favorite with your family and friends. I like to prepare this with a whole chicken, but you can certainly marinate chicken pieces and grill them in the rotisserie basket, if you prefer. Look for fish sauce in the Asian section of your supermarket.

One 4-pound chicken

Pungent Thai Marinade

1/4 cup chopped fresh
   cilantro leaves
1/4 cup chopped fresh basil
   leaves
1/2 cup chopped fresh mint
   leaves
1 tablespoon seeded and
   finely chopped jalapeño
   or serrano chile
2 cloves garlic, minced
2 teaspoons peeled and
   grated fresh ginger
1/4 cup canola oil
2 tablespoons light corn
   syrup
1/2 cup fish sauce
1/2 cup light soy sauce

Rinse the chicken inside and out under cold running water and pat dry. Place the chicken in a 2-gallon zipper-top plastic bag.

In a medium-size glass bowl, stir together the marinade ingredients until well blended. Pour the marinade over the chicken. Seal the bag, shake it gently to coat the chicken, and marinate the chicken in the refrigerator for at least 6 and up to 24 hours.

Remove the chicken from the bag, pat dry, and load it onto the spit rod assembly. Truss the chicken according to the manufacturer's directions, or tie the legs together and tie another string around the body and wings so the wings don't flop around during cooking. Roast until an instant-read meat thermometer inserted into the thickest part of the thigh registers 175 degrees, about 20 minutes per pound.

Remove the chicken from the spit rod, loosely cover with aluminum foil, and allow to rest for 10 to 15 minutes before carving.

Fresh Herb and Citrus Roasted Chicken

Serves 6   When this chicken came out of the rotisserie, my son Ryan said, "That looks good enough to eat," and he was right! The herbs and citrus zest combine to make this golden bird attractive as well as tasty.

One 3½- to 4-pound chicken

Fresh Herb and Citrus Marinade

Grated zest of 1 lemon
Grated zest of 1 orange
5 cloves garlic, minced
½ cup fresh lemon juice
¼ cup orange juice
1 teaspoon salt
½ teaspoon freshly ground black pepper
2 tablespoons chopped fresh thyme leaves
2 tablespoons chopped fresh sage leaves

Rinse the chicken inside and out under cold running water and pat dry. Place in a 2-gallon zipper-top plastic bag.

In a small mixing bowl, stir together the marinade ingredients. Pour over the chicken, seal the bag, and turn over to coat everything. Marinate in the refrigerator for at least 4 and up to 8 hours.

Remove the chicken from the marinade, pat dry, and load it onto the spit rod assembly. Truss the chicken according to the manufacturer's directions, or tie the legs together and tie another string around the body and wings so the wings don't flop around during cooking. Roast until an instant-read meat thermometer inserted into the thickest part of the thigh registers 175 degrees, about 20 minutes per pound.

Remove the chicken from the spit rod, cover loosely with aluminum foil, and let rest for 15 minutes before carving.

Athenian Chicken with Red Wine and Garlic

Serves 6 **This succulent roasted chicken is marinated in an herbed red wine marinade, which gives the chicken skin a reddish hue and infuses the meat with bold flavor. Tucking the garlic under the skin adds a mellow, nutty taste to the roasted meat.**

One 3½- to 4-pound chicken

Red Wine and Garlic Marinade

2 cups red wine (Burgundy is nice)

1½ teaspoons salt

1 teaspoon freshly ground black pepper

¼ cup olive oil

2 tablespoons chopped fresh oregano leaves

8 cloves garlic, cut into slivers

Rinse the chicken inside and out under cold running water and pat dry. Place in a 2-gallon zipper-top plastic bag.

In a medium-size mixing bowl, stir together the marinade ingredients. Pour over the chicken, seal the bag, and turn over to coat the chicken. Marinate in the refrigerator for at least 6 and up to 24 hours.

Remove the chicken from the marinade and pat dry. Beginning at the meatiest end of the chicken breast, lift up the skin and push the garlic slivers underneath, being careful not to tear the skin. Try and push some down towards the thigh area as well. Some of the slivers may overlap, but that is all right.

Load the chicken onto the spit rod assembly. Truss according to the manufacturer's directions, or tie the legs together and tie another string around the body and wings so the wings don't flop around during cooking. Roast until an instant-read meat thermometer inserted into the thickest part of the thigh registers 175 degrees, about 20 minutes per pound.

Remove the chicken from the spit rod, cover loosely with aluminum foil, and allow to rest for 10 to 15 minutes before carving.

Rosemary-Dijon Chicken

Serves 6   Fragrant rosemary and pungent Dijon mustard help make this chicken a star on any dinner table. You can use the marinade for whole chickens or chicken pieces; wings prepared this way make a terrific appetizer. We liked this hot, cold, or at room temperature.

One 3½- to 4-pound
    chicken

Rosemary-Dijon Marinade

¾ cup Dijon mustard
¼ cup red wine vinegar
2 tablespoons chopped
    fresh rosemary leaves
3 cloves garlic, minced
1½ teaspoons salt
1 teaspoon freshly ground
    black pepper

Rinse the chicken under cold running water and pat dry. Trim away any excess fat, and place the chicken in a 2-gallon zipper-top plastic bag.

In a medium-size mixing bowl, stir together the marinade ingredients until well combined. Pour the marinade over the chicken, seal the bag, and turn over to coat evenly. Marinate in the refrigerator for at least 3 and up to 6 hours, turning the chicken occasionally.

Remove the chicken from the marinade, pat dry, and load it onto the spit rod assembly. Truss the chicken according to the manufacturer's directions, or tie the legs together and tie another string around the body and wings so the wings don't flop around during cooking. Roast until an instant-read meat thermometer inserted into the thickest part of the thigh registers 175 degrees, about 20 minutes per pound.

Remove the chicken from the spit rod, cover loosely with aluminum foil, and allow to rest for 10 to 15 minutes before carving.

Cornish game hens, quail, duck, and goose are more tender and juicy after a soak in some brine. Hens and quail need only salt and water, while duck and goose like a sweeter brine.

Basic Brine for Birds

HENS AND QUAIL
1/2 cup salt
4 cups hot water

DUCK AND GOOSE
1 1/2 cups salt
3/4 cup firmly packed brown sugar
8 cups hot water

Mix the brine ingredients in a nonreactive bowl or pot, stirring to dissolve the salt and sugar, if any. Soak the bird(s) in the brine for the length of time specified in the recipe. (Note that if the recipe contains a lot of acid, such as orange juice, or a salty marinade or baste, then brining isn't necessary.)

Porcini Roasted Chicken

Serves 6   **Earthy dried porcini mushrooms are rehydrated and cook underneath the skin of this woodsy chicken, creating a beautiful pattern. Serve with a nice risotto and a salad of field greens.**

Porcini-Marsala Marinade

1¹/₂ ounces dried porcini mushrooms

1 cup hot chicken broth

¹/₄ cup olive oil

2 tablespoons Marsala

1¹/₂ teaspoons salt

¹/₂ teaspoon freshly ground black pepper

1 teaspoon dried thyme

One 3¹/₂- to 4-pound chicken

To make the marinade, place the dried mushrooms in a small mixing bowl, pour the broth over them, and let soften. This should take about 20 minutes. Drain the mushrooms and pat them dry. Cut into matchsticks. In another small mixing bowl, stir together the olive oil, Marsala, salt, pepper, and thyme. Pour the mixture into a 2-gallon zipper-top plastic bag.

Rinse the chicken inside and out under cold running water and pat dry. Trim away any excess fat. Add the chicken to the marinade, seal the bag, and turn over gently to coat. Marinate in the refrigerator for at least 4 and up to 8 hours, turning the chicken in the marinade occasionally.

Remove the chicken from the marinade and pat dry. Beginning at the meaty end of the breast, lift up the skin and slide the mushrooms underneath the skin, making an attractive pattern.

Load the chicken onto the spit rod assembly. Truss according to the manufacturer's directions, or tie the legs together and tie another string around the body and wings so the wings don't flop around during cooking. Roast until an instant-read meat thermometer registers 175 degrees when inserted into the thickest part of the thigh, about 20 minutes per pound.

Remove the chicken from the spit rod, cover loosely with aluminum foil, and allow to rest for 10 to 15 minutes before carving.

Game Hens Stuffed with Pancetta and Garlic

○ ● ○

Serves 4   Fragrant with garlic and smoky pancetta, these game hens will have you salivating while they are spinning. Serve with Grilled Wild Mushroom Salad (page 226).

3 Cornish game hens, brined
   for 4 hours (see page 30)
1¹/₂ teaspoons salt
1 teaspoon freshly ground
   black pepper

Parsley-Pancetta Paste

One ¹/₄-inch-thick slice
   pancetta, cut into
   matchsticks
6 cloves garlic, peeled
2 tablespoons olive oil
¹/₄ cup chopped fresh Italian
   parsley leaves

Wash the hens inside and out under cold running water and pat it dry. Remove any excess fat from the skin and cut off the wing tips and discard. Sprinkle the hens inside and out with the salt and pepper.

In a food processor, combine the paste ingredients and process until they reach a spreadable consistency. Starting at the meaty end of the breast, slip some of the paste under the skin of the hens. Load the hens onto the spit rod assembly side by side, spearing them through the center of the breast. Truss the hens with string, making sure that the legs are tied together tightly and the wings are secure.

Rub the breast area of the hens with any of the remaining paste. Roast until an instant-read meat thermometer registers 175 degrees when inserted into the thickest part of the thigh, about 15 minutes per pound.

Remove the hens from the spit rod, cover loosely with aluminum foil, and allow to rest for 10 to 15 minutes before carving.

Apricot-Curry Game Hens

Serves 4   These delectable hens are marinated in apricot nectar and spices, then turned on the rotisserie until they are golden brown. Spoon the lemony apricot sauce over the hens before you serve them. If you have a larger rotisserie, you can double the recipe.

Curried Apricot Marinade

1 cup apricot nectar
2 teaspoons rice vinegar or
   1 teaspoon white vinegar
2 teaspoons curry powder

3 Cornish game hens

Lemon-Apricot Sauce

1 tablespoon vegetable oil
2 tablespoons finely
   chopped shallot
   (1 medium-size)
Grated zest of 1 lemon
2 teaspoons fresh lemon
   juice
1 cup dried apricots,
   chopped
1/4 cup sugar

In a small mixing bowl, stir together the marinade ingredients. Pour the mixture into a 2-gallon zipper-top plastic bag, and place the hens in the bag. Seal the bag, and turn the hens in the marinade to coat. Refrigerate for at least 6 hours, or overnight.

Remove the hens from the marinade, pat dry, and load onto the spit rod assembly. Truss the hens with string, making sure that the legs are tied together tightly and the wings are secure. Roast the hens until a meat thermometer inserted into the thickest part of the thigh registers 175 degrees, about 15 minutes per pound.

While the hens are roasting, make the lemon-apricot sauce. In a 2-quart saucepan, heat the oil, add the shallot, and cook for 3 to 4 minutes, until translucent. Add the zest, lemon juice, apricots, and sugar, stirring to blend. Bring to a boil, then simmer for 20 minutes, until the mixture has thickened and the apricots have fallen apart. Remove the sauce from the heat and allow to cool. If you would prefer a completely smooth sauce, run it through the blender or food processor, or use an immersion blender. The sauce can be served warm or a room temperature. Refrigerate, covered, for up to 5 days, or freeze for up to 2 months.

When the hens are done, remove them from the spit rod assembly, and allow to rest, covered loosely with aluminum foil, for 10 minutes. Place the hens on a cutting board, and cut each hen in half, slicing through the breastbone.

Arrange the hens on a platter, garnish with the apricot sauce, and serve.

Hoisin-Five Spice Game Hens

Serves 4   These Asian-inspired birds will make your mouth water while you are waiting for them to be done. Rubbed with five-spice powder, and then glazed with Hoisin sauce, these make a great dinner any night of the week. I like to serve them like Peking Duck, with thin flour tortillas, green onions, and hoisin sauce, but they are also delicious with Asian Slaw (page 344) on the side. If you have a larger rotisserie, you can double the recipe.

2 tablespoons olive oil
2 tablespoons Chinese five-
   spice powder
3 Cornish game hens
$2/3$ cup hoisin sauce
2 tablespoons rice vinegar
1 tablespoon toasted
   sesame oil

In a small bowl, combine the oil and five-spice powder, stirring until they form a thick paste. Rub the paste on the game hens, and place the hens in a 2-gallon zipper-top plastic bag. Refrigerate the hens for 2 hours or overnight.

In a clean bowl, combine the hoisin, vinegar, and sesame oil, stirring until smooth. Refrigerate until ready to roast the hens.

Chopped green onions, white and light green parts, for garnish

Remove the hens from the bag, pat dry, and load onto the spit rod assembly. Truss the hens with string, making sure that the legs are tied together tightly and the wings are secure.

Roast until a meat thermometer inserted into the thickest part of the thigh registers 175 degrees, about 15 minutes per pound. During the last 15 minutes of cooking time, stop the machine 2 or 3 times and brush the birds liberally with the hoisin baste.

Remove the hens from the spit rod assembly and allow to rest, loosely covered with aluminum foil, for 10 minutes. When ready to serve, cut each hen in half, slicing through the breastbone. Serve garnished with green onions.

Honey-Thyme Rotisserie Quail

Serves 2 If you have a hunter in your family, the rotisserie is a great way to cook quail. Brining the quail before cooking is a good idea, as it will help to keep the little birds juicy and tender. Since quail have a tendency to dry out, wrapping them in bacon or pancetta also helps to keep them moist throughout the cooking time. You may have to ask your grocer to order quail for you, or try the frozen foods section of a gourmet market. This recipe is also terrific made with squab or Cornish hens. If you have a larger rotisserie, you can double the recipe.

4 jumbo quail (6 to 8 ounces each), brined for 4 to 6 hours (see page 30)

1/4 cup olive oil

1/2 cup All-American Barbecue Rub (page 286)

4 strips bacon

Honey-Thyme Baste

2 tablespoons honey

1/4 cup balsamic vinegar

2 tablespoons extra-virgin olive oil

1 teaspoon freshly ground black pepper

1 teaspoon fresh thyme leaves

Rinse the birds inside and out under cold running water and pat dry. With poultry shears or a sharp knife, cut off the neck, feet, and wing tips and discard.

In a small dish, combine the olive oil and rub. Brush each quail with some of the mixture inside and out.

Using the kabob rods, spear each quail diagonally through the breast at about a 45-degree angle (see illustration below). Wrap a strip of bacon around each one and secure the quail and bacon to the rod with cotton string. Load the kabob rods onto the spit rod assembly with the spring ends on the right.

In a small mixing bowl, combine the baste ingredients, stirring to blend. Brush each quail liberally with some of the mixture. Grill until the bacon is browned and the quail are cooked through, 20 to 25 minutes. The meat should not be pink when slashed with a knife.

Remove the quail from the skewers, cut off the string, and discard the bacon. Cover the birds loosely with aluminum foil and allow to rest for 5 minutes. Cut each quail in half through the breastbone and serve.

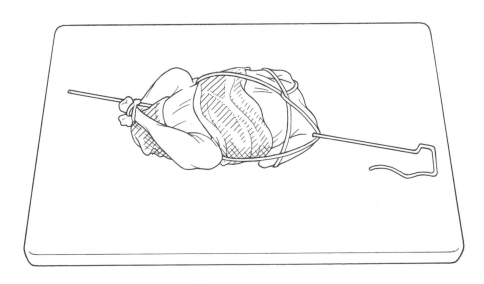

Dijon-Garlic Turkey

Serves 8   This turkey is marinated in aromatic herbs. The result is a tender, juicy turkey infused with the flavor of the herbs. The marinade can also be used for turkey breast or chicken, either whole or in pieces. Make sure to let the poultry marinate for at least 6 hours—overnight is even better. *Note:* This recipe is designed for the smaller rotisserie; if you have the larger one and want to cook up to a 16-pound bird, double the marinade and roast the turkey for 12 minutes per pound.

One 8- to 10-pound turkey

Dijon-Garlic Marinade

3/4 cup olive oil
1 1/4 cups red wine vinegar
1/4 cup Dijon mustard
2 tablespoons chopped
   fresh rosemary leaves
2 tablespoons chopped
   fresh thyme leaves
1 tablespoon chopped fresh
   sage leaves
4 cloves garlic, minced
2 teaspoons salt
1 teaspoon freshly ground
   black pepper

Wash the turkey inside and out under cold running water and pat it dry. Remove any excess fat from the skin and place in a 2-gallon zipper-top plastic bag.

In a small mixing bowl, combine the marinade ingredients, stirring to blend. Pour into the plastic bag, seal the bag, and turn over to coat the turkey. Marinate in the refrigerator for at least 6 hours or overnight, turning the bag frequently to distribute the marinade.

Remove the turkey from the marinade and pat dry. Cut off the wing tips and discard, or save to make stock.

Load the turkey onto the spit rod assembly. Truss according to the manufacturer's directions, or tie the legs together and tie another string around the body and wings so the wings don't flop around during cooking. Roast until an instant-read meat thermometer inserted into the thickest part of the thigh registers 175 degrees, about 12 minutes per pound.

Remove the turkey from the spit rod, loosely cover with aluminum foil, and allow it to rest for at least 20 minutes before carving.

Orange and Tea-Marinated Turkey

Serves 8   Turkey just loves to be marinated, and this gingery orange and tea marinade makes for a moist and juicy bird. Make sure to marinate the turkey for at least 6 hours and preferably overnight. This marinade also works wonders with duck. *Note:* This recipe is designed for the smaller rotisserie; if you have the larger one and want to roast a 16-pound bird, double the marinade.

Orange-Tea Marinade

4 cups hot water

5 orange pekoe tea bags
   (Lipton is fine)

2 teaspoons peeled and
   grated fresh ginger

Grated zest of 1 navel orange

¼ cup orange juice

2 teaspoons salt

One 8- to 10-pound turkey

To make the marinade, in a large mixing bowl, pour the hot water over the tea bags and allow to steep for 10 minutes. Squeeze the tea bags and discard. Stir in the ginger, orange zest and juice, and salt. Allow the marinade to cool to room temperature.

Wash the turkey inside and out under cold running water and pat it dry. Remove any excess fat from the skin and cut off the wing tips; discard or save to make stock. Place the turkey in a 2-gallon zipper-top plastic bag and pour the cooled marinade over the turkey. Seal the bag, turn over gently to coat the turkey, and refrigerate for 6 hours or overnight.

Remove the turkey from the marinade, pat dry, and load onto the spit rod assembly. Truss according to the manufacturer's directions, or tie the legs together and tie another string around the body and wings so the wings don't flop around during cooking. Roast until an instant-read meat thermometer inserted into the thickest part of the thigh registers 175 degrees, about 12 minutes per pound.

Remove the turkey from the spit rod assembly, cover loosely with aluminum foil, and allow the turkey to rest for at least 15 to 20 minutes before carving.

Rotisserie Thanksgiving Turkey

Serves 8   **Every year I travel around the country teaching my Do-Ahead Thanksgiving class at sold-out cooking schools. The turkey is what students fear the most, when in fact it's the easiest part of the meal—you just set it and forget it. This turkey comes off the spit with a golden brown skin and juicy, flavorful meat.**

One 8- to 10-pound turkey
2 teaspoons salt
1 teaspoon freshly ground
    black pepper
5 strips bacon

Wash the turkey inside and out under cold running water and pat it dry. Remove any excess fat from the skin, cut off the wing tips, and discard or save the tips to make stock. Season inside and outside with the salt and pepper.

Load the turkey onto the spit rod assembly. Truss according to the manufacturer's directions, or tie the legs together and tie another string around the body and wings so the wings don't flop around during cooking. Wrap the bacon around the turkey, securing it in place with string. Roast until an instant-read meat thermometer inserted into the thickest part of the thigh registers 175 degrees, about 12 minutes per pound.

Remove the turkey from the spit rod, loosely cover with aluminum foil, and allow to rest for at least 15 to 20 minutes. Discard the bacon and carve the turkey.

Cilantro-Honey-Lime Turkey Breast

○ ● ○

Serves 8 **Although you can use this same treatment with a whole turkey or chicken, I like it best on a whole turkey breast, which sometimes needs a little flavor boost. Make sure to marinate the turkey for at least six hours before cooking.**

One 4- to 5-pound turkey breast

Orange-Cilantro Marinade

1/4 cup canola oil

2 tablespoons fresh lime juice

Grated zest of 1 orange

1 teaspoon ground cumin

1 teaspoon sweet paprika

2 cloves garlic, minced

Leaves from 1 bunch fresh cilantro, chopped

2 teaspoons salt

1 teaspoon freshly ground black pepper

Cilantro-Honey-Lime Baste

1/2 cup honey

2 tablespoons fresh lime juice

Leaves from 1/2 bunch fresh cilantro, chopped

Rinse the turkey breast under cold running water and pat dry.

In a 2-gallon zipper-top plastic bag, combine the marinade ingredients, stirring to blend. Place the turkey in the bag, seal it, and turn over gently to coat the turkey. Marinate the turkey in the refrigerator for at least 6 and up to 24 hours, turning the bag frequently.

Remove the turkey from the marinade and pat dry. Load the turkey onto the spit rod assembly by pushing the spit rods through the meaty end of the breast. Tie the turkey tightly against the spit rod assembly with cotton string, making sure there is no loose skin.

Stir together the baste ingredients. Prick the skin of the turkey all over with a knife, and baste the turkey generously with the mixture. Roast until an instant-read meat thermometer inserted into the thickest part of the thigh registers 175 degrees, about 12 minutes per pound. About 30 minutes before the turkey will be done, turn off the rotisserie, baste the turkey with the honey-lime baste, and restart the machine. Repeat 3 more times, about every 8 minutes.

Remove the turkey from the spit rod, cover loosely with aluminum foil, and allow to rest for 15 to 20 minutes before carving.

Parsley, Sage, Rosemary, and Thyme Turkey Breast

○─◉─○

Serves 8   Turkey breasts tend to be dry, but prepared in the rotisserie they are succulent and juicy. These herbs make a pretty pattern under the skin, and flavor the meat nicely.

One 4- to 5-pound turkey breast
2 teaspoons salt
1 teaspoon freshly ground black pepper
3 tablespoons olive oil
1/4 cup firmly packed fresh Italian parsley leaves
5 fresh sage leaves
5 sprigs fresh thyme
5 sprigs fresh rosemary

Wash the turkey breast under cold running water and pat dry. Rub the turkey all over with the salt and pepper. Brush the underside of the turkey with some of the olive oil, then, carefully lifting up the skin, slide some of the herbs underneath the skin in a pattern. Save any remaining herbs for garnish.

Load the turkey breast onto the spit rod assembly by pushing the spit rods through the meaty end of the breast. Tie the breast tightly against the spit rods with cotton string, making sure there is no loose skin. Rub the breast with the remaining olive oil. Roast until an instant-read meat thermometer inserted into the thickest part of the breast registers 175 degrees, about 12 minutes per pound.

Remove the turkey from the spit rods, cover loosely with aluminum foil, and allow to rest for 10 minutes before carving.

Turkey Breast in the Rotisserie

The complaint that most people have about turkey breast is that it is sometimes dry, but in the rotisserie, as it spins, it self-bastes and comes out moist and tender. To ensure a juicy and flavorful roast, I sometimes grind thyme, sage, and a little olive oil into a paste and slip it under the skin of the turkey breast, so that the oil will further baste the meat and protect it from drying out while it is turning. You can substitute other herbs that you like; for a south of the border kick, use cilantro and ground cumin; or try dried herbes de Provence for some French flair.

Dark Wing Duck

○ ● ○

Serves 4   **This juicy duck, with its dark and crispy skin, is a terrific example of how the rotisserie can melt the fat off any meal. Make sure to marinate the duck for at least 24 hours, so that the flavors will marry with the meat.**

One 3$^1/_2$- to 4-pound duck

Soy-Garlic Marinade

$^1/_2$ cup soy sauce

3 cloves garlic, mashed

2 tablespoons rice wine

1 teaspoon peeled and grated fresh ginger

$^1/_4$ cup sesame seeds, toasted (see below), for garnish

4 green onions, white and light green parts, chopped, for garnish

Wash the duck inside and out under cold running water and pat dry. Cut off the wing tips, remove as much excess fat as possible, and then pierce the skin all over with the tip of a paring knife. Place the duck in a 2-gallon zipper-top plastic bag.

In a small mixing bowl, combine the marinade ingredients, stirring to blend. Pour the marinade over the duck, seal the bag, and turn it over to coat the duck. Marinate in the refrigerator for at least 24 hours, turning occasionally.

Load the duck onto the spit rod assembly. Truss according to the manufacturer's directions or tie the legs together and tie string around the wings to keep them from flopping during roasting, and roast until an instant-read meat thermometer inserted into the thickest part of the thigh registers 175 degrees, about 15 minutes per pound.

Toasting Sesame Seeds

To toast sesame seeds, pour them into a nonstick skillet and place them over medium heat. Shake the pan several times so the seeds color evenly. It should take about 5 minutes for the seeds become a golden color. Remove from the pan immediately to stop the cooking, and cool the seeds. Store the seeds in an airtight container in the freezer for up to 2 months.

Remove the duck from the spit rod, cover loosely with aluminum foil, and allow to rest for 10 minutes before carving.

Smart Turn

Most ducks are sold frozen. Before beginning the recipe, defrost the duck, remove the giblets, wash, and pat dry.

Twirling Duck à l'Orange

Serves 4 **You won't ever have to go out again to enjoy this classic French dish–duck glazed beautifully with a sweet and pungent orange sauce. If you have a larger rotisserie, you can prepare two ducks at once to serve eight. Make sure to marinate the duck for 24 hours for optimum flavor.**

One 3¹/₂- to 4-pound duck
1¹/₂ teaspoons salt
¹/₂ teaspoon freshly ground
    black pepper
4 navel oranges
1¹/₂ cups beef broth
¹/₄ cup sugar
¹/₄ cup red wine vinegar
2 teaspoons cornstarch
1 tablespoon Madeira wine

Wash the duck inside and out under cold running water and pat dry. Remove as much excess fat as possible, and cut off the wing tips. Season the duck inside and out with the salt and pepper and cut tiny slits in the skin all over. Place the duck in a 2-gallon zipper-top plastic bag and refrigerate while making the sauce.

Remove the zest in strips from 2 of the oranges and juice them. Cut the remaining 2 oranges into ¹/₂-inch-thick slices for a garnish and refrigerate. Combine the orange zest and juice, beef broth, sugar, and vinegar in a nonreactive 1-quart saucepan. Bring to a boil, reduce the heat to medium-low, and simmer until the mixture begins to reduce and concentrate its flavor, about 7 minutes. Remove from the heat and allow to cool. Pour half of the sauce over the duck in the bag, seal, and turn the bag over to coat the duck. Marinate in the refrigerator for 24 hours, turning occasionally. Refrigerate the remaining sauce.

Remove the duck from the marinade, pat dry with paper towels, and load onto the spit rod assembly. Truss according to the manufacturer's directions or tie the legs together and tie another string around the body and wings to keep the wings from flopping around during roasting. Roast until an instant-read meat thermometer inserted into the thickest part of the thigh registers 175 degrees, about 15 minutes per pound.

Remove the duck from the spit rod assembly, cover loosely with aluminum foil, and allow to rest for 10 minutes before carving. While the duck is resting, remove the reserved sauce from the refrigerator, place in a small saucepan, and bring it to a boil. Combine the cornstarch with the wine and stir into the boiling sauce. Return the sauce to a boil and remove from the heat when it begins to come clear.

Carve the duck, garnish each serving with some of the reserved orange slices, and pour some of the sauce over the duck.

Pear and Port Wine Duck

Serves 4 Duck is delicious on the rotisserie and this particular duck, with its port wine and sweet pear basting sauce, got two thumbs up during testing. The sauce is also wonderful on pork and chicken. If you have a larger rotisserie, you can double the recipe.

Pear and Port Wine Basting Sauce

1 tablespoon butter
$^1/_2$ cup chopped shallots
$^1/_2$ cup port wine
$^1/_2$ cup chicken broth
1 cup pear nectar
$^1/_3$ cup firmly packed dark brown sugar
1 teaspoon salt
1$^1/_2$ teaspoons freshly ground black pepper
1 tablespoon balsamic vinegar

One 4- to 5-pound duck, trimmed of excess fat and brined for 4 to 6 hours (see page 30)

To make the sauce, in a small saucepan, melt the butter over medium heat. Add the shallots and cook, stirring, until translucent, about 5 minutes. Stir in the port, broth, pear nectar, brown sugar, salt, pepper, and vinegar. Bring the sauce to a boil, reduce the heat to medium-low, and simmer until reduced and thickened, about 30 minutes. Keep the sauce simmering on the stove while roasting and basting the duck. If you are not using the sauce immediately, it can be refrigerated for 5 days or frozen for up to 1 month.

Cut off the wing tips and truss the duck according to the manufacturer's directions or tie the legs together and tie string around the wings to keep them from flopping during roasting. Load the duck onto the spit rod, prick the skin all over with a sharp knife, and brush the duck with the basting sauce. Roast briefly, stopping the machine every 10 minutes or so to baste the duck, until an instant-read meat thermometer inserted into the thickest part of the thigh registers 175 degrees, about 15 minutes per pound.

Remove the duck from the spit rod, cover loosely with aluminum foil, and allow to rest for 10 to 15 minutes before carving. Serve with any remaining sauce, giving it a final vigorous boil before using.

Never Fail Duck

Serves 4   When I was a new bride and learning to cook, I found this recipe in a women's magazine; it was simple and delicious. The red currant jelly is a perfect complement to the rich duck meat. I've added a few things to this recipe over the years and discovered that it's terrific for the rotisserie. This baste is also delicious with pork or goose. If you have a larger rotisserie, you can double the recipe.

Red Currant Basting Sauce

2 tablespoons butter
1/2 cup chopped onion
2 tablespoons dry sherry
1 1/2 cups red currant jelly
2 tablespoons fresh lemon juice
1 teaspoon salt
1/2 teaspoon freshly ground black pepper
1 teaspoon dried thyme

One 4- to 5-pound duck, trimmed of excess fat and brined for 4 to 6 hours (see page 30)

To make the sauce, melt the butter in a small saucepan over medium heat, add the onion, and cook, stirring until softened, about 3 minutes. Add the sherry, jelly, lemon juice, salt, pepper, and thyme and bring the mixture to a boil. Reduce the heat to medium-low and simmer for 15 minutes. Keep the sauce simmering while roasting and basting the duck. If you are not using it right away, let cool to room temperature and refrigerate for up to 5 days or freeze for up to 1 month.

Rinse the duck, cut off the wing tips, and load onto the spit rod assembly. Truss according to the manufacturer's directions, or tie the legs together and tie another string around the body and wings so the wings don't flop around during cooking. Prick the skin of the duck all over with a sharp knife, and brush with some of the basting sauce. Roast until an instant-read meat thermometer inserted into the thickest part of the thigh registers 175 degrees, about 15 minutes per pound, turning the machine off every 10 minutes or so to baste the duck.

Remove the duck from the spit rod, cover loosely with aluminum foil, and allow to rest 10 to 15 minutes before carving. Serve with any remaining basting sauce on the side, after giving it a final vigorous boil.

Spinning Plum Goose

Serves 6 I tried several different recipes for goose cooked in a rotisserie and liked this one the best of all. Goose can only be prepared in the larger rotisserie; it is too big for the compact or junior size. Brining the goose for 6 to 8 hours helps to make it tender and juicy.

Plum-Apricot Basting Sauce

1 cup plum jam
$^1/_2$ cup apricot preserves
$^1/_4$ cup balsamic vinegar
1 teaspoon dried sage
$^3/_4$ teaspoon freshly ground black pepper

One 12-pound goose, brined for 6 to 8 hours (see page 30)

To make the basting sauce, heat the ingredients together in a small saucepan, stirring, until the jam and preserves are melted. Keep the sauce at a simmer while roasting and basting the goose.

Rinse the goose and prick the skin all over with a sharp knife. Remove any visible fat from under the skin, trim the wing tips, and load the goose onto the spit rod assembly. Truss according to the manufacturer's directions, or tie the legs together and tie another string around the body and wings so the wings don't flop around during cooking. Brush with the basting sauce, and roast until an instant-read meat thermometer inserted into the thickest part of the thigh registers 175 degrees and the juices run clear when the drumstick is pierced with a sharp knife, about 12 minutes per pound. During the last 30 minutes of cooking time, stop the rotisserie briefly to baste the bird 3 times.

Remove the goose from the spit rod, cover loosely with aluminum foil, and allow to rest for at least 15 minutes before carving. Serve the goose with any remaining basting sauce, after giving it a final vigorous boil.

Boursin-Stuffed Chicken Breasts

Serves 6 **Creamy Boursin cheese, tucked under the skin of chicken breast and stuffed inside the center, imparts the wonderful flavor of garlic and herbs. This easy meal can be prepped ahead of time, then popped into the rotisserie for a fantastic, 20-minute entrée.**

6 boneless chicken breast halves, skin left on
1 teaspoon salt
¹/₂ teaspoon freshly ground black pepper
One 4¹/₂-ounce package Boursin cheese
6 thin slices prosciutto
2 tablespoons butter, melted
2 teaspoons sweet paprika

Place the chicken breasts halves between two pieces of waxed paper, skin side down, and pound with a meat mallet until uniformly thick—½ to ¼ inch. Remove the plastic wrap and sprinkle each breast half with some of the salt and pepper. Turn each breast half over and push some of the Boursin cheese underneath the skin of the chicken. Turn over again so the skin side is down. Lay a piece of prosciutto about the size of the breast over the chicken, cutting it to fit, then top with 1 tablespoon of the cheese in the middle of the breast. Working from the wider end, fold the breast over the cheese, then fold in the sides of the chicken and roll into a

Poultry Pieces in the Rotisserie

Cooking poultry pieces in the grill basket of the rotisserie is simple, and the results are delicious. Make sure that none of the pieces extend outside the basket, and to keep them in place, tuck pieces of crumpled aluminum foil into any spaces where the pieces might drift while rotating. I recommend leaving the skin on most pieces, even if your diet doesn't permit you to eat the skin, because it will protect the meat and baste it. You can remove the skin after the meat is cooked. To test for doneness, stick the sharp point of a knife into the thickest part of the meat; if the juices coming out run clear and are not tinged with pink, it's ready to eat. If they are still pink, you will need to continue to cook the meat until the juices run clear. A meat thermometer inserted into the thickest part should register 175 degrees when the bird is ready to eat.

neat package. At this point, you can refrigerate the chicken for up to 24 hours, covered with plastic wrap, or freeze for 1 month.

Blend together the butter and paprika.

Coat the rotisserie basket with nonstick cooking spray. Arrange the stuffed chicken breasts in the basket, brush the skin with the paprika butter, and close the lid tightly. Load the basket onto the spit rod assembly and grill until the chicken is golden brown and cooked through, 15 to 20 minutes. Remove the chicken from the basket and serve immediately.

Variation

For a quick sauce, melt 2 tablespoons of butter in a small saucepan over medium heat. Add any remaining prosciutto scraps and 1 chopped shallot and cook, stirring, until the shallot is soft. Add any remaining Boursin, ¼ cup heavy cream, and ½ cup white wine. Stir until the cheese melts and the sauce bubbles. Pour over the chicken rolls and serve immediately.

Chicken Breasts Stuffed with Prosciutto and Basil

Serves 6   Here is an elegant dish that can be prepared ahead of time, then popped into the rotisserie basket for a quick spin. The chicken has the heavenly aroma of basil and the pungent taste of prosciutto, making it one of our favorites.

6 boneless chicken breast halves, skin left on

1 1/2 teaspoons salt

1/2 teaspoon freshly ground black pepper

1/2 cup packed fresh basil leaves

1/4 cup olive oil

1/4 pound paper-thin slices prosciutto

Place the chicken breasts halves between two pieces of waxed paper, skin side down, and pound with a meat mallet until uniformly thick—1/2 to 1/4 inch. Sprinkle all over with the salt and pepper.

Brush the basil leaves with some of the olive oil and slip the leaves under the skin of the chicken, forming a nice pattern. Turn the chicken skin side down on a board and lay a piece of prosciutto over the meat, trimming the prosciutto to fit. Starting at the wider end, roll up the chicken, folding in the sides and forming a nice tight package. You may refrigerate the chicken, covered with plastic wrap, for up to 24 hours. You shouldn't need to secure the chicken breasts with toothpicks because the grill basket will hold them tightly.

Coat the grill basket with nonstick cooking spray. Load the chicken into the basket and close the lid tightly. Load the basket onto the spit rod assembly and grill until the chicken is golden brown on the outside and no longer pink near the center, 25 to 30 minutes.

Remove the chicken from the basket and slice each breast on the diagonal into 3 pieces. Serve immediately.

Honey-Mustard Chicken

Serves 6   This is a sweet and spicy way to grill chicken drumsticks and thighs. You can buy honey mustard at your grocery store or make the dill-flavored baste that I use here. This sauce is also delicious on shrimp, salmon, and turkey kabobs. As with most sweet basting sauces, make sure to

baste only during the last 30 minutes of cooking time so that the sugar doesn't burn onto the chicken.

2½ pounds mixed chicken drumsticks and thighs (3 of each), or all drumsticks or thighs
1½ teaspoons salt
½ teaspoon freshly ground black pepper

Honey-Mustard Baste

1 cup Dijon mustard
2 teaspoons fresh lemon juice
½ cup honey
2 teaspoons dillweed

Sprinkle the chicken evenly with the salt and pepper.

Coat the rotisserie basket with nonstick cooking spray and load the chicken pieces into the basket, closing the lid tightly. Make sure that none of the chicken is sticking out of the basket and place crumpled aluminum foil in any spaces where the chicken might drift while rotating. Load the basket onto the spit rod assembly and grill for 20 minutes.

While the chicken is cooking, in a small mixing bowl, blend together the baste ingredients.

After the chicken has cooked for 20 minutes, stop the rotisserie and brush the chicken with the honey-mustard baste. Restart the rotisserie and continue cooking for 30 minutes more, stopping to baste 3 more times, about every 8 minutes. Check to make sure that the chicken is cooked all the way through by piercing a thigh or drumstick with a sharp knife. If the juices run clear, the chicken is done.

Remove the chicken from the basket and serve immediately.

Tuscan Chicken

Serves 6   My grandmother's kitchen was filled with many flavors from her native Italy, and this chicken was one of them. Marinated in red wine vinegar, garlic, and rosemary, it perfumes the house with a mouthwatering aroma. Recently

the grandchildren got together for a family reunion, and we reminisced about the love she put into her cooking and this delicious dish, which we call "Grandma's Chicken."

8 skinless, boneless chicken thighs

Rosemary-Garlic Marinade

6 cloves garlic, mashed

1 1/2 teaspoons salt

1/2 teaspoon freshly ground black pepper

1/4 cup olive oil

2 tablespoons fresh rosemary leaves or 2 teaspoons dried

1/4 cup red wine vinegar

Place the chicken in a 2-gallon zipper-top plastic bag.

In a small mixing bowl, stir together the marinade ingredients. Pour over the chicken, seal the bag, and turn over to coat the chicken. Marinate in the refrigerator for at least 1 and up to 3 hours.

Remove the chicken from the marinade and pat dry with paper towels. Coat the rotisserie basket with nonstick cooking spray. Arrange the chicken in the basket and place crumpled aluminum foil in any spaces where the chicken might drift while rotating. Close the lid tightly. Load onto the spit rod assembly and grill until the chicken is golden brown and cooked through, 25 to 30 minutes.

Remove the chicken from the basket and serve immediately.

Rotisserie Buffalo Wings with Maytag Blue Cheese Dressing

Serves 6   Everyone loves these spicy hot wings and the rotisserie keeps them moist and tender. Make sure to pack the wings fairly tightly into the basket and put crumpled aluminum foil in the corners so the wings don't peek out of the basket.

18 chicken wing drumettes
1¹/₂ teaspoons salt
1 cup Louisiana hot sauce
¹/₄ cup vegetable oil
Maytag Blue Cheese
Dressing (recipe follows)

Place the chicken in a 2-gallon zipper-top plastic bag. In a small mixing bowl, combine the salt, hot sauce, and oil, stirring to blend. Pour the mixture over the wings, seal the bag, and turn over to coat the chicken. Marinate in the refrigerator for at least 6 and up to 24 hours.

Coat the rotisserie basket with nonstick cooking spray. Remove the chicken from the marinade, drain, and arrange in the basket so that the wings fit snugly. Close the lid tightly and load the basket onto the spit rod assembly. Grill the chicken wings until golden brown, 20 to 25 minutes.

Remove from the basket and serve immediately with the dressing on the side for dipping.

Maytag Blue Cheese Dressing

Makes 2 cups   Traditional Buffalo wings are served with blue cheese dressing and celery sticks to put out the fire. Maytag blue cheese is made in the same state that gave us the Maytag repairman. The cheese is aged in caves in Iowa for six months.

1¹/₂ cups mayonnaise
2 tablespoons red wine
vinegar
1 tablespoon Worcestershire
sauce
1 cup crumbled Maytag or
other good-quality blue
cheese
¹/₂ teaspoon freshly ground
black pepper

In a small mixing bowl, combine the mayonnaise, vinegar, and Worcestershire, stirring to blend.

Fold in the blue cheese and pepper and refrigerate for at least 2 hours. The dressing will keep, covered, in the refrigerator for up to 5 days.

Variation

If you would like a thinner dressing, thin with a few tablespoons of heavy cream.

Spicy Teriyaki-Glazed Chicken Wings

Serves 6   These mahogany-colored chicken wings are a great appetizer, but you can also substitute larger chicken pieces or a whole chicken in this recipe. I find that children love to pick up the small drumettes and eat them for dinner, so if you have small fry at your house, stick with the wings.

2 pounds chicken wing
    drumettes
1 recipe Spicy Teriyaki Sauce
    (page 314)

Place the wings in a 2-gallon zipper-top plastic bag and pour the teriyaki sauce over them. Seal the bag, shake gently to coat the meat evenly, and refrigerate at least 4 and up to 24 hours.

Coat the rotisserie basket with nonstick cooking spray. Drain the wings and pack them in the basket, making sure that none are sticking out. Tuck small crumpled pieces of aluminum foil snugly into the corners to keep the wings from shifting during the cooking process. Load the basket onto the spit rod assembly and grill until the chicken is cooked through, 30 to 45 minutes.

Remove the chicken from the basket and serve immediately.

Hot Coconut Chicken Satay

Serves 6   A satay consists of little skewers of beef, chicken, or seafood marinated in flavors from the Pacific Rim. Peanut sauce is the traditional accompaniment.

1 pound boneless, skinless chicken breasts, cut into $1/4$-inch-thick strips

Hot Coconut Marinade

$1/4$ cup unsweetened coconut milk

2 tablespoons soy sauce

$1/2$ cup chopped fresh cilantro leaves

1 tablespoon canola oil

1 tablespoon fresh lime juice

1 tablespoon firmly packed dark brown sugar

6 shakes Tabasco sauce

$1/4$ cup chopped fresh cilantro leaves for garnish

Ginger Peanut Sauce for dipping (recipe follows)

Place the chicken in a zipper-top plastic bag.

In a small mixing bowl, combine the marinade ingredients. Pour over the chicken in the bag, seal, turn over the bag to coat the chicken. Marinate in the refrigerator for at least 1 and up to 4 hours.

Remove the chicken from the marinade and pat dry. Thread the chicken onto the kabob rods and load onto the spit rod assembly with the spring ends on the right side. Grill until the chicken is cooked through, 5 to 8 minutes.

Remove the chicken from the skewers and serve, garnished with the ¼ cup of cilantro and accompanied by the dipping sauce.

Ginger Peanut Sauce

Makes about 3 cups   **This also tastes great with beef or seafood satay, or even as a sauce for noodles.**

1 cup chicken broth
$1/2$ cup unsweetened
   coconut milk
1 cup smooth peanut butter
$1/4$ cup firmly packed light
   brown sugar
$1/4$ cup soy sauce
2 teaspoons peeled and
   grated fresh ginger
6 shakes Tabasco sauce

In a 2-quart saucepan, stir together all the ingredients, and bring the mixture to a boil. Reduce the heat to medium-low, and simmer for 10 minutes, stirring until smooth. The sauce can be refrigerated, covered, for up to 3 days. To serve, reheat, thinning with additional chicken broth, if necessary. Or use it straight out of the refrigerator—it tastes good cold.

Rotisserie Kabobs and Satays

Skewers of poultry grilled on the kabob rods are not only easy, they are fun to make and even better to eat! When loading the kabob rods, make sure to leave about $1/2$ inch between pieces of food because they need a little air to circulate between them so that each one browns evenly. If you are doing veggies and meat at the same time, put the veggies on their own skewer; that way, if they cook faster, you can remove them before the meat is done. The best vegetables to grill on the kabob rods are red onion; green, red, and yellow peppers cut into 1-inch squares; and mushrooms. Make sure to load the kabob rods with the spring ends on the right, so that the kabobs will turn while cooking.

Grilled Pineapple-Cilantro Chicken Tenders

Serves 6 Chicken tenders are those little flaps of muscle underneath the chicken breast. They have a small tendon that runs through them lengthwise, which is easy to remove, and they are delicious when grilled on skewers. You can also try marinating chicken tenders in Spicy Teriyaki Sauce (page 314), bottled barbecue sauce, Honey-Mustard Baste (page 51), or Louisiana hot sauce for boneless Buffalo chicken "wings."

1 pound chicken tenders, tendons removed

Hot and Sweet Marinade

¼ cup pineapple juice
2 tablespoons vegetable oil
¼ cup chopped fresh cilantro leaves
2 cloves garlic, minced
2 tablespoons seeded and minced jalapeño
1 teaspoon salt
½ teaspoon freshly ground black pepper

Put the tenders in a zipper-top plastic bag.

In a small mixing bowl, combine the marinade ingredients. Pour the marinade over the chicken, seal the bag, and turn over to coat the chicken. Marinate in the refrigerator for up to 2 hours.

Remove the chicken from the marinade, drain, and thread onto the kabob rods. Load onto the spit rod assembly with the spring ends on the right side. Grill the chicken until cooked through, 5 to 8 minutes.

Remove from the skewers and serve immediately.

Calypso Jerk Chicken Kabobs

Serves 6   These kabobs are sprinkled with aromatic jerk seasoning, then basted with mango to give them a sweet and spicy flavor.

2 pounds boneless, skinless chicken breasts, cut into 1-inch chunks

$^1/_2$ cup Jerk Seasoning Rub (page 290)

Mango-Lime Glaze

1 cup mango purée (see Smart Turn)

2 tablespoons fresh lime juice

2 teaspoons light brown sugar

$^1/_4$ cup chopped fresh cilantro leaves for garnish

Sprinkle the chicken pieces with the jerk rub and toss to coat evenly. Thread the chicken onto the kabob rods, leaving ½ inch between each piece to allow for air circulation, and load onto the spit rod assembly with the spring ends on the right side. Grill for 10 minutes.

While the chicken is cooking, make the glaze: In a small saucepan, combine the ingredients and stir until the mixture comes to a boil. Reduce the heat to low and simmer while you grill and baste the kabobs.

After 10 minutes of cooking time, stop the rotisserie and brush the chicken with the glaze. Restart the rotisserie and continue to cook for 20 to 25 minutes more, stopping the rotisserie briefly 2 more times and brushing the kabobs with the sauce. Slash a piece of chicken to see if there is any pink left in the middle and remove the kabobs if they are cooked through.

Serve drizzled with some of the remaining glaze (after a vigorous boil) and garnished with the chopped cilantro.

Smart Turn

Two ripe mangoes, peeled, seeded, and puréed in the food processor, should yield 1 cup of purée. Some grocers sell frozen mango chunks. For a thinner sauce, you can substitute 1 cup mango nectar, which you will find in the juice aisle at your supermarket.

Miso-Glazed Shiitake Chicken Kabobs

Serves 6 **Meaty shiitake mushrooms skewered with miso-marinated chicken will make a real treat for your family.**

2 pounds boneless, skinless chicken breasts, cut into 1-inch chunks

Miso-Ginger Marinade

1/2 cup rice wine
1/4 cup canola oil
1/3 cup light-colored miso paste
1 tablespoon sugar
2 teaspoons peeled and grated fresh ginger

1/2 pound fresh shiitake mushrooms, cleaned and stems removed
1/2 red onion, cut into 1-inch pieces

Place the chicken in a 2-gallon zipper-top plastic bag.

In a small mixing bowl, combine the marinade ingredients. Pour the mixture over the chicken, seal the bag, and shake gently to coat the chicken. Marinate in the refrigerator for at least 2 and up to 6 hours.

Remove the chicken from the marinade and pat dry. Pour the marinade into a small saucepan and bring to a vigorous boil. Reduce the heat to medium-low and simmer while getting the kabobs ready.

Thread the chicken, mushrooms, and onion onto the kabob rods in that order, leaving 1/2 inch between each to allow for air circulation. Repeat until each rod is filled. Brush each skewer with some of the marinade and load the skewers onto the spit rod assembly with the spring ends on the right side. Return the marinade to a vigorous boil, then lower the heat and simmer. Grill the kabobs until the chicken is no longer pink inside, about 30 to 35 minutes, turning off the machine briefly a few times and brushing the chicken with the marinade.

Remove the kabobs from the skewers and serve immediately.

Chicken Kabobs Provençal

Serves 6   The sunny flavors of Provence infuse these tender chicken morsels, which are great served with a crisp white wine and a side of Fire-Roasted Caponata (page 311).

2 pounds boneless, skinless chicken breasts, cut into 1-inch chunks

Provençal Marinade

¹/₄ cup olive oil

2 tablespoons red wine vinegar

1 tablespoon fresh lemon juice

2 tablespoons dried herbes de Provence

1 teaspoon salt

¹/₂ teaspoon freshly ground black pepper

Place the chicken in a 2-gallon zipper-top plastic bag.

In a small mixing bowl, whisk together the marinade ingredients. Pour over the chicken, seal the bag, and shake gently to coat the chicken. Marinate in the refrigerator for at least 2 and up to 6 hours.

Remove the chicken from the marinade, pat dry, and thread onto the kabob rods, leaving ½ inch between each piece to allow for air circulation. Load the kabob rods onto the spit rod assembly, making sure the spring ends are on the right. Grill until the chicken is no longer pink in the center, 30 to 35 minutes.

Remove the chicken from the skewers and serve immediately.

Curried Chicken Kabobs

Serves 6 **This sweet curried chicken dish is really fun to serve with condiments such as chutney, coconut, chopped peanuts, chopped green onions, chopped cilantro, and Chile Peanut Dipping Sauce (page 149).**

2 pounds boneless, skinless chicken breasts, cut into 1-inch chunks

Sweet Curry Marinade

1/2 cup buttermilk

2 tablespoons firmly packed brown sugar

2 teaspoons curry powder

Pinch of cayenne

1/4 teaspoon ground coriander

Place the chicken in a 2-gallon zipper-top plastic bag.

In a small mixing bowl, stir together the marinade ingredients. Pour over the chicken, seal the bag, and shake gently to coat the chicken. Marinate in the refrigerator for at least 2 and up to 6 hours.

Remove the chicken from the marinade and pat dry. Thread the chicken onto the kabob rods, leaving 1/2 inch between each piece to allow for air circulation. Load the kabobs onto the spit rod assembly with the spring ends on the right side, and grill until the chicken is no longer pink in the center, 30 to 35 minutes.

Remove the chicken from the skewers and serve immediately.

Mango Madness Turkey Kabobs

Serves 6   The mango barbecue sauce for these kabobs turns good old turkey into a tropical feast! You can use chicken in place of the turkey, and the sauce also works well with shrimp.

2 pounds turkey tenderloin, cut into 1-inch pieces
2 tablespoons vegetable oil
1 teaspoon salt
$^1/_2$ teaspoon freshly ground black pepper

Mango Madness Barbecue Sauce

1 tablespoon vegetable oil
$^1/_4$ cup chopped onion
1 teaspoon garlic salt
1 teaspoon ground ginger
$^1/_4$ cup rice vinegar, red wine vinegar, or white wine vinegar
1 cup ketchup
1 cup mango purée (see Smart Turn, page 58)
1 tablespoon Worcestershire sauce
Pinch of cayenne pepper

Thread the turkey onto the kabob rods, leaving $^1/_2$ inch between each piece for air circulation. Brush with the vegetable oil and sprinkle with the salt and pepper. Load the skewers on the spit rod assembly with the spring ends on the right, and grill until the meat is cooked through, 20 to 25 minutes.

Make the sauce while the turkey is cooking. Heat the vegetable oil in a small skillet over medium heat, add the onion, and cook, stirring, until almost translucent, about 5 minutes. Add the remaining ingredients and bring the mixture to a boil. Reduce the heat to medium-low and simmer for 5 minutes.

Brush the sauce on the kabobs 2 or 3 times during the last 5 minutes of cooking, stopping the machine briefly each time. Remove the turkey from the skewers and serve with any remaining sauce (after a vigorous boil).

Pesto Chicken Burgers

Serves 6   Ground chicken is a leaner alternative to beef, but it tends be dry when made into a burger. The olive oil in the pesto moistens these burgers and gives them a wonderful flavor. They are great for a midweek dinner. Dress them up with condiments like sun-dried tomatoes and fresh mozzarella and serve them on crusty rolls.

2 pounds ground chicken
$\frac{1}{2}$ cup Basil Pesto (page 19) or store-bought pesto
$\frac{1}{4}$ cup dry bread crumbs
$\frac{1}{2}$ teaspoon freshly ground black pepper

In a large mixing bowl, mix together the chicken, pesto, bread crumbs, and pepper. Form the mixture into 6 patties about $\frac{1}{2}$ inch thick. Refrigerate the patties until ready to cook, up to 12 hours.

Coat the rotisserie basket with nonstick cooking spray, load the patties into the basket, and close the lid tightly. Load the basket onto the spit rod assembly and grill the burgers until cooked through, 15 to 18 minutes.

Remove from the basket and serve immediately.

Baste Your Way to Greatness

Bastes and barbecue sauces can make the difference between a ho-hum dinner and a five-star meal. Basting sauces should be boiled vigorously for a few minutes, then kept warm while you are basting the raw poultry. Make sure to boil the basting sauce again before serving with the finished dish, or set some aside for the sauce before you begin basting.

Turkey Club Burgers

Serves 6   **Turkey, bacon, and sun-dried tomatoes combine to make a great burger for a Sunday dinner. The bacon adds a smoky flavor and helps to moisten the turkey.**

2 pounds ground turkey
3 strips bacon, finely chopped
1/4 cup oil-packed sun-dried tomatoes, drained
2 green onions, chopped
1 large egg, beaten
1 cup fresh bread crumbs
6 hamburger buns
6 lettuce leaves
1 medium-size ripe tomato, sliced

Place the turkey in a large mixing bowl, stir in the bacon, sun-dried tomatoes, green onions, egg, and bread crumbs, and continue stirring until well blended. Form the mixture into 6 patties 3/4 inch thick.

Coat the rotisserie basket with nonstick cooking spray, load the patties into the basket, close the lid tightly, and load the basket onto the spit rod assembly. Grill the burgers until cooked through, 12 to 15 minutes.

Remove from the basket and serve on buns with lettuce and tomato.

No Fowl Play Here—Perfect Burgers in the Rotisserie

Poultry has a tendency to dry out, so if you decide to do burgers in the grill basket, make sure to compensate for the dryness by adding some type of fat to the burger mixture, such as ground bacon or mayonnaise, or mix in an egg. The fat will drain off as the burgers cook, and you will end up with a nice, moist burger. Burgers fit well in the grill basket and they can be made up ahead of time and refrigerated until you are ready to cook them.

Moo and Ewe

Imagine a rolled rib roast cooking on a spit. The meat is succulent and juicy inside, while the outside of the roast is crusted with roasted garlic and black peppercorns. Life doesn't get much better than that! The meats you choose to cook on the rotisserie should be tender cuts, because they cook from the outside in. So, cook rib-eye, sirloin, tenderloin, and ground beef and save the chuck roast and round steaks for the slow cooker.

Rolled boneless leg of lamb and racks of lamb are crusted, succulent, juicy, and tender when cooked in the rotisserie. Burgers, steaks, and lamb chops can be cooked in the basket attachment, leaving you free to attend to other part of the meal. The drippings from roasts and other meats are caught in a small drip pan and can be added to gravy or Au Jus (page 284) at the end of the cooking time.

For the most part, roasts, steaks, and chops can be seasoned with your favorite herbs and spices, then turned on the rotisserie according to the manufacturer's directions.

Moo and Ewe

Beef and lamb can be seasoned with any of the following pantry items when you are in a hurry and need to prepare dinner quickly. You can also try any of these no-brainers in ground beef or lamb burgers to perk up the flavor.

Spicy No-Brainers

- Seasoned Salt (page 285)
- Garlic salt
- Mrs. Dash (any flavor)
- Cavender's Greek seasoning
- Old Bay seasoning
- Creole Seasoning Rub (page 287)
- Dry soup mixes, such as Lipton's Beefy Onion, Onion, Fiesta Red Pepper with Herb, and Ranch Style and Knorr's Tomato Beef, Tomato Basil, and Leek Soup

Saucy No-Brainers

- Pesto (sun-dried tomato or basil, page 17 or 19)
- Bottled teriyaki sauce or Spicy Teriyaki Sauce (page 314) or Top Secret Teriyaki Sauce (page 315)
- Bottled barbecue sauce or homemade (see pages 319–324)
- Bottled Italian salad dressing
- Bottled Italian salad dressing mixed with an equal amount of soy sauce
- Bottled Caesar salad dressing
- Worcestershire sauce
- Garlic oil
- Dijon mustard

Cooking Beef, Veal, and Lamb Perfectly

Use an instant-read meat thermometer stuck into the thickest part of the meat and these suggested temperatures to cook your meat to perfection.

Internal Temperature	Degree of Doneness
140 degrees	Rare
145 degrees	Medium-rare
150 degrees	Medium
170 degrees	Well done

Tips for a Perfect Rotisserie Roast

Whether it's a prime rib roast or rack of lamb, you will need to try it on your spit rod assembly to make sure that the bones won't touch the heating element as the meat rotates. The compact model may be too small inside to turn a rack of lamb with long bones, or a prime rib with a bone, so make sure to check it out. If your roast is too big, then I suggest that you cut it off the bone; just follow the natural curvature of the meat against the bone with a very sharp knife. Tie the meat, then arrange it on the spit rod assembly. This is why I recommend seasoning the meat after you get it onto the spit rods; if you need to take it off again and bone it, you won't lose any of the seasonings.

Manufacturers recommend that you remove meat from the refrigerator about 30 minutes before you are ready to roast it so that it will come to room temperature. That way the rotisserie doesn't have to heat up the cold meat before roasting.

Herbed Roasted Tenderloin of Beef

Serves 6 to 8   Many of my students complain that filet is expensive, but the good news is that there is absolutely no waste on a filet. That said, the filet needs a little seasoning before it's roasted because there is no fat to flavor the meat. This filet is marinated, then turned on the rotisserie for a mouthwatering main course. You can roast the filet ahead of time, then serve it cold, if you like. It's great for holiday buffets.

Herb Marinade

¹/₃ cup olive oil
2 tablespoons red wine
   vinegar
¹/₄ cup soy sauce
4 cloves garlic, minced
1 teaspoon dried thyme
¹/₂ teaspoon dried sage
1 bay leaf
¹/₂ teaspoon freshly ground
   black pepper

One 3-pound beef tenderloin

In a small bowl, whisk together the marinade ingredients.

Place the roast in a 2-gallon zipper-top plastic bag and pour the marinade over the roast. Seal the bag, and turn it over to coat the roast. Marinate in the refrigerator for at least 8 and up to 24 hours.

When ready to cook, remove the roast from the marinade and pat dry. Load the roast onto the spit rod assembly, tying it in place if necessary. Roast until it reaches your preferred degree of doneness when tested with an instant-read meat thermometer, about 18 minutes per pound for medium-rare.

Remove the roast from the spit rod, cover loosely with foil, and allow to rest for 10 to 15 minutes before carving.

Smart Turn

Any meat that has been cooked with dry heat, such as in the rotisserie, will need to rest for at least 10 minutes before carving. This will ensure that the meat holds its juices and stays tender. Cover the meat loosely with aluminum foil, and set it aside; this will give you time for any last minute kitchen chores, such as making gravy or reheating veggies.

Beef tenderloin is simple to prepare in the rotisserie: there is no bone to get in the way and very little fat. Because of the absence of fat to baste it, though, tenderloin needs a little help in the flavor department and benefits from marinating. Here are a few marinades that work well with tenderloin, as well as beef kabobs.

Merlot Marinade   Makes about 2 cups

Hearty red wine will help to give your tenderloin a robust taste.

1 cup Merlot
1/4 cup olive oil
4 cloves garlic, peeled
2 teaspoons dried thyme
1 1/2 teaspoons salt
1/2 teaspoon freshly ground black pepper

In a small mixing bowl, whisk together all the ingredients.

Marinate the beef in the refrigerator for at least 6 and up to 24 hours. Drain and roast as directed on page 69.

Vidalia Onion Marinade   Makes about 3 cups

Sweet Vidalia onions mellow in red wine and balsamic vinegar to provide your tenderloin with a sweet and spicy flavor.

4 medium-size Vidalia onions, coarsely
    chopped
1 1/2 teaspoons salt
1/2 teaspoon freshly ground black pepper
1/2 cup olive oil
1 1/2 cups red wine
1/3 cup balsamic vinegar
1/4 cup firmly packed dark brown sugar
2 tablespoons fresh rosemary leaves,
    chopped

Place the onions in a medium-size mixing bowl and stir in the remaining ingredients.

Marinate the beef in the refrigerator for at least 6 hours or overnight. Drain and roast as directed on page 69.

Arugula Marinade   Makes about 2 cups

Spicy arugula and basil flavor this marinade, which is also terrific with chicken and pork.

3 cloves garlic, peeled
1/2 cup coarsely chopped onion
1 1/2 cups arugula
1/2 cup packed fresh basil leaves
1/2 cup olive oil
1/4 cup rice vinegar or white vinegar
1 teaspoon salt
1/2 teaspoon freshly ground black pepper

In a food processor, process the garlic, onion, arugula, and basil together until chopped. Add the remaining ingredients and process again until smooth.

Marinate the beef in the refrigerator for at least 4 hours up to 12 hours. Drain and roast as directed on page 69.

Lone Star Spit-Roasted Beef

Serves 6   A sirloin roast covered in spices is a great dinner from the rotisserie. The chiles in the rub give the beef a mellow, smoky outside, while the inside is tender and juicy.

One 3^1/$_3$- to 4-pound sirloin roast

^{1}/$_4$ cup Lone Star Rotisserie Rub (recipe follows)

Rub the beef all over with the rub, cover with plastic wrap, and refrigerate for at least 6 and up to 24 hours.

Bring the roast to room temperature and load onto the spit rod assembly, keeping the meat evenly distributed on the rods. Tie the roast if there are any pieces that dangle. Roast until it reaches your preferred degree of doneness when tested with an instant-read meat thermometer, about 18 minutes per pound for medium-rare.

Remove the roast from the spit rods, cover loosely with aluminum foil, and allow to rest for 10 to 15 minutes before carving.

Lone Star Rotisserie Rub

Makes ^{1}/$_2$ cup   A little kick of chili powder and cayenne gives this Texas-style rub a lot of personality. Use on chicken, beef, or pork.

^{1}/$_4$ cup chili powder

2 tablespoons kosher salt

2 tablespoons firmly packed light brown sugar

^{1}/$_2$ teaspoon cayenne pepper

1 tablespoon ground cumin

2 teaspoons garlic powder

1 teaspoon dry mustard

Combine the ingredients in an airtight jar. Store, tightly covered, in a cool, dry place for up to 6 months.

Santa Maria Barbecue

Serves 6   Here in the West we have a tradition called Santa Maria barbecue, which is a tri tip, or triangle sirloin roast, that is dry rubbed for flavor, then cooked over an open flame. It's usually served with guacamole, tortillas, sour cream, salsas, and refried beans. The rotisserie does a great job of cooking this tasty roast; you can do two at one time on the large rotisserie.

Two 1-pound tri tip or sirloin tip roasts, tied together (see Smart Turn)

Santa Fe Spice Rub

4 cloves garlic, mashed
1 teaspoon sweet paprika
1 teaspoon salt
1/2 teaspoon freshly ground black pepper
1/2 teaspoon ground cumin
1/2 teaspoon chili powder
2 tablespoons olive oil

Place the roast on a piece of plastic wrap that is twice the size of the roast. In a small mixing bowl, stir together the rub ingredients. Rub the mixture all over the roast, roll the roast up in the plastic wrap, and refrigerate overnight.

Load the roast onto the spit rod assembly and roast until it reaches your preferred degree of doneness when tested with an instant-read meat thermometer, about 15 minutes per pound for medium-rare.

Remove the roast from the spit rod, cover loosely with aluminum foil, and allow to rest for 10 minutes before carving. Remove the strings from the meat and slice on the diagonal against the grain into thin slices.

Smart Turn

To tie the roasts together, lay one on a flat surface with the pointed end on your left. Lay the other roast on top of the first roast so that base of the triangle is over the pointed end of the bottom roast. Beginning at one end, roll the roasts together and tie them tightly (see Figures 1 and 2, below).

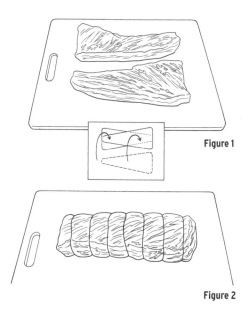

Figure 1

Figure 2

Roasted Garlic Prime Rib Roast

Serves 6 to 8   This prime rib roast, crusted in garlic and spices, is a delicious entree when cooked in the rotisserie, as it self bastes and retains its juices. Use the drippings in the pan to make Au Jus (page 284) and serve with Garlic Smashed Potatoes (page 342).

6 cloves garlic, peeled

2 teaspoons salt

1 teaspoon freshly ground
black pepper

One 4- to 5-pound bone-in
prime rib roast

Place the garlic in a small mixing bowl and mash with the salt and pepper until it forms a paste. Cut several slits in the fat of the roast and push some of the paste into the slits. Rub the rest of the paste over the roast.

Load the roast onto the spit rod assembly, starting at the meaty end of the roast. Maneuver the rods between the bones, keeping the meat evenly distributed on the rods. Roast until the meat reaches your preferred degree of doneness when tested with an instant-read meat thermometer; 18 minutes per pound for rare (internal temperature of 140 degrees), 20 minutes per pound for medium (160 degrees), and 22 minutes per pound for well done (which I don't recommend, as the meat will be dry and tough; 170 degrees).

Remove the meat from the spit rod, cover loosely with aluminum foil, and allow to rest for 15 minutes before carving. To carve the roast, slice along the bones to remove them, then place the roast on a cutting board and cut into ½-inch-thick slices.

Creole Mustard-Crusted Rib Roast

Serves 6 to 8　Spicy Creole mustard and seasonings give this roast a nice crispy crust, as well as flavoring the meat.

¼ cup Creole Seasoning Rub
(page 287)

½ cup Creole mustard or
whole-grain mustard

One 4- to 5-pound bone-in
prime rib roast

In a small mixing bowl, combine the seasoning and mustard, stirring to blend.

Make slits all over the roast and spread the mustard mixture all over the roast. Cover tightly with plastic wrap and refrigerate for at least 12 hours or overnight.

Remove the roast from the refrigerator 30 minutes before you are ready to begin cooking. Load the roast onto the spit rod assembly, starting at the meaty end of the roast. Maneuver the rods between the bones, keeping the meat evenly distributed on the rods. Roast until it reaches your preferred degree of doneness when tested with an instant-read meat thermometer, 18 minutes per pound for rare (internal temperature of 140 degrees), 20 minutes per pound for medium (160 degrees), and 22 minutes per pound for well done (which I don't recommend, as the meat will be dry and tough).

Remove the roast from the spit rod, cover loosely with aluminum foil, and allow to rest for at least 15 minutes before carving.

Garlicky Lemon Pepper Prime Rib

Serves 6 to 8   **The bright flavor of lemon zest combined with coarsely ground black pepper gives this roast a terrific flavor. This rub works well with chicken and pork as well.**

Garlicky Lemon Pepper Rub

Grated zest of 2 lemons
$1/4$ cup coarsely cracked
     black peppercorns
$1^1/2$ teaspoons salt
1 teaspoon sweet paprika
$1/4$ cup olive oil
4 cloves garlic, minced

One 4- to 5-pound bone-in
     prime rib roast

In a small mixing bowl, combine the rub ingredients.

Load the roast onto the spit rod, starting at the meaty end of the roast. Maneuver the rods between the bones, keeping the meat evenly distributed on the rods. Make slits all over the roast and spread the rub evenly over the meat. Roast until it reaches your preferred degree of doneness when tested with an instant-read meat thermometer, 18 minutes per pound for rare (internal temperature of 140 degrees), 20 minutes per pound for medium (160 degrees), and 22 minutes per pound for well done (which I don't recommend, as the meat will be dry and tough; 170 degrees).

Remove the roast from the spit rod, cover loosely with aluminum foil, and allow to rest for at least 15 minutes before carving.

Lemon-Thyme Roasted Veal

Serves 6   Although veal can be expensive, it makes a delicious dinner when cooked in the rotisserie. Here small slits in the meat are stuffed with piquant lemon zest and savory fresh thyme. Season the meat the night before to give the flavors a chance to permeate the meat.

Lemon-Thyme Rub

1½ teaspoons salt

½ teaspoon freshly ground black pepper

2 cloves garlic, minced

Leaves from 6 sprigs fresh thyme

Grated zest of 1 lemon

One 3-pound boneless rolled veal leg or shoulder roast

2 tablespoons olive oil

In a small mixing bowl, stir together the rub ingredients. Make 8 slits in the roast about ½ inch deep. Push the seasoning mixture into the slits. Rub the roast with the olive oil, cover with plastic wrap, and refrigerate overnight.

Load the roast onto the spit rod assembly and tie it securely, if necessary. Roast about 15 minutes per pound for medium, or until an instant-read meat thermometer inserted in the thickest part registers 150 degrees. (The middle should still be pink, but not red.)

Remove the roast from the rod, cover loosely with aluminum foil, and allow to rest for 10 minutes. Remove the string from the roast and carve. Any juices in the drip pan can be used to make an Au Jus (page 284).

Tarragon-Dijon Rolled Veal Shoulder Roast

Serves 6   Veal cooked on the rotisserie can be a wonderful meal for your family. This rolled shoulder is fragrant with Dijon mustard, garlic, and tarragon leaves, blended and spread all over the roast. You can generally buy veal shoulder already boned and rolled, but it's not too difficult to do it yourself.

Tarragon-Dijon Slather

$1/2$ cup Dijon mustard
2 tablespoons olive oil
4 cloves garlic, minced
$1^1/2$ teaspoons salt
$1/2$ teaspoon freshly ground black pepper
2 tablespoons fresh tarragon leaves

One 3-pound boneless rolled veal shoulder roast

In a small mixing bowl, combine the slather ingredients, stirring to blend. Spread the mixture all over the roast, cover tightly with plastic wrap, and marinate in the refrigerator for at least 8 hours or overnight.

Load the veal onto the spit rod assembly and roast about 15 minutes per pound for medium, or until an instant-read meat thermometer inserted into the thickest part of the meat registers 150 degrees. (The middle should still be pink, but not red.)

Remove the roast from the spit rod, cover loosely with aluminum foil, and allow to rest for 15 minutes before carving.

Herb-Crusted Leg of Lamb

Makes 6 servings   Fragrant with garlic and herbs, this roast develops a delicious crust when cooked in the rotisserie.

Garlic-Herb Paste

4 cloves garlic, peeled

2 tablespoons fresh
    rosemary leaves

1 tablespoon fresh thyme
    leaves

2 teaspoons salt

1 teaspoon freshly ground
    black pepper

2 tablespoons olive oil

One 3-pound boneless rolled
    leg of lamb, marinated in
    Garlic Marinade (page
    79) for 6 hours

Place the paste ingredients in a food processor, mini-chopper, or mortar and process or mash together with a pestle until it forms a paste. Smear the paste over the lamb, making sure to cover the entire roast.

Load the roast onto the spit rod assembly and cook for 15 minutes per pound for medium, or until an instant-read meat thermometer inserted into the thickest part registers 155 degrees.

Remove the roast from the spit rod assembly and let it rest for 10 to 15 minutes, loosely covered with aluminum foil. Remove the string and carve the roast. Any drippings in the rotisserie pan can be used to make an Au Jus (page 284).

Moroccan-Style Roast Leg of Lamb

Makes 6 servings   Sweet and pungent spices will transport you to the Casbah while this roast is turning on your rotisserie.

Sweet Moroccan Spice Paste

3 cloves garlic, minced

2 tablespoons firmly packed light brown sugar

$1/2$ teaspoon sweet paprika

$1/4$ teaspoon ground coriander

$1/4$ teaspoon ground cumin

2 tablespoons olive oil

One 3-pound boneless rolled leg of lamb, marinated in Garlic Marinade (see below) for 6 hours

In a small mixing bowl, combine the paste ingredients. Rub the mixture over the lamb, coating it well.

Load the lamb onto the spit rod assembly and cook for 15 minutes per pound for medium, or until an instant-read meat thermometer inserted into the thickest part registers 155 degrees.

Remove the roast from the spit rod assembly and allow to rest for 10 to 15 minutes, loosely covered with aluminum foil, before carving.

Marinating Rolled Roast Leg of Lamb

A rolled leg of lamb roast—sold in the supermarket tied and ready to twirl—is terrific on the rotisserie; you literally set it and forget it for about an hour. I recommend marinating the lamb in this red wine vinegar mixture first for about six hours before proceeding with the recipe of your choice.

Garlic Marinade for Leg of Lamb   Makes $3/4$ cup

$1/2$ cup olive oil

$1/4$ cup red wine vinegar

4 cloves garlic, minced

1 teaspoon salt

$1/2$ teaspoon freshly ground black pepper

In a small mixing bowl, stir together the marinade ingredients. Pour over the lamb, seal the bag, and turn over to coat the roast. Marinate the lamb in the refrigerator for at least 6 and up to 24 hours, occasionally turning over the bag.

Remove the lamb from the marinade and pat dry. Proceed with the rest of your recipe.

Santa Fe-Style Rolled Leg of Lamb

Makes 6 servings   **The flavors of the Southwest permeate this delectable roast. Serve it fajita style, sliced thinly and wrapped in tortillas. Accompany with Salsa Fresca (page 297).**

Chile-Lime Paste

¹/₄ cup olive oil

¹/₂ cup finely chopped fresh
   cilantro leaves

1 dried ancho chile, crushed

2 tablespoons fresh lime
   juice

5 cloves garlic, minced

2 teaspoons ground cumin

2 tablespoons firmly packed
   light brown sugar

One 3-pound boneless rolled
   leg of lamb

In a small mixing bowl, blend together the paste ingredients. Remove the string from the roast and spread the roast out flat on a cutting board. Spread half of the paste over the roast, roll the roast up, and spread the rest of the paste over the outside. Tie with cotton string. Cover the roast with plastic wrap and refrigerate for at least 6 and up to 12 hours.

Remove the lamb from the refrigerator, unwrap it, and load onto the spit rod assembly. Roast for 15 minutes per pound for medium, or until an instant-read meat thermometer inserted into the thickest part registers 155 degrees.

Remove the roast from the spit rod and allow it to rest for 10 to 15 minutes, loosely covered with aluminum foil, before carving.

Lemon-Rosemary Rolled Leg of Lamb

Makes 6 servings   **Infused with the sunny flavors of the Mediterranean, this roast pairs well with rice pilaf and Cucumber-Yogurt Sauce (page 317).**

Mediterranean Marinade

Grated zest of 2 lemons

2 tablespoons fresh lemon juice

1/2 cup olive oil

6 cloves garlic, minced

2 tablespoons chopped fresh rosemary leaves

1 1/2 teaspoons salt

1 teaspoon freshly ground black pepper

One 3-pound boneless rolled leg of lamb

In a small mixing bowl, combine the marinade ingredients. Untie the lamb and place it in a 2-gallon zipper-top plastic bag. Pour the marinade over the top of the lamb, seal the bag, and turn over to coat. Marinate in the refrigerator for at least 6 and up to 12 hours.

Drain the lamb, pat it dry with paper towels, and roll it back up. Tie with cotton string. Arrange the lamb on the spit rod assembly and roast for 15 minutes per pound for medium, or until an instant-read meat thermometer inserted into the thickest part registers 155 degrees.

Remove the meat from the spit rod assembly and allow it to rest for 10 to 15 minutes, loosely covered with aluminum foil, before carving.

Nona's Leg of Lamb Roast

Makes 6 servings   My Italian grandmother made this lamb as a midweek meal and used the leftovers to create a ravioli filling for Sunday dinner.

6 cloves garlic, minced

2 teaspoons salt

1 teaspoon freshly ground
  black pepper

2 tablespoons olive oil

6 sprigs fresh thyme leaves

6 sprigs fresh rosemary

One 3-pound boneless rolled
  leg of lamb

In a small mixing bowl, combine the garlic, salt, pepper, and olive oil. Unroll the leg of lamb and spread the inside with half of the garlic mixture. Arrange the thyme and rosemary evenly on top, then roll the roast, and tie with cotton string. Spread the remaining garlic mixture over the outside of the roast, cover with plastic wrap, and marinate in the refrigerator for at least 6 and up to 12 hours.

Remove the roast from the refrigerator, remove the plastic wrap, and load onto the spit rod assembly. Roast the lamb for 15 minutes per pound for medium, or until an instant-read meat thermometer inserted into the thickest part registers 155 degrees.

Remove the lamb from the spit rod assembly and allow it to rest for 10 to 15 minutes, loosely covered with aluminum foil, before carving.

Balsamic Dijon Rack of Lamb

Serves 6 **This elegant dinner is simple when you use your rotisserie. Depending upon the size of your machine, you can roast up to four racks. Marinate the racks for at least 12 hours before cooking. Serve this with Apple-Mint Chutney (page 307).**

Balsamic-Dijon Slather

¹/₂ cup balsamic vinegar
¹/₃ cup Dijon mustard
5 cloves garlic, peeled
¹/₄ cup fresh rosemary
    leaves
2 teaspoons salt
1 teaspoon freshly ground
    black pepper

One 4-pound rack of lamb

In a food processor or minichopper, combine the slather ingredients and pulse until the garlic is chopped. Spread the mixture all over the rack of lamb. Cover with plastic wrap and refrigerate overnight.

Load the rack of lamb onto the spit rod assembly and roast 15 to 18 minutes per pound for medium, or until an instant-read thermometer inserted into the thickest part of the meat registers 155 to 160 degrees.

Remove the rack from the spit rod assembly, cover loosely with aluminum foil, and let rest for 10 minutes before carving.

Mint Chimichurri Rack of Lamb

Serves 6 Chimichurri is an Argentine hot pepper, parsley, and garlic sauce, but for this roast we'll substitute mint for the parsley and tone down the heat just a little. This is very nice served with Apple-Mint Chutney (page 307).

Mint Chimichurri Marinade

1 cup packed fresh mint leaves

4 cloves garlic, peeled

1 tablespoon rice vinegar or white vinegar

¼ cup olive oil

6 to 7 fresh oregano leaves

⅛ teaspoon cayenne pepper

1 teaspoon salt

One 4-pound rack of lamb

In a food processor, combine the marinade ingredients and process until smooth.

Make ½-inch slits all over the meat and transfer it to a 2-gallon zipper-top plastic bag. Pour the marinade over the roast, turn it to coat the meat evenly, and seal the bag. Marinate in the refrigerator for at least 12 and up to 24 hours.

Remove the roast from the marinade (no need to pat dry) and load onto the spit rod assembly. Roast 15 to 18 minutes per pound for medium, or until an instant-read meat thermometer inserted into the thickest part of the meat registers 155 degrees.

Remove the rack from the spit rod, cover loosely with aluminum foil, and allow the lamb to rest for at least 10 minutes before carving.

All-American Barbecued Beef Ribs

Serves 4   **Meaty beef ribs are a great dish to cook in the rotisserie; since they don't have to be watched, you are free to do other kitchen tasks. Threading ribs onto the rotisserie is a bit tricky, but the end result is worth it—follow the instructions and you won't have a problem.**

1 rack of beef ribs (about
   1¹/₂ pounds)
3 tablespoons All-American
   Barbecue Rub (page
   286)
1 cup All-American Barbecue
   Sauce (page 324)

Season the ribs with the barbecue rub, massaging it well into the meat. Cover with plastic wrap and refrigerate for at least 2 and up to 8 hours.

Arrange the spit rod assembly in the resting area of the rotisserie. Place 4 empty kabob rods next to each other in the holes around the wheel with the spring ends on the left side. Using another kabob rod, thread it through the first rib. Take the last kabob rod and thread it through the last rib (see Figure 1). Wrap the ribs around the empty kabob rods already arranged in the spit rod assembly until you come to the end (see Figure 2). Insert the kabob rods attached to the ribs into the gear wheel, with the spring ends on the left. Roast the ribs for 30 minutes, stopping the machine to baste the ribs with the barbecue sauce during the last 7 to 10 minutes.

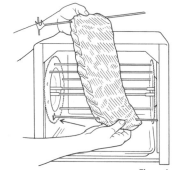

Figure 1

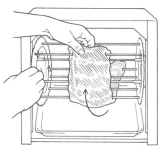

Figure 2

Remove the ribs from the spit rods, cut into individual ribs, and serve with the remaining barbecue sauce (after a vigorous boil) on the side.

Variations

If you love meaty beef ribs and want to try other sauces and rubs, here are a few:

Rub the ribs with Fiesta Rub (page 291) for a south of the border flavor.

Try Chinese five-spice powder as the rub, then baste with Hoisin Barbecue Sauce (page 319).

Tennessee Mopping Sauce (page 325) makes great beef ribs.

Grecian Formula Rub (page 291) is also great on beef ribs.

Prosciutto- and Basil-Wrapped Filet Mignon

Serves 6   Flavors of Italy transform these filets into a savory dish for your family or friends. Try serving this with Bruschetta Salsa (page 300) on the side.

$1/4$ cup olive oil

$1^1/2$ teaspoons salt

$1/2$ teaspoon freshly ground black pepper

Six 1-inch-thick filet mignon steaks

15 to 18 fresh basil leaves

$1/4$ pound thinly sliced prosciutto

Pour the olive oil onto a dinner plate, and season it with the salt and pepper. Dip each steak into the oil mixture, turning to coat evenly. Place 3 or 4 basil leaves around the outside edge of each filet, using the oil as "glue." Then wrap the outside of the filet with a slice of prosciutto that has been cut to fit (it may overlap itself a bit, and that's fine). Secure the prosciutto and basil with 1 or 2 toothpicks. At this point, you may cover the steaks with plastic wrap and refrigerate until you are ready to grill, up to 24 hours later.

Arrange the steaks in the rotisserie basket and close the lid tightly. Load the basket onto the spit rod assembly and grill until the steaks are the desired degree of doneness, about 15 minutes for medium-rare.

Remove the filets from the basket, remove the toothpicks from each one, and serve immediately.

Filet Mignon Stuffed with Caramelized Onions

Serves 6   Using the rotisserie basket, it's easy to stuff meats, and then grill them, and you can avoid the hassle of losing the entire filling through the grates of an outdoor grill. Caramelized onions flavored with thyme give these filets a savory surprise center.

3 tablespoons olive oil

3 teaspoons salt

1½ teaspoons freshly ground black pepper

Six 1-inch-thick filet mignons

½ cup (1 stick) butter

6 large onions, sliced ¼ inch thick

1 tablespoon sugar

1½ teaspoons dried thyme

Pour the olive oil onto a dinner plate and season with 1½ teaspoons of the salt and ¾ teaspoon of the pepper, stirring to blend. In the side of each filet, cut a slit that reaches about halfway through to the middle. Dip the filets into the oil mixture and turn to coat evenly. Cover the filets with plastic wrap and refrigerate while you prepare the onions.

In a large sauté pan (don't use a nonstick pan), melt the butter over medium-high heat. Add the onions, stirring to coat with the butter. Sprinkle with the sugar, the remaining 1½ teaspoons salt, ¾ teaspoon pepper, and the thyme and cook, stirring occasionally so that the onions do not burn. As the onions cook, they will begin to turn a light caramel color; this should take about 20 minutes. When the onions have caramelized, remove them from the heat and let cool to room temperature. Stuff some of the mixture into the pocket of each filet. At this point, you may refrigerate the filets for up to 12 hours.

When ready to grill, arrange the meat in the rotisserie basket, close the lid tightly, and load onto the spit rod assembly. Grill until cooked to your taste, about 15 minutes for medium-rare.

Remove from the rotisserie basket and serve immediately.

Wild Blue Mushroom–Stuffed Filet Mignon

Serves 6   Cremini mushrooms and Maytag blue cheese are two of my favorite flavors, so when I stuffed a filet mignon with them, I was in heaven. You can make the stuffing ahead of time and have a great dinner in 20 minutes.

3 tablespoons olive oil
2 teaspoons salt
1 teaspoon freshly ground
     black pepper
Six 1-inch-thick filet mignon
     steaks
¼ cup (½ stick) butter
¼ cup finely chopped
     shallots

Pour the olive oil on a dinner plate and season with 1 teaspoon of the salt and ½ teaspoon of the pepper, stirring to blend. In the side of each of the filets, cut a slit reaching about halfway through. Dip the filets in the oil mixture, turning to coat evenly. Cover the steaks with plastic wrap and refrigerate until ready to use, for up to 24 hours.

In an 8-inch sauté pan, melt the butter over medium heat. Add the shallots and cook, stirring, until translucent, 4 to 6 minutes. Add the mushrooms, the remaining 1 teaspoon of salt, and ½ teaspoon of pepper and cook, stirring, until the liquid from the mushrooms in the pan evaporates, about 5

½ pound cremini
  mushrooms, finely
  chopped
¼ pound Maytag or other
  quality blue cheese,
  crumbled

minutes. Remove the mushrooms from the pan and allow to cool to room temperature, draining off any excess moisture. Stir in the blue cheese, place the mixture on a piece of plastic wrap, and form into a log about 1 inch in diameter. Refrigerate until firm.

When the blue cheese and mushroom mixture is firm, cut six ½-inch-thick pieces off the log and stuff one into the pocket of each filet. Close the pocket with a toothpick to hold it in place.

Load the filets into the rotisserie basket and close the lid tightly. Load the basket onto the spit rod assembly and cook the steaks to your desired level of doneness, about 15 minutes for medium-rare.

Remove the steaks from the basket, take out the toothpicks, and serve immediately.

Bloody Mary Steaks

Serves 4   The marinade for this succulent sirloin is a
Bloody Mary, that great eye-opening drink often served with
brunch. A savory and spicy tomato flavor permeates the
meat, which is tasty served with rice or pasta. If you have a
larger rotisserie, you can double the recipe.

Four 1-inch-thick ribeye
steaks, trimmed of fat
Bloody Mary Marinade
(page 293)

Place the steaks in a 2-gallon zipper-top plastic bag. Pour
the marinade over the steaks, seal the bag, and turn over to
coat the steaks. Marinate in the refrigerator for at least 2 and
up to 6 hours.

Remove the steaks from the marinade, pat dry with paper
towels, and arrange them in the rotisserie basket, closing the
lid tightly. Load the basket onto the spit rod assembly and
grill the steaks until they reach the desired degree of doneness, about 15 minutes for medium-rare.

Remove the steaks from the basket and serve immediately.
If you would like to serve the remaining marinade on the side
as a sauce, bring it to a boil while the steaks are cooking,
reduce the heat to medium-low, and simmer for 10 minutes.

Margarita Steaks

Serves 4   The flavors of the classic margarita make a great marinade for sirloin, giving it a fresh taste of lime and tequila. Use this marinade for steaks or beef kabobs. If you have a larger rotisserie, you can double the recipe.

2 pounds sirloin steak

Margarita Marinade

¹/₂ cup tequila, preferably
    Cuervo Gold
¹/₄ cup fresh lime juice
2 tablespoons orange juice
3 cloves garlic, minced
1¹/₂ teaspoons salt
¹/₂ teaspoon freshly ground
    black pepper
Pinch of cayenne pepper

Place the steaks in a 2-gallon zipper-top plastic bag. In a small mixing bowl, combine the marinade ingredients. Pour it over the steak, seal the bag, and turn over to coat. Marinate in the refrigerator for at least 2 and up to 6 hours.

Remove the steaks from the marinade, pat dry with paper towels, and arrange them in the rotisserie basket, closing the lid tightly. Load the basket onto the spit rod assembly and cook until the steaks have reached the desired degree of doneness, about 15 minutes for medium-rare.

Remove from the basket and serve immediately.

Pepper-Crusted New York Steaks

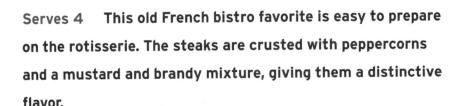

Serves 4   **This old French bistro favorite is easy to prepare on the rotisserie. The steaks are crusted with peppercorns and a mustard and brandy mixture, giving them a distinctive flavor.**

4 New York strip steaks

Cracked Pepper-Dijon Slather

2 tablespoons Dijon mustard

2 cloves garlic, mashed

2 teaspoons brandy

2 teaspoons coarsely cracked black peppercorns

1 teaspoon salt

Place the steaks on a cutting board. In a small mixing bowl, stir together the slather ingredients, and brush the steaks with it on both sides. Cover with plastic wrap, and marinate in the refrigerator for at least 2 and up to 4 hours.

Arrange the steaks in the rotisserie basket, closing the lid tightly. Load the basket onto the spit rod assembly and cook the steaks until the desired degree of doneness is reached, about 15 minutes for medium-rare.

Remove the steaks from the basket and serve immediately.

Alamo T-Bones

Serves 4 **Massaged with a Texas-style beef rub, these hearty T-bones are just what the doctor ordered for a down-home barbecue in the middle of winter. Pleasantly spicy, the rub not only flavors but tenderizes the meat. Serve this with Refried Bean Bake (page 339) and Southwestern Rice (page 352). If you have a large rotisserie, you can double the recipe.**

Alamo Spice Rub

1 tablespoon sweet paprika

1 tablespoon firmly packed dark brown sugar

2 teaspoons chili powder

1½ teaspoons freshly ground black pepper

1½ teaspoons dried oregano

1 teaspoon ground cumin

½ teaspoon cayenne pepper

Two 1-pound T-bone steaks

2 tablespoons vegetable oil

In a small mixing bowl, combine the spice rub ingredients, stirring well to blend.

Brush the T-bones with the vegetable oil, then dredge the steaks in the rub until they are evenly and well coated on each side. Cover the steaks with plastic wrap and marinate in the refrigerator for at least 4 and up to 8 hours.

Arrange the steaks in the rotisserie basket and close the lid tightly. Load the basket onto the spit rod assembly and cook to the desired degree of doneness, about 15 minutes for medium-rare.

Remove the steaks from the basket and allow to rest for 5 to 7 minutes, loosely covered with aluminum foil, before serving.

Veal Chops with Rosemary and Garlic

Serves 4   My grandmother used to season her meats the day before cooking them with something akin to a dry rub, but with a little olive oil and mashed garlic added to it. As the meat cooked, the flavors intensified.

6 cloves garlic, peeled
1 tablespoon fresh rosemary
   leaves
1 teaspoon salt
1/2 teaspoon freshly ground
   black pepper
2 tablespoons olive oil
Four 1-inch-thick bone-in
   veal chops

In a minichopper or mortar, combine the garlic, rosemary, salt, pepper, and oil and process or mash with a pestle until a liquidy paste is formed. Brush the veal chops liberally with the mixture, cover with plastic wrap, and refrigerate for at least 24 hours.

Place the veal in the rotisserie basket and close the lid tightly. Load the basket onto the spit rod assembly and cook the chops until they are still a little pink in the middle and juicy, about 30 minutes.

Remove the chops from the basket and serve immediately.

Spit-Roasted Lamb Chops with Garlic and Mint

Serves 6   Lamb chops come out crisp on the outside and tender on the inside when cooked on the rotisserie. These lamb chops are flavored with mint and garlic.

8 loin lamb chops, trimmed of excess fat

Mint and Garlic Marinade

2 tablespoons olive oil

1½ teaspoons salt

½ teaspoon freshly ground black pepper

3 cloves garlic, mashed

¼ cup chopped fresh mint leaves

2 tablespoons white wine

Place the lamb chops in a 2-gallon zipper-top plastic bag. In a small mixing bowl, combine the marinade ingredients. Pour over the chops, seal the bag, and turn it over to coat the meat. Marinate in the refrigerator for at least 2 and up to 6 hours.

Remove the chops from the marinade and pat dry with paper towels. Arrange in the rotisserie basket, closing the lid tightly. Load the basket onto the spit rod assembly and cook to the desired degree of doneness, 25 to 30 minutes medium.

Remove the chops from the basket and serve immediately.

Skewering Your Way to Culinary Greatness

Kabobs are great in the rotisserie because the little spring mechanism turns them while they roast, so that they are cooked evenly, without the usual hot spots you would encounter on the grill. For the recipes in this chapter, I've left off the veggies; we found that the vegetables didn't cook very well with the meat and elected to prepare separate skewers of vegetables that would cook at the same time (see A Garden in the Rotisserie, pages 207–258). If you have a small rotisserie, the recipes featured here will work well; if you have the large rotisserie, you can double the recipes to serve eight if you wish.

For beef kabobs I've used top sirloin because it is so flavorful and absorbs a marinade well. If you want to use a less expensive cut of meat, like London broil, increase the marinating time by several hours.

Asian Beef Skewers

Serves 4 to 6 **Fragrant with ginger and garlic, these skewers are terrific served with Perfect Sticky Rice (page 350).**

Hoisin-Soy Marinade

$1/2$ cup soy sauce

2 tablespoons rice wine

2 tablespoons vegetable oil

2 cloves garlic, mashed

$1^1/2$ teaspoons peeled and minced fresh ginger

2 tablespoons hoisin sauce

$1^1/2$ pounds top sirloin, trimmed of excess fat and cut into 1-inch chunks

In a small mixing bowl, combine the marinade ingredients, stirring until well combined.

Place the beef in a zipper-top plastic bag, and pour the marinade over it. Seal the bag, and turn it over to coat the beef. Marinate in the refrigerator for at least 2 and up to 6 hours.

When you are ready to cook the beef, pour the marinade into a small saucepan and bring to a boil. Reduce the heat to medium-low and simmer for 10 minutes.

Remove the beef from the marinade and pat dry. Thread the meat onto the kabob rods and load them onto the spit rod assembly with the spring ends on the right side. Grill the kabobs to the desired degree of doneness, 15 to 20 minutes, brushing with some of the marinade twice during the cooking time and at the end.

Remove the beef from the skewers and serve immediately.

Tijuana Tilly's Beef Kabobs

Serves 4 to 6   **A little southwestern flavor perks up these kabobs. Serve fajita-style with tortillas, salsa, guacamole, and sour cream.**

Spicy Tequila Marinade

¹/₄ cup vegetable oil

2 tablespoons fresh lime juice

¹/₄ cup tequila, preferably Cuervo Gold

3 cloves garlic, mashed

¹/₂ teaspoon ground cumin

¹/₈ teaspoon chili powder

¹/₄ cup chopped fresh cilantro leaves

1 teaspoon salt

1¹/₂ pounds top sirloin, trimmed of excess fat and cut into 1-inch chunks

In a small mixing bowl, combine the marinade ingredients, stirring to blend.

Place the beef in a zipper-top plastic bag, and pour in the marinade. Seal the bag, and turn over to coat the beef. Marinate in the refrigerator for at least 4 and up to 8 hours.

Remove from the marinade and pat dry. Thread the meat onto the kabob rods and load onto the spit rod assembly with the spring ends on the right side. Grill to the desired degree of doneness, 15 to 20 minutes.

Remove the kabobs from the skewers and serve immediately.

Midwest Barbecue Beef Kabobs

Serves 4 to 6   Reminiscent of the barbecue served in Kansas City, these skewers are perfect with corn on the cob.

BBQ-Style Marinade

1 teaspoon salt

1/2 teaspoon freshly ground black pepper

2 cloves garlic, minced

1 1/2 teaspoons sweet paprika

2 tablespoons firmly packed light brown sugar

1/2 cup vegetable oil

2 teaspoons red wine vinegar

1 tablespoon Worcestershire sauce

1/2 teaspoon dry mustard

1 1/2 pounds top sirloin, trimmed of excess fat and cut into 1-inch chunks

In a small mixing bowl, combine the marinade ingredients, stirring to blend.

Place the beef in a zipper-top plastic bag. Pour in the marinade, seal the bag, and turn over to coat. Marinate in the refrigerator for at least 4 and up to 6 hours.

Remove the beef from the marinade and pat dry. Thread the beef onto the kabob rods and load them onto the spit rod assembly with the spring ends on the right side. Grill to the desired degree of doneness, 15 to 20 minutes.

Remove the kabobs from the skewers and serve immediately.

Texas Two-Step Beef Kabobs

Serves 4 to 6   Hot and spicy, these kabobs will tickle your taste buds. Serve with Lone Star beer for a total Texas experience.

Kickin' Texas Marinade

2 cloves garlic, minced

1½ teaspoons salt

½ teaspoon freshly ground black pepper

½ teaspoon chili powder

½ teaspoon ground cumin

¼ cup vegetable oil

1½ pounds top sirloin, trimmed of excess fat and cut into 1-inch chunks

In a small mixing bowl, combine the marinade ingredients.

Place the beef in a zipper-top plastic bag and pour in the marinade. Seal the bag, and turn over to coat the beef. Marinate in the refrigerator for at least 2 and up to 4 hours.

Remove the beef from the marinade and pat dry. Thread the kabobs onto the skewers and load the skewers onto the spit rod assembly with the spring ends on the right side. Grill to the desired degree of doneness, 15 to 20 minutes.

Remove the kabobs from the skewers and serve immediately.

Bella Tuscany Beef Kabobs

Serves 4 to 6   Fragrant with rosemary and garlic, these skewers will transport you to the hills of Tuscany.

Tuscan Marinade

1 teaspoon salt

½ teaspoon freshly ground black pepper

3 cloves garlic, mashed

1 tablespoon fresh rosemary leaves, chopped

2 tablespoons olive oil

2 teaspoons fresh lemon juice

1½ pounds top sirloin, trimmed of excess fat and cut into 1-inch chunks

In a small mixing bowl, stir together the marinade ingredients.

Place the beef in a zipper-top plastic bag, and pour in the marinade. Seal the bag, and turn it over to coat the beef. Marinate in the refrigerator for at least 2 and up to 6 hours.

Remove the beef from the marinade and pat dry. Thread the beef onto the kabob rods and load them onto the spit rod assembly with the spring ends on the right side. Grill to the desired degree of doneness, 15 to 20 minutes.

Remove the kabobs from the rods and serve immediately.

Burgundy Beef Kabobs

Serves 4 to 6   Hearty Burgundy helps to further tenderize and flavor the rich sirloin. Serve this dish with sautéed mushrooms, onions, and potatoes.

Burgundy Marinade

1 cup red Burgundy wine

1/2 cup Campbell's condensed beef broth

1/4 cup olive oil

1 teaspoon salt

1/2 teaspoon freshly ground black pepper

2 cloves garlic, mashed

1 teaspoon dried thyme

1 bay leaf

1 1/2 pounds top sirloin, trimmed of excess fat and cut into 1-inch chunks

In a medium-size mixing bowl, stir together the marinade ingredients.

Place the beef in a zipper-top plastic bag, and pour in the marinade. Seal the bag and turn it over to coat the beef. Marinate in the refrigerator for at least 2 and up to 8 hours.

Remove the beef from the marinade and pat dry. Pour the marinade into a small saucepan, bring to a boil, and reduce the heat to medium-low. Simmer for 10 minutes.

Pat the beef dry and thread onto the skewers. Load the skewers onto the spit rod assembly with the spring ends on the right side. Grill the kabobs to the desired degree of doneness, 15 to 20 minutes.

Remove the kabobs from the rods and brush with a little of the reduced marinade before serving.

Jalapeño-Garlic Beef Satay

Serves 6   Great toppers for a Thai beef salad, these skewers are great for appetizers or dinner. If you have a small rotisserie, you will need only half the recipe. In that case, I recommend that you purchase and slice the quantity of flank steak that is called for and then freeze half for another recipe (see Bul Goki, page 103). Serve with Sweet and Pungent Dipping Sauce (page 102) or Ginger Peanut Sauce (page 56).

One 1- to 1¼-pound flank
    steak, trimmed of
    excess fat

Jalapeño-Garlic Marinade

½ cup soy sauce
2 tablespoons firmly packed
    light brown sugar
2 cloves garlic, minced
1 teaspoon ground coriander
2 tablespoons fresh lemon
    juice
1 tablespoon vegetable oil
1 tablespoon seeded and
    finely chopped jalapeño

Cut the flank steak crosswise into thin strips. Place the strips in a 13 x 9-inch glass dish.

In a small mixing bowl, stir together the marinade ingredients. Pour over the steak and cover the dish tightly with plastic wrap. Marinate in the refrigerator for 2 and up to 6 hours.

Remove the steak from the marinade, pat dry with paper towels, and thread onto the kabob rods. Load the kabob rods onto the spit rod assembly with the spring ends on the right side. Grill the steak until just cooked through, 3 to 5 minutes.

Remove the strips from the skewers and serve immediately.

Sweet and Pungent Dipping Sauce

Makes about 6 tablespoons   A nice accompaniment for a satay, this has fish sauce as an ingredient. Fish sauce can be found in the Asian section of your grocery store. I like the brand called Thai Three Crab.

2 tablespoons vegetable oil
2 tablespoons fish sauce,
    preferably imported
1 teaspoon sugar
1 teaspoon peeled and
    minced fresh ginger
1 teaspoon seeded and finely
    chopped jalapeño
1 tablespoon rice wine

Whisk together all the ingredients in a small mixing bowl. Store in a tightly covered glass jar in the refrigerator until ready to use. It will keep for up to 1 week.

Bul Goki

Serves 6   *Bul goki* is the national dish of Korea. Thinly sliced beef is marinated in a sweet soy and sesame marinade, then grilled over open flames and served with condiments, which usually include another national dish, a hot and spicy cabbage dish called *kimchee*. You can serve this delicious and easy dish at home, accompanied by sticky rice, Hot Ginger Pickled Cucumbers (page 357), and Crunchy Cabbage Salad with Cashews (page 348). If you have a small rotisserie, make half the recipe. The marinade is also delicious with kabobs or T-bones.

One 1¼-pound flank steak, trimmed of excess fat

Sweet Sesame Marinade

½ cup soy sauce
¼ cup firmly packed light brown sugar
1 tablespoon vegetable oil
2 tablespoons rice wine
1 tablespoon toasted sesame oil
4 green onions, white and light green parts, chopped
2 cloves garlic, mashed
¼ cup sesame seeds

Slice the flank steak crosswise into thin strips and place in a zipper-top plastic bag.

In a small mixing bowl, whisk together the marinade ingredients. Pour over the steak, seal the bag, and turn over to coat the meat. Marinate in the refrigerator for at least 1 and up to 8 hours.

Remove the meat from the marinade, pat dry with paper towels, and thread onto the kabob rods. Load the skewers onto the spit rod assembly with the spring ends on the right side. Grill until the meat is cooked through, 3 to 5 minutes.

Remove the strips from the skewers and serve immediately.

Spiedini of Veal and Sausages

Serves 6   *Spiedini* is Italian for "grilled skewers" and these little treats of spicy sausage, sage leaves, and tender veal are delicious. Serve them as an appetizer or as a main course; either way, they are terrific.

1 pound sweet Italian sausage links, cut into 1-inch pieces

³/₄ pound veal, cut from the leg or shoulder, trimmed of excess fat and cut into 1-inch chunks

12 fresh sage leaves

1 teaspoon salt

¹/₂ teaspoon freshly ground black pepper

¹/₄ cup olive oil

2 tablespoons white wine

Alternate the sausage, veal, and sage leaves on the kabob rods and lay them in a shallow dish that will hold them in single layer. In a small mixing bowl, combine the salt, pepper, olive oil, and wine, stirring to blend and dissolve the salt. Pour the mixture over the skewers, cover with plastic wrap, and marinate in the refrigerator for at least 2 and up to 8 hours, turning occasionally.

Load the kabob rods onto the spit rod assembly with the spring ends to the right. Grill until the sausage is cooked through, 10 to 15 minutes.

Remove the meat and sage leaves from the skewers and serve immediately.

Classic Lamb Shish Kebab

Serves 6 Lamb is such an overlooked meat, but it really shines when marinated, and then skewered. This shish kebab is an adaptation of one that I made when I first got married. Serve this with rice pilaf and field greens salad with feta cheese and walnuts.

1¹/₂ pounds boneless leg of lamb, trimmed of excess fat and cut into 1-inch cubes

Aegean Marinade

¹/₂ cup olive oil
Grated zest of 1 lemon
¹/₄ cup fresh lemon juice
3 cloves garlic, mashed
1 teaspoon dried oregano
¹/₂ teaspoon dried thyme
1 teaspoon salt
¹/₂ teaspoon freshly ground black pepper

Place the lamb in a zipper-top plastic bag.

In a small mixing bowl, stir together the marinade ingredients. Pour the marinade over the lamb, seal the bag, and turn over to coat the meat. Marinate in the refrigerator for at least 4 hours or overnight.

Remove the meat from the marinade and pat dry with paper towels. Thread the meat on the kabob rods and load the skewers onto the spit rod assembly with the spring ends on the right side. Grill until the lamb registers 150 degrees on an instant-read meat thermometer, about 20 minutes. (The meat will be slightly pink in the center.)

Remove the kabobs from the skewers and serve immediately.

Mom's Old-Fashioned Meat Loaf

Serves 6   Simple, homey meat loaf bastes itself on the rotisserie. Serve with Garlic Smashed Potatoes (page 342) on the side.

1$\frac{1}{2}$ pounds ground chuck
$\frac{1}{2}$ cup finely chopped onion
1 teaspoon dried thyme
1 teaspoon salt
$\frac{1}{2}$ teaspoon freshly ground
    black pepper
$\frac{1}{2}$ cup fresh bread crumbs
$\frac{1}{4}$ cup chopped fresh
    parsley leaves
1 large egg
$\frac{1}{4}$ cup ketchup
All-American Barbecue
    Sauce (optional, page
    324), warmed

In a large mixing bowl, stir together all the ingredients except the sauce until well blended.

Coat the rotisserie basket with nonstick cooking spray, then pack the meat loaf mixture into the basket and close the lid tightly. Load the basket onto the spit rod assembly and cook until a meat thermometer inserted into the center registers 175 degrees, 40 to 50 minutes.

Take the basket out of the rotisserie and allow the meat loaf to rest for 5 minutes, covered loosely with aluminum foil, before removing from the basket. Turn out the meat loaf onto a cutting board and slice thinly. Accompany with the sauce on the side, if desired.

Rotisserie Meat Loaf

The rotisserie basket produces a rectangular meat loaf with a nice crust on all sides, and with the added benefit that the fat drips off the meat loaf into the drip pan. In this chapter you will find three different ways to flavor your meat loaf on the rotisserie. I recommend that you coat the basket with nonstick cooking spray first so that the meat loaf releases easily from the basket. You can make up the meat loaf mixture in the morning, then roast it in the evening. Or roast it on the weekend and freeze it for a midweek meal; meat loaf freezes well (it keeps for about 2 months).

Southwestern Chipotle Meat Loaf

Serves 6 Smoky chipotle chiles, cumin, and cilantro make this south of the border entrée a delicious change of pace.

$^1/_4$ cup milk

Four soft 6-inch corn tortillas, cut into 1-inch squares

$^1/_2$ pound lean ground pork

1 pound ground beef

1 large egg

$^1/_4$ cup finely chopped red onion

1 teaspoon salt

$^1/_2$ teaspoon freshly ground black pepper or a pinch of cayenne pepper

$^1/_4$ teaspoon ground cumin

1 canned chipotle chile in adobo sauce, drained and minced, plus 1 teaspoon adobo sauce

2 tablespoons chopped fresh cilantro leaves, plus extra for garnish

Accompaniments

Sour cream

Guacamole

Salsa Fresca (page 297)

In a small mixing bowl, pour the milk over the tortillas and let them soak for 5 to 10 minutes while preparing the rest of the meat loaf.

In a large mixing bowl, stir together the pork, beef, egg, onion, salt, pepper, cumin, chipotle and sauce, and cilantro until well blended. Squeeze the excess moisture out of the tortilla squares and add to meat loaf mixture, stirring until blended.

Coat the rotisserie basket with nonstick cooking spray, and pack the basket with the meat loaf mixture. Close the lid tightly. Load the basket onto the spit rod assembly and roast until an instant-read meat thermometer inserted into the center of the meat registers 175 degrees, 40 to 50 minutes.

Remove the basket from the rotisserie and allow the meat loaf to rest for 5 minutes, covered loosely with aluminum foil. Turn out the meat loaf onto a cutting board and slice thinly. Garnish with the cilantro and serve the sour cream, guacamole, and salsa on the side.

Spicy Meatball Meat Loaf

Serves 6   **My mom's meatball recipe also makes an awesome meat loaf.**

1 cup fresh bread crumbs
$^1/_2$ pound lean ground pork
$^1/_2$ pound ground veal
$^1/_2$ pound ground beef
$^1/_2$ cup freshly grated
    Parmesan cheese
2 cloves garlic, mashed
2 tablespoons grated lemon
    zest
1 teaspoon dried oregano
1 teaspoon salt
Pinch of red pepper flakes
1 large egg
Quick Marinara (optional,
    page 318), warmed

In a large mixing bowl, stir together all the ingredients except the sauce until well blended.

Coat the rotisserie basket with nonstick cooking spray, and pack the meat loaf mixture into the basket. Close the lid tightly. Load the basket onto the spit rod assembly and roast until an instant-read thermometer inserted in the center of the meat registers 175 degrees, 40 to 50 minutes.

Remove the basket from the rotisserie and allow the meat loaf to rest for 10 minutes, loosely covered with aluminum foil. Turn out the meat loaf onto a cutting board, slice thinly, and serve with the sauce on the side, if desired.

Burgers are tender and juicy when prepared in the rotisserie basket, and they offer a great opportunity to try out new tastes on your family. The burgers in this chapter are seasoned with flavors from the Southwest, Asia, and the Mediterranean. Feel free to buy ground meat that is 15 to 20 percent fat, because the fat melts away in the rotisserie. Ground chuck has a great beefy flavor, or you could mix chuck and sirloin together for hamburger heaven.

Southwestern Burgers

Serves 6 **Smoky chipotles help spice up these burgers. Serve these in corn tortillas with guacamole.**

1½ pounds ground chuck
1 tablespoon drained and finely chopped canned chipotle chile in adobo sauce
2 tablespoons finely chopped red onion
2 cloves garlic, minced

Combine the ground chuck, chile, onion, and garlic in a large mixing bowl, stirring until the chile, onion, and garlic are distributed uniformly throughout the beef. Shape the beef into 6 patties about ¾ inch thick. Refrigerate until ready to cook, up to 6 hours.

Arrange the burgers in the rotisserie basket, close the lid tightly, and load onto the spit rod assembly. Cook the burgers until they reach the desired degree of doneness, 20 to 25 minutes.

Remove the burgers from the basket and serve immediately.

Pacific Rim Burgers

Serves 6   Flavors of the Orient transform these burgers into a delicious surprise for lunch or dinner. Serve with additional hoisin sauce and chopped green onions.

1 pound ground beef
1/2 pound lean ground pork
1 clove garlic, minced
4 green onions, white and light green parts, finely chopped
1 tablespoon hoisin sauce
2 tablespoons soy sauce
1 teaspoon toasted sesame oil

In a large mixing bowl, blend together all the ingredients. Form the mixture into 6 patties about ¾ inch thick. Refrigerate until ready to cook, up to 4 hours.

Arrange the patties in the rotisserie basket, close the lid tightly, and load onto the spit rod assembly. Grill the burgers until they reach the desired degree of doneness, 20 to 25 minutes.

Remove the burgers from the basket and serve immediately.

Great Caesar's Burgers

Serves 6   With all the ingredients of a Caesar salad, these burgers are really tasty on onion rolls.

1¹/₂ pounds ground beef
2 cloves garlic, minced
1 tablespoon Worcestershire sauce
1 teaspoon fresh lemon juice
1 teaspoon anchovy paste

In a large mixing bowl, combine all the ingredients, stirring until well blended. Form the mixture into 6 patties about ¾ inch thick. Refrigerate until ready to cook, up to 4 hours.

½ cup dry bread crumbs

½ cup freshly grated
Parmesan cheese

1 large egg

Arrange the patties in the rotisserie basket and close the lid tightly. Load the basket onto the spit rod assembly and grill to the desired degree of doneness, 22 to 26 minutes.

Remove the burgers from the basket and serve immediately.

Mamma Mia's Burgers

Serves 6 **Similar to a meatball, these burgers are terrific served in crusty rolls with marinara and grated cheese.**

1½ pounds ground beef

1 cup fresh bread crumbs

2 cloves garlic, minced

2 teaspoons grated lemon
zest

¼ cup chopped fresh Italian
parsley leaves

1½ teaspoons salt

½ teaspoon freshly ground
black pepper

½ cup freshly grated
Parmesan cheese

1 large egg

6 crusty rolls

1 cup Quick Marinara
(page 318), warmed

In a large mixing bowl, combine all the ingredients except the marinara and stir until well combined. Shape the mixture into 6 patties about ¾ inch thick. Refrigerate until ready to cook, up to 4 hours.

Arrange the patties in the rotisserie basket, close the lid tightly, and load onto the spit rod assembly. Grill the burgers to the desired degree of doneness, 22 to 25 minutes.

Remove the burgers from the basket and serve on crusty rolls topped with the marinara sauce.

Greek Burgers

Serves 6   **Lamb and beef combine with fresh herbs and feta cheese to make a moist and spicy burger. Serve these in pita with Cucumber-Yogurt Sauce (page 317).**

1 pound ground beef
1/2 pound ground lamb
1/2 cup dry bread crumbs
2 cloves garlic, minced
2 teaspoons chopped fresh
    oregano leaves
2 teaspoons chopped fresh
    mint leaves
1 teaspoon freshly ground
    black pepper
1/4 cup crumbed feta cheese

In a large mixing bowl, combine all the ingredients, stirring until well blended. Shape the mixture into 6 patties about 3/4 inch thick. Refrigerate until ready to cook, up to 4 hours.

Arrange the patties in the rotisserie basket and grill until the burgers reach the desired degree of doneness, 22 to 25 minutes.

Remove the burgers from the basket and serve immediately.

Steak and Salsa Burgers

Serves 6   Spicy chorizo sausage gives these burgers a real flavor punch. Serve with guacamole, sour cream, and additional Salsa Fresca on the side.

1$^{1}/_{2}$ pounds ground beef

2 links chorizo sausage, minced

$^{1}/_{4}$ cup Salsa Fresca (page 297)

$^{1}/_{2}$ cup crushed tortilla chips

1 large egg, beaten

Place all the ingredients in a large mixing bowl and stir until well combined. Form the mixture into 6 patties about ¾ inch thick. Refrigerate until ready to cook, up to 4 hours.

Arrange the patties in the rotisserie basket, close the lid tightly, and load the basket onto the spit rod assembly. Grill the burgers to the desired degree of doneness, 18 to 22 minutes.

Remove the burgers from the basket and serve immediately.

Zorba's Gyros

Serves 6   Gyros are a savory combination of lamb and spices served on pita with lettuce, tomato, and a delicious cucumber and yogurt sauce. In this version, lamb and ground beef are made into patties, which are grilled in the rotisserie basket.

1 cup fresh bread crumbs
1 pound ground lamb
1 pound ground beef
(15 percent fat)
1 large egg
1^1/$_2$ teaspoons salt
^{3}/$_4$ teaspoon freshly ground
black pepper
4 cloves garlic, minced
2 tablespoons dried oregano
Six 6-inch pitas

Garnishes

Shredded lettuce
Sliced tomatoes
Pitted Kalamata olives
Cucumber-Yogurt Sauce
(page 317)

Place the bread crumbs, lamb, beef, egg, salt, pepper, garlic, and oregano in a food processor and pulse 4 to 5 times, until the mixture is well combined. Shape the mixture into 6 patties about ¾ inch thick. Refrigerate until ready to cook, up to 4 hours.

Coat the rotisserie basket with nonstick cooking spray and arrange the patties in the basket. Close the lid tightly and load the basket onto the spit rod assembly. Grill the gyros until they are cooked medium-well, 18 to 20 minutes.

Remove the patties from the basket and serve in pita bread with lettuce, tomato, olives, and the sauce.

Whole Hog

I consider pork to be a great "host," if you will. It likes to take on flavors that are introduced to it, and a variety of tastes marry well with the meat. Fruit and fruit juices pair nicely with pork in marinades and bastes. Flavors from Asia, the Southwest, and the Mediterranean all work well with pork, and your family will love the tender meat that comes from the rotisserie; this is one main course that will keep them coming back for more!

Cuts of pork that roast nicely in the rotisserie are pork tenderloins, pork loin roasts, ham (boneless and bone-in), pork chops, kabobs, burgers, and sausages. The recipes in this chapter specify certain cuts of pork, but a pork loin roast can be cooked with a basting sauce suggested for a pork tenderloin and vice versa, so you should feel free to mix and match the basting sauces for the different cuts.

I prefer to use boneless roasts on the rotisserie because sometimes the butcher will leave the bones long enough to hit against the heating element of the rotisserie. Pork shoulder roasts, which are delicious from the rotisserie, tend to cook a bit unevenly with the bone left in, whether on an electric rotisserie or an outdoor grill. If you buy a bone-in roast, you may want to cut it off the bone yourself or have the butcher do it for you. A 5-pound bone-in roast will yield about 3 pounds of meat off the bone, which will serve 6 nicely. Pork shoulders benefit from an overnight rub of herbs and spices, like All-American Barbecue Rub (page 286).

A pork loin has the smaller pork tenderloin on one side of the bone, and the loin roast or chops are on the other side (imagine a pork T-bone steak). Pork loin is solid meat, like the tenderloin, but a bit chewier, and thus benefits from brining. Pork tenderloin is the pork equivalent of filet mignon. There is almost no fat on it, but there is something called "silverskin," which is the tendon sheath, and you should remove this before you put the roast on the spit rod, otherwise, the roast will have a tendency to curl up when it's cooked. To remove the silverskin, take a sharp knife, and beginning at one end, slip the knife under the silverskin, loosen it from the meat, and cut it away from the meat down the length of the roast. Discard the silverskin. Pork tenderloins generally weigh between $3/4$ and $1^1/4$ pounds each, and since there is no waste, one tenderloin will serve 3 people nicely. Pork butt and fresh ham do not cook evenly enough and, therefore, I don't recommend trying them.

In recent years, the pork producers have been raising leaner pigs, which has led to some complaints of dry pork chops or roasts. The easiest way to prevent this is to brine the pork before cooking. A brine is a saltwater solution that sometimes contains sugar and spices. It helps to break down the protein in the meat to make it tender and juicy.

Whole Hog

These are some items that you may already have in your pantry to rub on pork roasts and chops for a quick meal. I suggest that you roll the meat in a tablespoon or two of oil first (either vegetable or olive oil), then rub on the spices and roast according to the manufacturer's directions.

Spicy No-Brainers

- Creole Seasoning Rub (page 287)
- Lemon Pepper Rub (page 286)
- Crushed fresh garlic, salt, and pepper
- Mrs. Dash (any flavor)
- Chinese five-spice powder
- Chili powder
- Curry powder
- Italian herbs
- Herbes de Provence Rub (page 289)
- Old Bay seasoning
- Dry soup mixes, such as Lipton's Onion Soup and Golden Onion Soup, and Knorr's Tomato Basil Soup
- Lipton's Ranch Dressing mix

Saucy No-Brainers

Pork slathered in a prepared sauce and popped in the rotisserie makes a tasty and quick dinner. If the sauce is high in sugar content, then baste only during the last 10 to 15 minutes of cooking; otherwise, the sauce will burn on the pork.

- Bottled barbecue sauce or Old-Fashioned Barbecue Sauce (page 323)
- Bottled teriyaki sauce or Spicy Teriyaki Sauce (page 314) or Top Secret Teriyaki Sauce (page 315)
- Apple butter or other fruit preserve thinned with a little apple or lemon juice
- Orange marmalade
- Dijon mustard
- Honey mustard
- Tabasco Chipotle Sauce
- Stonewall Kitchen sauce (any flavor)
- Hoisin sauce
- Chinese char sui sauce
- Bottled Italian salad dressing
- Kraft's bottled Catalina salad dressing

Brining is a great technique for keeping lean pork chops juicy and tender when they are cooked in a dry heat, such as the rotisserie. There are lots of different recipes for brining; a simple soy sauce marinade will suffice in some cases or you can use a combination of water, salt, and sugar to marinate the pork. Bruce Aidells, the sausage king, adds molasses to his brine, and many cooks add things like garlic and ginger to the brine to help intensify the flavor. It is possible to brine meat for too long a period, so don't exceed the number of hours suggested in the recipes. This will ensure that the meat has had time to cure, but won't end up mushy.

Basic Pork Brine

2 tablespoons sea salt
1/2 cup sugar
4 hot cups water

Dissolve the salt and sugar in the water, then soak the pork in the brine for as long as directed in the recipe.

Remove from the brine, rinse well, dry thoroughly with paper towels, and proceed with the recipe.

Peach and Ginger Pork Roast

Serves 6 to 8 **Pork loin roasts are delicious on the rotisserie and the gingery, peachy aroma of this one had my family watching the window of the rotisserie until it was done. The sauce is also terrific brushed on ribs or chops.**

One 3-pound pork loin roast, brined for 4 to 6 hours (see page 119)
2 tablespoons vegetable oil
1½ teaspoons salt
1 teaspoon freshly ground black pepper
2 cloves garlic, minced
2 teaspoons peeled and grated fresh ginger
½ cup chopped onion
2 cups peeled, pitted, and coarsely chopped ripe peaches
2 teaspoons fresh lemon juice
2 teaspoons ground ginger
2 tablespoons firmly packed light brown sugar

Brush the roast with 1 tablespoon of vegetable oil and rub all over with the salt, pepper, garlic, and fresh ginger. Load the roast onto the spit rod assembly and roast until an instant-read meat thermometer inserted into the thickest part registers 160 degrees, about 20 minutes per pound.

While the pork is roasting, heat the remaining 1 tablespoon vegetable oil in a small saucepan over medium heat. Add the onion and cook, stirring, until softened, about 3 minutes. Add the peaches, lemon juice, ground ginger, and brown sugar and simmer until the mixture reduces and thickens, 15 to 20 minutes. Keep the sauce simmering.

During the last 20 minutes of cooking time, stop the rotisserie and brush the roast all over with the peach sauce. Restart the rotisserie and continue cooking, stopping to baste the roast every 5 minutes or so.

When the roast is done, remove it from the rotisserie, cover loosely with aluminum foil, and allow to rest for 15 minutes. Carve the roast and serve with any remaining peach sauce on the side (after a vigorous boil).

Smart Turn

When fresh peaches aren't available, unsweetened frozen peaches, thawed, can be substituted. You can also use canned peaches in thin syrup, but the flavor won't be as peachy.

Sugar and Spice Pork Roast

Serves 6 to 8 This simple roast is coated with fragrant spices and brown sugar to give it a deliciously crusty outside, while staying juicy inside. It's great to serve as part of a buffet dinner, but easy enough to serve to your family during the week, dressed up with scalloped potatoes and sautéed spinach.

Sugar and Spice Rub

1 teaspoon ground cumin

1 1/2 teaspoons fennel seeds

1/2 teaspoon ground cinnamon

1 teaspoon ground coriander

2 tablespoons firmly packed dark brown sugar

2 tablespoons Dijon mustard

1 1/2 teaspoons salt

3/4 teaspoon freshly ground black pepper

One 3-pound pork loin roast, brined for 4 hours (see page 119)

In a small mixing bowl, combine the rub ingredients until blended.

Load the pork roast onto the spit rod assembly, coat it all over with the rub, and roast until an instant-read meat thermometer inserted into the thickest part registers 160 degrees, about 20 minutes per pound.

Remove the pork from the spit rod, cover loosely with aluminum foil, and let rest for 15 minutes before carving.

Fourth of July Fireworks Pork Loin

Serves 6 to 8   A spicy rub made with chipotle-flavored Tabasco makes this fiery pork roast light up the dinner table. Carve the pork into thin slices and serve with tortillas, refried beans, and Salsa Fresca (page 297).

Fireworks Spice Rub

2 teaspoons Tabasco
   Chipotle Pepper Sauce
1 tablespoon canola oil
1 teaspoon garlic salt
2 teaspoons sweet paprika
1 teaspoon ground cumin
1/2 teaspoon dried oregano

One 3-pound pork loin roast,
   brined for 4 to 6 hours
   (see page 119)

In a small bowl, stir together the rub ingredients.

Place the pork roast on a large piece of plastic wrap and spread the rub evenly over the pork. Roll the pork in the plastic and marinate in the refrigerator for at least 4 and up to 12 hours.

Load the roast onto the spit rod assembly and roast until an instant-read meat thermometer inserted into the thickest part registers 160 degrees, about 20 minutes per pound.

Remove the roast from the spit rod, cover loosely with aluminum foil, and let rest for 15 minutes before carving.

Apricot-Mustard Pork Loin Roast

Serves 6 Piquant dried apricots and spicy Dijon mustard combine to make a tasty coating for this pork roast. The sauce can be made a few days ahead of time; it's also terrific on ribs, chops, ham, and chicken.

Apricot-Mustard Baste

1¹/₂ cups dried apricots
²/₃ cup water
¹/₂ cup firmly packed light brown sugar
¹/₂ cup Dijon mustard
2 teaspoons fresh lemon juice

1¹/₂ teaspoons salt
¹/₂ teaspoon freshly ground black pepper
2 cloves garlic, minced
One 3-pound pork loin roast, brined for 4 to 6 hours (see page 119)

To make the baste, in a 1¹/₂-quart saucepan, combine the apricots and water and bring to a boil. Reduce the heat to medium-low and simmer the apricots until they begin to fall apart and the mixture thickens, about 20 minutes. Remove the pan from the stove and stir in the brown sugar, mustard, and lemon juice. Allow the mixture to cool.

In a small bowl, combine the salt, pepper, and garlic, stirring to form a paste. Spread the paste evenly over the pork, cover tightly with plastic wrap, and refrigerate for at least 4 and up to 24 hours.

Bring the apricot baste to a simmer. Spread a little over the roast and keep it at a simmer while the pork cooks. Load the pork onto the spit rod assembly. Roast until an instant-read meat thermometer inserted in the thickest part registers 160 degrees, about 20 minutes per pound. During the last 30 minutes of cooking time, stop the rotisserie to brush the meat with the apricot baste every 10 minutes.

Remove the meat from the spit rod, brush one more time with the apricot baste, cover loosely with aluminum foil, and allow the roast to rest for 15 minutes before carving.

Reheat any remaining baste and serve alongside the sliced pork roast.

Tuscan Herbed Pork Roast

Serves 6 Tuscan cooking is defined by its simplicity, and this dish is no exception. Slits in the roast hold pockets of sunny lemon zest, rosemary, and garlic to season the inside of the roast, while red wine bastes the outside to give it a nicely caramelized crust.

Tuscan Herb Paste

4 cloves garlic, peeled

1¹⁄₂ tablespoons fresh rosemary leaves or 1¹⁄₂ teaspoons dried

Grated zest of 2 lemons

2 teaspoons salt

1 teaspoon freshly ground black pepper

One 3-pound pork loin roast, brined for 4 to 6 hours (see page 119)

1 cup red wine

In a minichopper, food processor, or mortar, grind the paste ingredients together.

With a sharp knife, make slits ¹⁄₂ inch deep all over the roast, then insert some of the paste into each slit. Rub any excess on the outside of the pork.

Load the roast onto the spit rod assembly and brush with some of the wine. Roast until an instant-read meat thermometer inserted in the thickest part registers 160 degrees, about 20 minutes per pound, turning off the machine to baste with the wine every 20 minutes and then restarting it.

Remove the roast from the spit rod, cover loosely with aluminum foil, and allow it to rest for 15 minutes before carving.

Glazed Pork Loin Stuffed with Drunken Plums

Serves 6 to 8   **This dish is a little unusual in that the pork is stuffed with dried plums plumped in Armagnac, coated with a brown sugar and mustard glaze, and roasted on the spit. When the pork is carved, there is a mosaic of fruit to complement the flavor of the pork. You will need to begin this dish the evening before you plan to make it.**

12 dried plums (prunes, see
    Smart Turn, page 126)
1/2 cup Armagnac or Cognac
One 3-pound pork loin roast
1 1/2 teaspoons salt
1/2 teaspoon freshly ground
    black pepper
2 tablespoons olive oil
1/4 cup Dijon mustard
1/2 cup firmly packed light
    brown sugar

Cut the plums in half, put them in a small mixing bowl, and pour the Armagnac over the plums. Set them aside until they have softened, about 1 hour. Drain the plums, saving the liquid.

Use a kabob rod or long skewer to poke a hole all the way through the meat, beginning at the cut end of the roast. Using your index finger, make the hole larger and stuff the prunes into the hole (you should be able to get 4 halves into the hole, working from each end). Make three other holes and repeat this procedure. Set the remaining plums aside for garnish.

In a 2-gallon zipper-top plastic bag, combine the soaking liquid from the plums, the salt, pepper, and olive oil. Add the pork to the bag, seal, and shake gently to coat the pork. Marinate in the refrigerator overnight.

Remove the roast from the bag and pat dry with paper towels. Load the roast onto the spit rod assembly, coat it with the mustard, then pat the brown sugar over the mustard to form a crust. Roast until an instant-read meat thermometer inserted into the thickest part of the meat registers 160 degrees, about 20 minutes per pound.

Carefully remove the roast from the spit rod assembly, cover loosely with aluminum foil, and let rest for 15 minutes before carving.

Serve the roast surrounded with the remaining plums.

Smart Turn

The prune people have renamed them "dried plums"— sounds a little bit more appetizing.

Why You Need an Instant-Read Thermometer

Pork tenderloins are not all created equal in size, weight, and thickness. It is important to test the meat with an instant-read meat thermometer before removing it from the rotisserie.

Aloha Pork Roast

Serves 6 to 8   Crusted with macadamia nuts and marinated in tropical fruit juices, this magnificent roast is fragrant with ginger and orange zest. Try using the same technique with chops in the rotisserie basket.

South Seas Marinade

$1/2$ cup pineapple juice

$1/4$ cup orange juice

$1/4$ cup unsweetened coconut milk

$1/4$ cup soy sauce

One 3-pound pork loin roast

Honey-Orange Glaze

2 teaspoons peeled and grated fresh ginger

Grated zest of 2 oranges

$1^1/2$ teaspoons salt

$1/2$ teaspoon freshly ground black pepper

2 tablespoons honey

1 cup chopped macadamia nuts

In a 2-gallon zipper-top plastic bag, combine the marinade ingredients. Add the roast, seal the bag, and shake gently to coat the meat. Marinate in the refrigerator for at least 6 and up to 24 hours.

In a small bowl, combine the glaze ingredients.

Remove the roast from the marinade, pat dry, and load onto the spit rod assembly. Coat the roast with the glaze mixture, then pat the nuts onto the glaze, making sure to cover the entire pork loin. Roast until an instant-read meat thermometer inserted into the thickest part registers 160 degrees, about 20 minutes per pound.

Remove the roast from the spit rod, cover loosely with aluminum foil, and allow to rest for 15 minutes before carving.

Asian Pork Tenderloin

Serves 6   Pork tenderloins are a great rotisserie dinner; they take very little time and absorb flavors well. This tenderloin is brined in an Asian-inspired marinade for an hour, then roasted for 20 minutes, until the outside is crisp and the inside is tender and juicy. A nice side of Asian Slaw (page 344) and sticky rice will complete your meal. Any leftovers can be turned into a salad or stir-fry noodle dish later in the week.

2 pork tenderloins (about 2 pounds total), silverskin removed

Simple Asian Marinade

2 tablespoons vegetable oil

2 cloves garlic, minced

2 tablespoons rice wine or rice vinegar

1/2 cup soy sauce

1 teaspoon peeled and grated fresh ginger

1/4 cup sesame seeds

1/2 cup water

Place the pork in a 2-gallon zipper-top plastic bag.

In a small mixing bowl, combine the marinade ingredients. Pour over the pork, seal the bag, and shake it gently to coat the pork. Marinate in the refrigerator for at least 1 and up to 2 hours.

Remove the pork from the marinade, pat dry, and thread each tenderloin onto the spit rod assembly.

Pour the water into the drip pan and roast until an instant-read meat thermometer inserted in the thickest part of the meat registers 160 degrees, about 10 minutes per pound.

Remove the meat from the spit rod assembly, cover loosely with aluminum foil, and allow to rest for 10 to 15 minutes before carving.

Smart Turn

Adding water to the drip pan helps to keep the tenderloins from drying out during cooking.

Cranberry-Pecan Pork Tenderloin

Serves 6 to 8   Flavored with tangy cranberries and crusted with pecans, this pork roast not only looks appealing, but the crunchy exterior and succulent meat are also a winning combination.

Cranberry-Orange Sauce

2 teaspoons butter

$1/2$ cup finely chopped onion

2 teaspoons peeled and grated fresh ginger

One $15\frac{1}{2}$-ounce can whole-berry cranberry sauce

$1/4$ cup orange juice

$1/4$ cup firmly packed light brown sugar

1 teaspoon dried thyme

2 pork tenderloins (about 2 pounds total), silverskin removed and brined for 1 hour (see page 119)

$1\frac{1}{2}$ cups chopped pecans

To make the sauce, in a small saucepan, melt the butter over medium heat. Add the onion and ginger, and cook, stirring, until the onion is softened, about 4 minutes. Add the cranberry sauce, orange juice, brown sugar, and thyme. Bring the mixture to a boil, reduce the heat to medium-low, and simmer until the sauce is thickened, about 20 minutes. At this point, the sauce may be refrigerated for up to 2 weeks. Reheat the sauce over medium heat when you are ready to use it, and keep it warm.

Lay the pork on a large piece of plastic wrap or waxed paper. Remove ½ cup of the sauce from the saucepan and brush the pork all over with it. Sprinkle the nuts onto the plastic wrap and roll the meat in the nuts until evenly covered.

Carefully load the pork onto the spit rod assembly, replacing any stray pecans. Roast until an instant-read meat thermometer inserted in the thickest part of the meat registers 160 degrees, about 10 minutes per pound.

Gently remove the pork from the spit rods, cover loosely with foil, and allow to rest for 15 minutes before carving.

Serve the pork with the reserved warmed cranberry sauce on the side.

Red Roasted Pork Tenderloin Shanghai Style

○ ● ○

Serves 6 to 8   Although not a Christmas red, this pork tenderloin roast is gloriously colored and seasoned with the flavors of Chinese cuisine. I like to think that somewhere in Shanghai someone is cooking something similar over an open fire, turning it slowly to caramelize the outside. The dish is great as an appetizer or main course, and leftovers taste wonderful rolled up in flour tortillas with some Asian Slaw (page 344) and slathered with leftover basting sauce. Try the same recipe with pork roast, chops, or ham.

Red Wine and Hoisin Basting Sauce

1 cup red wine

1/2 cup rice wine or rice vinegar

2 cups soy sauce

1/4 cup hoisin sauce

1/4 cup ketchup

3 cloves garlic, minced

1 teaspoon peeled and minced fresh ginger

1/2 teaspoon Chinese five-spice powder

2 tablespoons firmly packed dark brown sugar

To make the sauce, in a 1½-quart saucepan, combine the basting sauce ingredients and bring the mixture to a boil. Reduce the heat to medium-low, simmer until the mixture has thickened, about 20 minutes, and keep it warm. At this point, you may refrigerate the sauce for up to 2 weeks.

Load the pork onto the spit rod assembly, remove ½ cup of the baste, and brush the tenderloins with some of it. (Keep the rest warm for serving.) Roast until an instant-read meat thermometer inserted into the thickest part of the meat registers 160 degrees, about 20 minutes per pound, stopping the machine briefly every 10 minutes to baste the pork.

2 pork tenderloins (about 2
pound total), silverskin
removed and brined for
1 hour (see page 119)
4 green onions, white and
light green parts,
chopped

Remove the tenderloins from the spit rods, cover loosely with aluminum foil, and allow to rest for 15 minutes. Before carving, brush liberally with some of the warm basting sauce.

Serve the sauce alongside the roast and garnish with the chopped green onions.

Twirling Picnic

Serves 8   A picnic, or pork shoulder, roast is the basis for some great barbecue in the South, which you can recreate that in your rotisserie. This kind of roast is covered with a layer of fat, which is where pork rinds come from. In the rotisserie the fat turns into a crispy crust and insulates the meat, which becomes tender and juicy on the spit. The basting sauce here is just a suggestion; you can use whatever sauce suits you and your family. I do recommend that you go heavy on the rub, though. You will need to apply it at least 12 hours ahead of time.

One 3- to 5-pound pork shoulder roast, boned (have your butcher do this for you)

1/4 cup All-American Barbecue Rub (page 286)

Garlic-Herb Baste

1/4 cup All-American Barbecue Rub (page 286)

1/4 cup chopped fresh parsley leaves

1 tablespoon dried sage, crumbled

2 teaspoons dried thyme, crumbled

6 cloves garlic, chopped

1/2 cup beer

1/2 cup beef broth

Lay the shoulder out on a cutting board or other flat surface and sprinkle the barbecue rub evenly over both sides of the roast. Using cotton string, roll up the roast with the fat on the outside. Cover tightly with plastic wrap and refrigerate for at least 12 and up to 24 hours.

To make the baste, in a small saucepan, stir together the ingredients and bring to a boil. Reduce the heat to medium-low and simmer for 15 minutes. Cover and refrigerate until you are ready to roast the pork, then reheat the basting sauce to a simmer.

Load the roast onto the spit rod assembly and baste it with a little of the sauce. Roast until an instant-read meat thermometer inserted into the thickest part registers 160 degrees, about 20 minutes per pound, turning off the machine to baste it with the sauce every 20 minutes or so and restarting it.

Remove the pork from the spit rod, cover loosely with aluminum foil, and allow to rest for 15 minutes. Meanwhile, bring the basting sauce to a vigorous boil.

Carve the roast and drizzle with some of the warm basting sauce.

Smart Turn

Sometimes the meat pulls away from the crackling coating, and slicing becomes impossible. If that happens, make the best of it and cut the meat into chunks or pull the meat from the crackling, the way they do in the South.

Honey-Glazed Ham

Serves 8   Every year the purveyors of spiral sliced ham run advertisements that make your mouth water, including beauty shots of a glistening ham with a crackly coating. Your rotisserie can help you to achieve the same crispy coating, and for a lot less than that ham from the store. Basting with a combination of honey and raw sugar during the last 30 minutes of cooking time will give you that delicious, crunchy glaze.

One 5-pound fully cooked boneless or bone-in ham

Spiced Honey Glaze

1/2 cup honey

2 teaspoons fresh lemon juice

1 teaspoon ground cinnamon

1/8 teaspoon ground cloves

1/2 cup raw sugar crystals

Load the ham onto the spit rod assembly and roast until an instant-read thermometer inserted into the thickest part of the ham registers 160 degrees, about 13 minutes per pound.

While the ham is cooking, combine the glaze ingredients in a small bowl and stir until smooth.

About 30 minutes before the ham is done, stop the machine and brush the ham with the honey glaze. Then sprinkle the sugar crystals evenly over the glaze. Restart the machine and continue roasting.

Remove the ham from the spit rod, being careful not to knock off any of the crust. Cover loosely with aluminum foil and allow it to rest for 10 minutes before carving.

Red Hot Ham

Serves 8   **This Southern-inspired dish will make you a kid again because the glaze tastes like cinnamon-flavored Red Hot candies. The ham turns a delectable red on the outside and the cinnamon flavor permeates the meat.**

Tangy Cinnamon Glaze

1¹/₂ cups cranberry juice
    cocktail
8 cinnamon sticks
2 tablespoons firmly packed
    light brown sugar

One 5-pound fully cooked
    boneless or bone-in ham
¹/₄ cup plus 2 tablespoons
    firmly packed light
    brown sugar

To make the glaze, in a small saucepan over medium heat, combine the ingredients. Stir, bring to a simmer, and reduce the heat to low. Allow to steep over low heat for 1 hour. Remove from the heat and set aside.

Load the ham onto the spit rod assembly, brush it with some of the glaze, and roast until an instant-read meat thermometer inserted into the thickest part of the ham registers 160 degrees, about 15 minutes per pound.

Thirty minutes before the ham is done, turn off the rotisserie, baste with the glaze, and pat the brown sugar evenly all over the ham. Restart the rotisserie and continue cooking, stopping every 10 minutes to baste the ham with the glaze.

Remove the ham from the spit rod assembly, baste with any remaining glaze, and cover loosely with aluminum foil. Let the ham rest for 15 minutes before carving.

Maple-Glazed Ham

Serves 8   Maple syrup and smoky ham pair for a spectacular roast on the rotisserie. The sauce can be prepared ahead of time and kept in the refrigerator for up to a week.

Maple Syrup Glaze

1 cup pure maple syrup
2 tablespoons fresh lemon
    juice
1 teaspoon ground cinnamon

One 5-pound fully cooked
    boneless or bone-in ham

In a measuring cup, stir together the glaze ingredients.

Load the ham onto the spit rod assembly and brush with some of the glaze. Roast for 15 minutes per pound, stopping the machine every 10 minutes to brush the ham with the glaze and then restarting it. The ham is done when an instant-read thermometer inserted into the thickest part of the ham registers 160 degrees and the glaze is golden brown.

Remove the ham from the spit rod, baste with any remaining glaze, and cover loosely with aluminum foil. Let rest for 15 minutes before carving.

In my opinion, there is nothing better than biting into a juicy, tender rib slathered with barbecue sauce. The rotisserie is a great place to cook ribs, and the rib recipes in this chapter are terrific examples of how this simple cooking method makes extraordinary food. Baby back ribs are best when they are simmered for 15 minutes, then placed on the rotisserie. You can brine meaty, country-style ribs or you can simmer them for 15 to 20 minutes as well. Remember to baste the ribs during the last 15 to 20 minutes of cooking time, then baste them again when they are cut into serving portions.

Pork Rib Boil

You can just boil your ribs in salted water, but this mixture gives them a little pizzazz before they go onto the rotisserie.

4 quarts water
$1/3$ cup soy sauce
2 cloves garlic, quartered
3 dime-size pieces fresh ginger
3 black peppercorns

In a 5-quart stockpot, stir together all the ingredients.

Add the ribs to the pot and bring the liquid to a boil. Reduce the heat to medium-low and gently simmer for 15 minutes for baby back ribs and 15 to 20 minutes for country-style ribs.

Remove the pork from the liquid and pat dry. Refrigerate the ribs if you are not cooking them immediately.

Rotisserie Baby Back Ribs

Serves 6 **Tender baby back ribs are delicious on the rotisserie. The secret to moist and tender ribs is to simmer them first, then grill them in the rotisserie. The compact models can do one rack of ribs comfortably; the larger models will accommodate two.**

2 racks baby back ribs, boiled in Pork Rib Boil (page 136)

2 to 3 cups basting or barbecue sauce of your choice (see A Whole Lot of Saucin' Going On, pages 281-336), kept simmering on the stove

Arrange the spit rod assembly in the resting area of the rotisserie. Place 4 empty kabob rods next to each other in the holes around the wheel with the spring ends on the left side. Using another kabob rod, thread it through the first rib. Take the last kabob rod and thread it through the last rib (see Figure 1). Wrap the ribs around the empty kabob rods already arranged in the spit rod assembly until you come to the end (see Figure 2). Insert the kabob rods attached to the ribs into the gear wheel, with the spring ends on the left. For two racks of ribs, thread both racks at the same time, as described above.

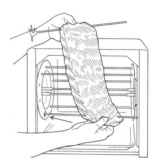

Figure 1

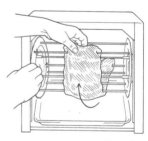

Figure 2

Brush the ribs with some of the barbecue sauce and grill for 17 to 22 minutes, stopping the machine to baste the ribs every 5 to 7 minutes. The ribs are done when they are crisp and the meat is pulling away from the bone.

Remove the racks from the rods, cut the ribs into individual portions, and brush with additional sauce.

Country-Style Pork Ribs

Serves 6   Meaty, country-style pork ribs are terrific on the rotisserie. They should be brined for a few hours before loading them onto the kabob rods, so that they stay moist and tender during the cooking time. If you prefer not to brine the ribs, you can use the Pork Rib Boil (page 136). If you go that route, your ribs will cook a little faster on the rotisserie, so check them for doneness after 30 minutes. The meat should no longer be pink in the center when it's done.

2$\frac{1}{2}$ pounds country-style pork spare ribs, brined for 4 hours (see page 119)

2 tablespoons olive oil

1 teaspoon salt

$\frac{1}{2}$ teaspoon freshly ground black pepper

1 to 2 cups basting or barbecue sauce of your choice (see A Whole Lot of Saucin' Going On, pages 281-336), kept at a simmer

Brush the ribs with some of the olive oil and sprinkle them evenly with the salt and pepper. Thread the ribs onto the kabob rods; some ribs may be very long and take up one rod, others may be short enough so you can fit two on a rod. Load the rods onto the spit rod assembly with the spring ends on the right side. Brush the meat with some of the basting sauce.

Grill the ribs for 20 minutes. Stop the machine, brush the ribs with more sauce, and restart the machine. Cook for 20 minutes more, stopping the machine to baste the meat every 5 minutes.

Remove the ribs from the rods and drizzle with additional sauce before serving.

Grilled in the rotisserie, pork chops are a quick and easy dinner. You can cook bone-in or boneless pork chops; the best thickness is about $3/4$ to 1 inch for even cooking. I recommend that you brine chops for 2 hours before grilling to help ensure that they don't dry out. Bone-in chops have a tendency to stick out of the basket, so be careful to position them so there aren't any bones protruding.

Plum Crazy Pork Chops

Serves 6   This sweet and savory pork dish can be prepared using chops, pork loin roast, tenderloin, or ham (see the Smart Turn). Here I use boneless pork chops, which have been brined for an hour before cooking. The result is tender, juicy meat, with a delectable plum basting sauce.

**Plum-Mustard
Basting Sauce**

2 tablespoons butter
$1/2$ cup finely chopped onion
1 cup plum preserves
2 tablespoons fresh lemon
  juice
2 tablespoons Dijon mustard
$1/4$ cup ketchup

8 boneless pork chops,
  1 inch thick, brined for
  1 hour (see page 119)

To make the sauce, in a small saucepan, melt the butter over medium heat. Cook the onion, stirring, until it begins to soften, about 3 minutes. Stir in the preserves, lemon juice, mustard, and ketchup. Bring to a simmer, reduce the heat to low, and continue to simmer the mixture until it is thick, about 15 minutes.

Measure out $1/4$ cup of the sauce, brush the chops with it, and keep the rest of the sauce warm.

Coat the rotisserie basket with nonstick cooking spray, arrange the chops in the basket, and close the lid tightly. Load the basket onto the spit rod assembly and grill the pork chops until an instant-read thermometer inserted into the thickest part of a chop registers 160 degrees, about 20 minutes.

Remove the chops from the basket, arrange on a serving plate, and brush with the reserved sauce. Serve immediately.

Smart Turn

For ham or roasts, baste with the sauce every 10 minutes during the last 30 minutes of cooking.

Caribbean Pork Chops with Tropical Salsa

Serves 6   Spicy jerk seasoning and cooling fruit nectar combine to turn your kitchen into a tropical paradise. The marinade will act as a brine, so make sure to marinate the chops for at least 2 hours before cooking.

8 center-cut, ³/₄-inch-thick boneless pork chops

Rummy Guava-Mango Marinade

3 tablespoons olive oil
¹/₄ cup guava nectar
¹/₄ cup mango nectar
2 tablespoons Jerk Seasoning Rub (page 290)

Place the chops in a 2-gallon zipper-top plastic bag.

In a medium-size glass mixing bowl, whisk together the marinade ingredients. Pour the marinade over the pork in the bag, seal the bag, and shake gently to coat the chops. Marinate in the refrigerator for at least 2 and up to 6 hours.

When ready to cook, drain the marinade into a medium-size saucepan and bring to a boil. Lower the heat, and simmer the marinade.

Coat the rotisserie basket with nonstick cooking spray. Place the chops in the basket and close the lid tightly. Load the basket onto the spit rod assembly and grill until an instant-

¼ cup dark rum

¼ cup soy sauce

2 tablespoons dark corn syrup

All-Purpose Fruit Salsa for garnish (recipe follows)

read meat thermometer inserted into the thickest part of a chop registers 160 degrees, 30 to 40 minutes.

Remove the chops from the basket and drizzle with some of the warm marinade. Serve garnished with the fruit salsa.

Smart Turn

Kern's, a division of Nestlé, sells canned nectars. You may find them in your supermarket on the shelves with other canned juices or with refrigerated juices.

All-Purpose Fruit Salsa

Makes 1¼ cups   **This basic formula for fruit salsa can be used for most soft fruits, such as peaches, mangoes, plums, cantaloupe, nectarines, and watermelon. It doesn't work with pears, apples, or other harder fruits. If you would like a little heat, turn it up by adding 1 to 2 teaspoons of finely chopped jalapeño or a few shakes of Tabasco.**

1 cup seeded and diced ripe mango, cantaloupe, plums, or peaches (½-inch dice)

¼ cup finely chopped red onion

2 tablespoons vegetable oil

2 tablespoons fresh lime juice, or to taste

Salt and freshly ground black pepper to taste

1 teaspoon sugar

¼ cup chopped fresh herbs (cilantro, basil, and mint are great choices)

In a small glass mixing bowl, stir together the fruit and onion. Sprinkle the vegetable oil and lime juice over the fruit, season with salt, pepper, and the sugar, and toss to combine. Sprinkle the fresh herbs over the mixture in the bowl and toss again.

The salsa is best if made 4 hours before serving and refrigerated. If you need to store it overnight, drain it before you serve it because the salt and lime juice will cause the fruit and vegetables to sweat their moisture.

Old-Fashioned Stuffed Pork Chops

○ ● ○

Serves 6 **This is an old-fashioned dish with a new twist. Pork chops are stuffed with a traditional bread stuffing seasoned with thyme and sage, then grilled in the rotisserie basket and basted with a Madeira wine and apricot glaze. It's a great dish for company, but also homey enough to serve during the week to the best company of all, your own family. You can make the stuffing the night before, then stuff the pork chops right before grilling.**

Madeira Marinade

2 tablespoons vegetable oil
2 tablespoons orange juice
1 teaspoon grated orange
    zest
2 tablespoons soy sauce
2 tablespoons Madeira wine
1 teaspoon freshly ground
    black pepper

8 center-cut, ³/₄-inch-thick
    boneless pork chops
Old-Fashioned Bread
    Stuffing (recipe follows)
Madeira-Apricot Basting
    Sauce (page 144), kept
    simmering on the stove

In a 2-gallon zipper-top plastic bag or glass baking dish, stir together the marinade ingredients.

Cut a pocket in the side of each pork chop about 1½ to 2 inches deep and 3 inches long. Add the pork chops to the marinade, seal the bag, and gently shake to coat the chops. Marinate in the refrigerator for at least 2 and up to 4 hours.

Remove the chops from the marinade and pat dry. Stuff each pocket with about ¼ cup of stuffing, pressing the filling firmly into the pockets.

Coat the rotisserie basket with nonstick cooking spray, place the chops in the basket, and close the lid tightly. Load the basket onto the spit rod assembly and grill the chops for 25 minutes. Stop the machine, brush with the basting sauce, and restart the machine. Cook the chops until an instant-read meat thermometer inserted into the thickest part of a chop registers 160 degrees, about another 20 minutes, stopping the machine to baste the chops 2 more times.

Remove the chops from the basket and garnish with the remaining basting sauce.

Old-Fashioned Bread Stuffing

Makes about 3 cups   This is comfort food to savor on its own or stuff into pork chops or a roasting chicken. Double the recipe for chicken, or to have extra stuffing when grilling pork chops, since they don't hold very much. Bake the additional stuffing in the oven for 20 to 30 minutes. Most rotisserie manufacturers don't recommend stuffing chicken or pork for fear the stuffing will fall out, but I find that if I don't cram in too much, the stuffing remains inside the meat and is delicious.

2 tablespoons butter
$\frac{1}{2}$ cup finely chopped onion
2 ribs celery, finely chopped
$1\frac{1}{2}$ teaspoons dried thyme
$\frac{1}{2}$ teaspoon dried sage,
    crumbled
3 cups stale French bread
    cubes, without crusts
$\frac{1}{2}$ cup hot chicken broth

In a small sauté pan, melt the butter over medium heat. Add the onion, celery, thyme, and sage, and cook, stirring, until the vegetables are soft and translucent, about 6 minutes.

Remove the pan from the heat, transfer the vegetables to a large mixing bowl, add the bread cubes, and toss to combine. Add the chicken broth, a few tablespoons at a time, until the stuffing holds together. The amount of broth will depend upon the bread and its absorption.

Cover and refrigerate the stuffing until you are ready to use it. It will keep, refrigerated, for 3 days.

Madeira-Apricot Basting Sauce

Makes about 2½ cups

This sweet and tangy sauce is a great baste for pork, ham, and poultry.

1 tablespoon butter
1 medium-size shallot, minced
Leaves from 3 sprigs fresh thyme
1 cup apricot jam
1 cup Madeira wine
Pinch of ground nutmeg
½ teaspoon freshly ground black pepper
2 tablespoons chicken broth
½ cup dried apricots, thinly sliced
¼ cup chopped fresh parsley leaves

In a small saucepan, melt the butter over medium heat. Add the shallot and thyme and cook, stirring, until the shallot is golden, about 5 minutes. Stir in the apricot jam, wine, nutmeg, pepper, and broth and bring to a boil. Reduce the heat to low and simmer for 20 to 30 minutes, stirring occasionally.

Stir in the dried apricots and parsley and simmer for an additional 5 minutes.

Remove the sauce from the heat and use immediately or store, covered, in the refrigerator for up to 5 days or freeze for up to 2 months. Reheat the sauce when you are ready to use it.

Honey-Lime Basted Pork Chops

Serves 6   **These golden chops are flavored with clean-tasting lime juice and smooth honey while grilling in the rotisserie. The result is a chop that is crispy, juicy, sweet, and tender. Make sure to brine the chops for 2 hours before grilling.**

2 tablespoons olive oil
1 tablespoon All-American Barbecue Rub (page 286)
8 center-cut, ³/₄-inch-thick pork chops, brined for 2 hours (page 119)

Honey-Lime Glaze

¹/₄ cup fresh lime juice
¹/₂ cup honey
2 teaspoons dried thyme
Pinch of cayenne
¹/₈ teaspoon ground cumin

¹/₄ cup chopped fresh cilantro leaves for garnish
1 or 2 limes for garnish, each cut into 8 wedges

Pour the olive oil into a shallow dish and mix with the barbecue rub. Dip the chops into the spice mixture and turn to coat evenly.

Coat the rotisserie basket with nonstick cooking spray, lay the chops in the basket, and close the lid tightly. Load the basket onto the spit rod assembly and grill the chops for 10 minutes.

While the chops are grilling, combine the glaze ingredients in a small mixing bowl.

When the chops have cooked 10 minutes, stop the machine and baste the chops with the glaze. Restart the machine and continue to grill the chops until an instant-read meat thermometer inserted in the thickest part registers 160 degrees, about another 25 minutes, stopping the machine 3 more times to baste.

Remove the chops from the basket, garnish with the cilantro and lime wedges, and serve.

Santa Fe Pork Kabobs

Serves 6   **Marinated with lime and fragrant with cumin and chili powder, these kabobs will liven up a weeknight meal. Serve with flour tortillas and a fruit salsa on the side.**

Santa Fe Chili Rub

2 teaspoons chili powder

$^1/_2$ teaspoon ground cumin

1 clove garlic, minced

2 tablespoons fresh lime juice

2 tablespoons canola oil

1 teaspoon light brown sugar

1 teaspoon salt

$^1/_2$ teaspoon freshly ground black pepper

$^1/_4$ cup chopped red onion

2 pounds pork loin or shoulder meat, trimmed of excess fat and cut into 1-inch pieces

$^1/_4$ cup chopped red onion for garnish

$^1/_2$ cup chopped fresh cilantro leaves for garnish

In a medium-size glass mixing bowl or a 2-gallon zipper-top plastic bag, combine the rub ingredients. Add the pork to the mixture, toss to coat, and cover the bowl with plastic wrap or seal the bag. Marinate in the refrigerator for at least 2 and up to 6 hours.

When ready to cook, drain the pork and thread onto the kabob rods, leaving ¼ inch between each piece of meat for air to circulate. Load the kabobs on the spit rod assembly with the spring ends on the right. Grill until an instant-read meat thermometer inserted into the thickest piece of meat reads 160 degrees, about 30 minutes.

Remove the meat from the skewers, garnish with the red onion and cilantro, and serve.

Nona's Pork Spiedini

—○ ● ○—

Serves 6 My grandmother cooked some really memorable meals when I was a child, and this skewered pork dish, prepared outdoors over an open flame, was pure heaven. Nona dry-marinated the pork overnight in the refrigerator, then brushed the kabobs with olive oil and let the fire do the rest. She would serve this over a salad of tossed greens and fresh tomato slices dressed with oil and red wine vinegar. You will need to marinate the pork for at least 12 hours.

2 pounds pork loin or shoulder meat, trimmed of excess fat and cut into 1-inch cubes

2 teaspoons salt

1 teaspoon freshly ground black pepper

1 tablespoon crumbled fresh rosemary leaves

4 cloves garlic, chopped

1 tablespoon chopped fresh sage leaves

¼ cup olive oil

Place the pork in a large mixing bowl or 2-gallon zipper-top plastic bag and sprinkle it with the salt, pepper, rosemary, garlic, and sage, tossing to coat the cubes evenly. Cover the bowl with plastic wrap or seal the bag and marinate in the refrigerator for at least 12 and up to 24 hours.

Load the pork onto the kabob rods, leaving ¼ inch between each piece for air to circulate, and brush each skewer with some of the olive oil. Load the kabob rods onto the spit rod assembly with the spring ends on the right. Grill until an instant-read meat thermometer inserted into the thickest piece registers 160 degrees, 30 to 35 minutes.

Remove the pork from the skewers and serve immediately.

Pork kabobs cooked on the rotisserie are simple and give you a jump on a quick dinner during the week. Marinate or brine the pork, thread it onto the kabob rods, then load them onto the spit rod assembly with the spring ends on the right. In little more than half an hour, you will have a gourmet meal fit for a king. Kabobs can be served on a bed of rice, sautéed veggies, smashed potatoes, or fruit salsas.

Indonesian Pork Satay

Serves 6 Flavored with peanuts and coconut, these skewers are insanely easy, and the results are terrific. Serve with Asian Slaw (page 344), Chile Peanut Dipping Sauce (page 149), and jasmine rice.

Peanut-Ginger Marinade

1/2 cup soy sauce

1/4 cup unsweetened coconut milk

2 tablespoons smooth peanut butter

2 cloves garlic, minced

2 teaspoons fresh lime juice

To make the marinade, in a 2-quart saucepan, whisk the ingredients together over medium heat until the peanut butter thins out and the brown sugar dissolves. Remove from the heat and let cool to room temperature.

Place the pork in a zipper-top plastic bag. Pour the marinade into the bag, seal, and shake it gently to coat the pork. Marinate in the refrigerator for at least 2 and up to 6 hours.

2 teaspoons peeled and
grated fresh ginger
1 tablespoon firmly packed
light brown sugar

2 pounds pork loin or
shoulder meat, trimmed
of excess fat and cut into
1-inch chunks
1/2 cup salted roasted
peanuts, chopped, for
garnish
1/4 cup unsweetened
shredded coconut
(available in health food
stores) for garnish
1/4 cup chopped fresh
cilantro leaves for
garnish
Chile Peanut Dipping Sauce
(optional)

Remove the pork from the marinade and pat dry. Load the pork onto the kabob rods, leaving ¼ inch between each piece for air to circulate. Load the kabob rods onto the spit rod assembly with the spring ends on the right side. Grill until an instant-read meat thermometer inserted into the thickest pieces registers 160 degrees, 30 to 35 minutes.

Remove the pork from the skewers, garnish with chopped peanuts, coconut, and cilantro, and serve. Pass the Chile Peanut Dipping Sauce separately, if desired.

Chile Peanut Dipping Sauce

Makes about 2⅓ cups into a delightful feast.

This spicy little sauce turns an ordinary satay into a delightful feast.

1 cup chicken broth
3/4 cup smooth peanut
butter
1/4 cup firmly packed light
brown sugar
1/4 cup unsweetened
coconut milk
2 tablespoons soy sauce
1 tablespoon peeled and
grated fresh ginger
5 shakes Tabasco sauce

Place all the ingredients in a medium-size saucepan. Bring to a boil, whisking until the brown sugar and peanut butter dissolve, then reduce the heat to medium-low and simmer for 2 minutes.

Remove the sauce from the heat and serve warm. Refrigerate any leftover sauce for up to 5 days. Reheat, thinning with chicken broth as needed.

Spinning Sausages and Peppers

Serves 6 One of my favorite combinations is Italian sausages with peppers and onions. They can all be cooked on the rotisserie kabob rods and loaded into crusty rolls for a great meal while watching football.

8 Italian sausages
1 medium-size red bell pepper, seeded and cut into 1-inch squares
1 medium-size green bell pepper, seeded and cut into 1-inch squares
1 large red onion, quartered
2 tablespoons olive oil
1 1/2 teaspoons salt
1/2 teaspoon freshly ground black pepper
6 crusty rolls
2 cups Quick Marinara (optional, page 318), warmed
1/2 cup grated mozzarella or Monterey Jack cheese (optional)

Cut each sausage crosswise in half and prick with a sharp knife in several places.

Place the bell peppers, onion, olive oil, salt, and pepper in a large mixing bowl and toss to coat the vegetables.

Thread the kabob rods, alternating sausage pieces with peppers and onion, and load the kabob rods onto the spit rod assembly with the spring ends on the right side. Grill until the vegetables are charred and the sausages cooked through, 30 to 35 minutes.

Remove the meat and vegetables from the skewers and serve in crusty rolls, topped with the marinara and grated cheese, if desired.

Sausages are terrific on the rotisserie, whether they be hot dogs, bratwurst, Italian sausages, or smoked sausages. Load them into the basket or onto the kabob rods, depending upon how many you have and what your preference is.

When using kabob rods, skewer the sausage down the center of each rod lengthwise and load the kabob rods onto the spit rod assembly. If you are grilling in the basket, place the sausages in the basket, close the lid tightly, and load onto the spit rod assembly. If you only have a few in the basket, remember to tuck some aluminum foil into the corners so you don't end up with flying sausages.

Cajun Turbo Dogs

Serves 6 to 8 **This is just the thing to serve to the guys when you are watching football games. Boil the sausages in Abita Brewery's Turbo Dog dark ale or another dark brew, rub them with Cajun spices, and then grill on the rotisserie until browned. Serve with lots of cold beer and coarse-grained mustard.**

Two 12-ounce bottles Turbo Dog or other dark ale
2 pounds hot dogs, Polish sausage, or bratwurst
2 tablespoons Creole Seasoning Rub (page 287)

Pour the ale into a large saucepan, add the sausages, and bring to a boil. Reduce the heat to medium-low, and simmer for 4 to 6 minutes. Remove the sausages from the liquid and prick with a sharp knife.

Spread the Creole seasoning on a plate and roll the sausages in it.

Coat the rotisserie basket with nonstick cooking spray and arrange the sausages in the basket, closing the lid tightly. Load the basket onto the spit rod assembly and grill the sausages until evenly browned, about 30 minutes.

Remove the sausages from the basket and serve.

Variation

Turbo Dog Bites: Cut the sausages into 1-inch-thick rounds and follow the directions above, but load the bites onto the kabob rods instead of the basket and grill for 30 minutes.

Milwaukee Beer Brats

Serves 6 **These brats are boiled in beer before they are grilled. The sauerkraut in the drip pan catches the flavor of the sausages while they are cooking. This is couch potato food supreme, and a great Saturday night supper.**

One 12-ounce can dark beer

1 teaspoon caraway seeds

8 bratwurst links

One 15 1/2-ounce can sauerkraut, rinsed and drained

In a 10-inch skillet, combine the beer, caraway seeds, and bratwurst. Bring the beer to a boil, reduce the heat to medium-low, and simmer for 10 minutes.

Spread the sauerkraut over the bottom of the rotisserie drip pan, and pour ¼ cup of the beer in the skillet over the sauerkraut. Place the cover on the drip pan and position the pan in the rotisserie.

Coat the rotisserie basket with nonstick cooking spray, drain the bratwurst, and load them into the basket, closing the lid tightly. Load the basket onto the spit rod assembly and grill until the sausages are golden brown, 20 to 25 minutes.

Remove the sausages from the grill basket and serve on a bed of sauerkraut.

Hot Doggers

Serves 6   When I was a kid, one of my favorite things was a hot dog split open, slathered with mustard, and stuffed with cheddar cheese. My dad loved them too. He would cook them on the barbecue, and there were many times when he'd eat them before they got to the table.

10 jumbo all-beef hot dogs, split in half lengthwise, but not all the way through

1/4 cup brown mustard

1 cup grated cheddar cheese

Brush the interior of the hot dog liberally with the mustard.

Sprinkle some of the cheese over the mustard and close up the hot dog.

Coat the rotisserie basket with nonstick cooking spray and put the hot dogs into the basket, closing the lid tightly. Load the basket onto the spit rod assembly and grill the hot dogs until browned, 15 to 17 minutes.

Remove the hot dogs from the basket and serve. The cheese may be a little drippy, so spoon some of it over the dogs if you lose any.

Burgers are great grilled in the basket, and pork burgers are moist and flavorful. The compact rotisserie basket will hold 5 comfortably, and the larger size will hold 8. Burgers can be prepared in the morning and refrigerated until you are ready to grill later in the day. Remember to coat the basket with nonstick cooking spray for easy clean up.

Rasta Pork Barbecue Burgers

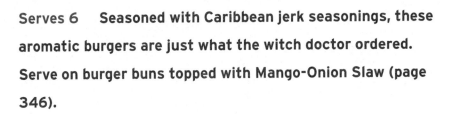

Serves 6   Seasoned with Caribbean jerk seasonings, these aromatic burgers are just what the witch doctor ordered. Serve on burger buns topped with Mango-Onion Slaw (page 346).

1½ pounds lean ground pork
¼ cup minced onion
1 teaspoon dried thyme
½ teaspoon ground allspice
1 teaspoon dark brown sugar
1 teaspoon salt
½ teaspoon freshly ground
black pepper
½ teaspoon dried sage
⅛ teaspoon cayenne pepper
2 cloves garlic, mashed

In a large mixing bowl, stir together all the ingredients until well blended. Form the mixture into 6 burger patties, about ¾ inch thick. Refrigerate the burgers until you are ready to grill, up to 12 hours.

Coat the rotisserie basket with nonstick cooking spray and arrange the burgers in the basket, closing the lid tightly. Load the basket onto the spit rod assembly and grill until an instant-read meat thermometer inserted into a burger registers 160 degrees, 25 to 30 minutes.

Remove the burgers from the basket and serve immediately.

Old-Fashioned Ham Loaf Burgers

Serves 6   Ham loaf was a staple in the Midwest during the '50s. Smoky and sweet, these burgers are delicious served on challah buns with Mom's Pretty in Pink Slaw (page 345). They're a great way to recycle that Easter ham.

2 cups chopped smoked ham
1/4 cup packed fresh parsley
    leaves
1/4 cup ketchup
1 teaspoon dry mustard
1 cup fresh bread crumbs
1 teaspoon salt
1/2 teaspoon freshly ground
    black pepper
1/8 teaspoon ground nutmeg
1/4 teaspoon ground ginger
1 pound lean ground pork
1/2 cup firmly packed light
    brown sugar
1/4 cup Dijon mustard

In a food processor, combine the ham and parsley and pulse on and off until finely chopped. Transfer to a large mixing bowl. Stir the ketchup, mustard, bread crumbs, salt, pepper, nutmeg, ginger, and ground pork into the ham and parsley mixture and continue mixing until well combined. Form the mixture into 6 patties about ¾ inch thick. Refrigerate until ready to cook, up to 12 hours.

In a small mixing bowl, stir the brown sugar and mustard together.

Coat the rotisserie basket with nonstick cooking spray. Brush each burger with some of the brown sugar mixture, arrange the burgers in the basket, and close the lid tightly. Load onto the spit rod assembly and grill until an instant-read meat thermometer inserted into a burger registers 160 degrees, 22 to 25 minutes.

Remove the burgers from the basket and serve immediately.

Pineapple Teriyaki Pork Burgers

Serves 6   Pineapple slices and teriyaki sauce give these burgers a taste of the islands. Serve them with Cold Sesame Noodle Salad (page 359) or Asian Slaw (page 344).

1½ pounds lean ground pork

¼ cup chopped green onions, white and light green parts only

½ teaspoon freshly ground black pepper

½ cup Spicy Teriyaki Sauce (page 314), Top Secret Teriyaki Sauce (page 315), or store-bought teriyaki sauce

Six ½-inch-thick slices pineapple

In a large mixing bowl, stir together the pork, green onions, pepper, and ¼ cup of the teriyaki sauce until well blended. Form the mixture into 6 patties about ¾ inch thick. Refrigerate the patties until ready to cook, up to 12 hours.

Coat the rotisserie basket with nonstick cooking spray and lay the burgers in the basket. Cover each with a slice of pineapple, close the lid tightly, and load the basket onto the spit rod assembly. Grill until an instant-read meat thermometer inserted into a burger registers 160 degrees, 22 to 25 minutes.

Remove the burgers from the basket, baste with some of the remaining ¼ cup of teriyaki sauce, and serve immediately.

Honey Dijon Pork Burgers

Serves 6   **Zesty Dijon mustard mixed with honey gives these pork burgers a sweet and spicy kick. These also make great cocktail meatballs.**

1½ pounds lean ground pork
1 teaspoon salt
½ teaspoon freshly ground
  black pepper
1 teaspoon dried sage
½ cup chopped shallots
½ cup Dijon mustard
2 tablespoons honey
1 tablespoon fresh lemon
  juice

In a large mixing bowl, combine the pork, salt, pepper, sage, and shallots, stirring until well blended.

In a small mixing bowl, blend together the mustard, honey, and lemon juice. Add 2 tablespoons of the mixture to the pork and stir to combine. Refrigerate the remaining honey mustard. Form the pork mixture into 6 patties ¾ inch thick. Refrigerate the burgers until ready to cook, up to 12 hours.

Coat the basket of the rotisserie with nonstick cooking spray and lay the burgers in the basket. Set aside ¼ cup of the honey mustard and brush each burger with a little of the remainder. Close the lid tightly and load the basket onto the spit rod assembly. Grill until an instant-read meat thermometer inserted into a burger registers 160 degrees, 22 to 25 minutes.

Remove from the grill basket and serve immediately, with the reserved honey mustard on the side.

Wonton Burgers

Serves 6   These burgers mimic the filling in wontons, a spicy pork and shrimp mixture, with a soy and sesame oil baste to perk up the flavor.

1 pound lean ground pork
1 teaspoon cornstarch
1/2 cup soy sauce
2 teaspoons rice wine or
   rice vinegar
1/4 pound shrimp, peeled,
   deveined, and coarsely
   chopped
4 green onions, white
   and green parts kept
   separated and chopped
3 tablespoons toasted
   sesame oil

In a large mixing bowl, combine the pork, cornstarch, 2 tablespoons of the soy sauce, the rice wine, shrimp, chopped white parts of the green onions, and 1 tablespoon of the sesame oil, and stir to blend.

Stir together the remaining 1/4 cup plus 2 tablespoons of soy sauce and 2 tablespoons of sesame oil.

Form the pork mixture into 6 patties 3/4 inch thick. Refrigerate the patties until ready to use, up to 12 hours.

Coat the rotisserie basket with nonstick cooking spray and lay the burgers in the basket. Brush the burgers with the soy-sesame mixture, close the lid, and load the basket onto the spit rod assembly. Grill until an instant-read meat thermometer inserted into a burger registers 160 degrees, 22 to 25 minutes.

Remove the burgers from the basket and serve immediately, sprinkled with the remaining chopped green onion tops.

Fish Tales

The rotisserie is the perfect place to grill fish and some types of shellfish. The basket is great for scallops, shrimp, and fish steaks or fillets. Fish kabobs will become one of your favorites; because the fish is rotated, there is no danger of overcooking one side, or having it stick to the grill, as is sometimes the case outdoors. Instead, the fish comes out succulent and juicy, not dry. This is the perfect method for those who have been hesitant to try cooking fish and shellfish at home. Grill crab cakes and salmon burgers in no time at all, without using any oil; you won't even notice that you are cooking lighter.

Fish cooks quickly, and since not all fish is exactly one inch thick and not all shrimp are exactly the same size, take care to watch what you're cooking while you're cooking it. Don't be afraid to stop the rotisserie, check to see if it's done before, or after, my suggested cooking times. The best fish to cook on the rotisserie are those that have firm flesh and are at least three-quarters of an inch thick. I recommend tuna, salmon, swordfish, halibut, sea bass, escolar, mahimahi, mako shark, and monkfish. Shrimp, lobster, and scallops are also great in the rotisserie, cooked either in the basket or as kabobs.

Whole fish are generally too large to cook in the compact rotisserie. If you have the larger size, you can grill small whole fish, such as trout with its tail removed, in the basket. The rotisserie really is best, though, for fillets, steaks, kabobs, burgers, and shellfish.

Fish fillets and steaks can be cooked in the basket. I like to brush them with some oil before cooking to keep them from drying out. You can also cut thin slices of citrus (lemon, lime, or orange) and lay them on top of the fish to help keep them moist. Basting sauces flavor fish and keep it moist throughout the cooking time.

Kabobs are simple to make and cook in a jiffy. Whether you cook all of one kind of fish, or alternate different types on the kabob rods, the rods turn them so that they are cooked evenly. Like fish fillets and steaks, kabobs benefit from a good basting sauce.

Fish burgers are a great way to transform leftover cooked fish, crab, or shrimp into yummy meals. Make sure to coat the grill basket with a nonstick cooking spray so that the burgers can be easily removed from the basket after they are cooked.

When you get fish home from the market, make sure that you wash it thoroughly in cold water and pat it dry. Store the fish, covered in plastic wrap, in the refrigerator until you are ready to use it. If you are using frozen fish, make sure to defrost it overnight in the refrigerator, then wash in cold water and pat dry.

Fish Tales

Fish and shellfish can be lightly coated with any of the following prepared seasonings, rubs, or bastes, and grilled according to the manufacturer's directions.

Spicy No-Brainers

When using spices, rub whatever you're going to prepare with some oil first so that they will stick to the fish or shellfish.

- Old Bay seasoning
- Creole Seasoning Rub (page 287)
- Cavender's Greek seasoning
- Herbes de Provence Rub (page 289)
- Lemon Pepper Rub (page 286)
- Mrs. Dash (any flavor)
- Dried *fines herbes*
- Seasoned Salt (page 285)

Saucy No-Brainers

- Bottled Caesar salad dressing
- Bottled Italian salad dressing
- Bottled teriyaki sauce or Spicy Teriyaki Sauce (page 314) or Top Secret Teriyaki Sauce (page 315)
- Garlic oil

Smart Turn

Some people complain about odors in the house when they cook fish. With the rotisserie the best way to get rid of the odors is to put a few lemon slices in the drip pan along with about ¼ cup of water. The lemon tends to neutralize the odor from the fish.

Salt-Crusted Fish

Serves 4 **This is an old-fashioned way to cook, but it works wonderfully on the rotisserie. You will need a larger rotisserie to prepare this because the smaller one does not have a big enough basket to accommodate whole fish.**

4 whole small fish (about 1 pound each), such as snapper, sunfish, or trout, cleaned, gutted, and head and tail removed

1½ teaspoons salt

½ teaspoon freshly ground black pepper

1 large onion, thinly sliced

1 tablespoon fresh thyme leaves

¼ cup fresh lemon juice

¼ cup extra-virgin olive oil

4 cups kosher salt

1 to 2 cups warm water, as needed

Sprinkle the inside of the fish with the salt and pepper. Lay some of the onion inside the fish and sprinkle the onion with the thyme. Cut several deep slits through the skin of the fish, parallel to the bone. Whisk together the lemon juice and olive oil and pour some of the mixture into the slits.

In a large mixing bowl, stir together the kosher salt and 1 cup of the water, adding more salt or water as necessary to make a paste. Spread the paste over the fish so that it has a nice crusting of salt on both sides.

Coat the grill basket with nonstick cooking spray. Put the fish into the grill basket and close the lid tightly. Load the basket onto the spit rod assembly and grill until the crust is hardened and browned, 25 to 35 minutes. Slash into the thickest part of the fish to see if the flesh is opaque and flakes away from the bone.

Remove the fish from the basket, and scrape the salt off the skin. Run a knife along the backbone of the fish, cutting the flesh away from the bone. Remove the skin, and serve the fillet.

Miso-Glazed Sea Bass

Serves 6 Miso, a soybean product found in the Asian section of the supermarket, is a staple in the Japanese kitchen. Here it is used to glaze meaty sea bass for a savory entrée. Serve this with Ginger-Glazed Bok Choy (page 214).

Miso Glaze

1/3 cup white miso or 1 box Kikkoman Shiro Miso soup mix

1/4 cup rice wine

3 tablespoons sugar

2 tablespoons vegetable oil

2 tablespoons soy sauce

4 shakes Tabasco sauce

2 pounds sea bass fillets

3 green onions, white and light green parts, chopped, for garnish

2 tablespoons sesame seeds for garnish

In a small mixing bowl, stir together the glaze ingredients.

Place the sea bass in a 2-gallon zipper-top plastic bag, pour the glaze over it, and seal the bag. Turn it over to coat the fish and marinate in the refrigerator for at least 1 and up to 4 hours.

When ready to cook, coat the rotisserie basket with nonstick cooking spray, remove the fish from the marinade, and pat it dry. Arrange the fish in the basket and close the lid tightly. Load the basket onto the spit rod assembly and grill until the fish is cooked through, 18 to 22 minutes.

Remove the fish from the basket, garnish with the green onions and sesame seeds, and serve immediately.

Smart Turn

Sea bass can tolerate a longer cooking time than most fish; the standard rule of 10 minutes of cooking time for each inch of flesh doesn't apply. Cooking the fish thoroughly ensures that it is tender and flaky throughout; if it is undercooked, it can be tough and chewy.

Lemon-Dill Halibut

Serves 6 **Halibut is one of my favorite fishes because it has a mild flavor and adapts well to any method of cooking.**

Lemon-Dill Butter

2 tablespoons vegetable oil

1/2 cup (1 stick) butter, melted

3 tablespoons fresh lemon juice

2 tablespoons chopped fresh dill

1 teaspoon sweet paprika

2 pounds halibut fillets

Combine the ingredients for the flavored butter in a shallow dish. Dip the fillets in the mixture, coating them evenly on both sides. Place the fish in the rotisserie basket and close the lid tightly. Place the remaining lemon-dill butter in a small saucepan, bring to a simmer, and keep at a simmer over low heat.

Load the basket onto the spit rod assembly and grill until cooked through, 15 to 22 minutes, turning off the machine to baste the fish with the hot lemon-dill butter 2 or 3 times.

Remove the fish from the basket to a serving platter and pour the remaining hot lemon-dill butter over the fish. Serve immediately.

Halibut with Tequila-Lime Baste

Serves 4   Halibut is a great fish on the rotisserie; it cooks evenly and loves to be basted, and what could be better than a little tequila and lime to spice things up? Sometimes at our house, we'll grill the fish, then make them into tacos, tucking the fish into soft corn tortillas and garnishing with a cabbage salad, guacamole, and Salsa Fresca (page 297). If you have a larger rotisserie, you can double the recipe.

Tequila-Lime Baste

1/2 cup olive oil
1/4 cup fresh lime juice
1/4 cup tequila, preferably
   Cuervo Gold
1 1/2 teaspoons kosher salt
Pinch of cayenne pepper

Four 6-ounce halibut fillets
1/4 cup chopped fresh
   cilantro leaves for
   garnish

In a small mixing bowl, whisk together the baste ingredients. Dip the fillets into the mixture and turn them over to coat evenly.

Coat the rotisserie basket with nonstick cooking spray, put the halibut into the basket, and close the lid tightly. Give the fillets one last baste and load the basket onto the spit rod assembly. Grill until the fish flakes when it's pierced with a knife, 20 to 25 minutes.

Remove the fish from the basket, garnish with the chopped cilantro, and serve immediately.

Monkfish with Jalapeño-Cilantro Butter

Serves 4 to 6   Monkfish is referred to as poor man's lobster because it is such a rich and succulent fish. It tends to be irregularly shaped, so the best way to cook it on the rotisserie is to cut it into kabobs. If you get several pieces that are the same thickness, you can certainly do them in the grill basket.

Jalapeño-Cilantro Butter

- 1/2 cup (1 stick) butter
- 1/4 cup chopped shallots
- 1 tablespoon seeded and finely chopped jalapeño
- 1 teaspoon salt
- Pinch of cayenne pepper
- 2 teaspoons fresh lime juice
- 1/4 cup chopped fresh cilantro leaves

- 1 1/2 pounds monkfish, membranes removed and cut into 1-inch pieces

To make the flavored butter, in a small saucepan, melt the butter over medium heat, then add the shallots and cook, stirring, until softened, about 3 minutes. Add the jalapeño and cook 1 or 2 minutes more, then add the salt, cayenne, lime juice, and cilantro. At this point, you can refrigerate the flavored butter for up to 4 days. Keep at a simmer.

Thread the monkfish onto the kabob rods and brush with some of the flavored butter. Load the kabob rods onto the spit rod, making sure that the spring ends are on the right side. Grill until the fish is flaky when pierced with a knife, 20 to 25 minutes, stopping the machine every 7 to 10 minutes to baste the fish.

Remove the fish from the skewers and serve immediately.

Sesame Salmon Steaks

Serves 4   Salmon is one of those great fish that tastes wonderful no matter how you prepare it. Here the salmon is glazed with soy and sesame oil for a smoky flavor. The dish is finished with green onions and sesame seeds for additional color and texture. If you have a larger rotisserie, you can double the recipe.

Sesame-Soy Basting Sauce

¹/₂ cup soy sauce
2 tablespoons rice wine
1 tablespoon toasted sesame oil

Four 6-ounce salmon steaks or 2 pounds salmon fillets
2 tablespoons toasted sesame oil
4 green onions, white and light green parts, chopped, for garnish
¹/₄ cup sesame seeds for garnish

To make the sauce, in a small saucepan, heat the soy sauce, rice wine, and 1 tablespoon of the sesame oil over medium heat until it simmers. Keep the sauce at a simmer.

Coat the rotisserie basket with nonstick cooking spray, lay the salmon in the basket, and close the lid tightly. Brush the salmon with some of the basting sauce and load the basket onto the spit rod assembly. Grill the salmon until the fish is flaky when pierced with a knife, 20 to 25 minutes, stopping the machine to baste the salmon 2 or 3 times during the cooking.

Remove the salmon from the grill basket, drizzle with the remaining sesame oil, sprinkle with green onions and sesame seeds, and serve immediately.

Five-Spice Salmon

Serves 6   Chinese five-spice powder—a mixture of ground star anise, cinnamon, Szechuan peppercorns, fennel seeds, and cloves—takes center stage here. This is nice served on a bed of Ginger-Glazed Bok Choy (page 214).

¼ cup vegetable oil
3 tablespoons Chinese five-spice powder
2 pounds salmon fillets

In a 13 x 9-inch baking dish, combine the vegetable oil and five-spice powder. Dip the salmon fillets into the oil mixture and turn to coat well. Cover with plastic wrap and marinate in the refrigerator for at least 1 and up to 8 hours.

When ready to cook, coat the rotisserie basket with nonstick cooking spray. Place the salmon in the basket and close the lid tightly. Load the basket onto the spit rod assembly and grill until just cooked through, 20 to 25 minutes.

Remove the salmon from the basket and serve immediately.

Sweet Hot Mustard-Glazed Salmon

Serves 6   This sweet and tangy glaze seals in the natural flavor of the salmon and gives it a spicy coating as well. The glaze also makes a nice dipping sauce for cooked shrimp.

Honey Dijon Glaze

1 cup Dijon mustard

$^1/_2$ cup honey

1 tablespoon fresh lemon
   juice

1$^1/_2$ pounds salmon fillets

In a small mixing bowl, stir the glaze ingredients until smooth.

Coat the rotisserie basket with nonstick cooking spray and place the salmon fillets inside, skin side against the basket. Brush the glaze liberally over the flesh of the salmon, close the lid tightly, and load the basket onto the spit rod assembly. Grill until just cooked through, 15 to 20 minutes. Meanwhile, heat the remaining glaze in a small saucepan until it reaches a simmer.

Remove the salmon from the basket, brush each fillet with some of the hot glaze, and serve immediately.

Daikon-Crusted Salmon

Serves 6 Daikon, a member of the radish family, becomes crispy on the outside of the salmon, while the fish remains tender and moist inside.

1¹/₂ cups peeled and coarsely grated daikon

1 teaspoon salt

¹/₂ teaspoon freshly ground black pepper

2 tablespoons Dijon mustard

1 tablespoon firmly packed dark brown sugar

2 pounds salmon fillets

¹/₄ cup sesame seeds for garnish

4 green onions, white and light green parts, chopped, for garnish

In a small mixing bowl, combine the daikon, salt, and pepper, tossing to blend, and set aside. In another small bowl, blend together the mustard and brown sugar.

Coat the rotisserie basket with nonstick cooking spray and lay the salmon in the basket, skin side against the basket. Brush the fillets with the mustard mixture, then pat some of the daikon onto the fillets so that you have about a ½-inch-thick crust. Close the basket lid tightly, load it onto the spit rod assembly, and grill until the salmon is cooked through and the daikon begins to turn golden, 15 to 18 minutes. Don't worry if some of the daikon falls off during the cooking; the mustard "glue" will hold on enough for a nice presentation.

Carefully remove the salmon from the basket and serve immediately, garnished with the sesame seeds and green onions.

Teriyaki-Style Salmon

Serves 6   **Salmon is a great fish to cook on the rotisserie and this Japanese sauce gives it a sweet and salty flavor. Serve with sticky rice and a green salad with ginger dressing.**

Teriyaki Marinade

1/2 cup soy sauce

2 cloves garlic, minced

2 teaspoons peeled and
   minced fresh ginger

2 tablespoons firmly packed
   light brown sugar

3 tablespoons rice wine

1 tablespoon rice vinegar

2 tablespoons vegetable oil

2 pounds salmon fillets

1 tablespoon toasted
   sesame oil

2 tablespoons sesame seeds

4 green onions, white and
   light green parts,
   chopped

To make the marinade, combine the ingredients in a small saucepan and bring to a boil. Reduce the heat to medium-low, and simmer for 5 minutes. Remove from the heat and let cool to room temperature.

Place the salmon in a 2-gallon zipper-top plastic bag. Pour in half of the marinade, seal the bag, and turn it over to coat the fish. Marinate in the refrigerator for at least 20 minutes and up to 2 hours. Refrigerate the remaining marinade separately.

Coat the rotisserie basket with nonstick cooking spray. Remove the salmon from the marinade, pat it dry, and arrange in the basket. Close the lid tightly, and load the basket onto the spit rod assembly. Grill until the salmon is just cooked through, 15 to 20 minutes.

While the salmon is cooking, take the reserved marinade out of the refrigerator and stir in the sesame oil, sesame seeds, and green onions.

Remove the salmon from the basket, drizzle some of this marinade over each serving, and serve immediately.

Roasted Salmon with Mustard-Chive Butter

Serves 4   This beautiful fish is glazed with a mustard and butter combination that complements the richness of the salmon. You can also cut the salmon into kabobs and baste them with the mustard butter. Or try this technique with halibut or sea bass. If you have a larger rotisserie, you can double the recipe.

1¹/₂ to 2 pounds salmon
    fillets
1 teaspoon Old Bay
    seasoning

Mustard-Chive Butter

¹/₂ cup (1 stick) butter,
    melted
2 tablespoons Dijon mustard
¹/₄ cup chopped fresh chives

Sprinkle the salmon evenly with the Old Bay seasoning. Coat the grill basket with nonstick cooking spray and lay the fillets in the basket.

In a small mixing bowl, stir together the ingredients for the mustard butter. Brush the flavored butter over the salmon, close the lid to the basket tightly, and load the basket onto the spit rod assembly. Heat the remaining butter so that it is bubbling gently. Grill the salmon until it flakes when pierced with a knife in the thickest part, 20 to 25 minutes, stopping the machine twice during the cooking time to baste the fish.

Remove the fish from the basket, top with any remaining mustard butter, and serve immediately.

Salmon with Nectarine Salsa

Serves 4   Salmon is so widely available in the grocery store that it's a great choice for dinner any night of the week. The sweet and spicy salsa gives this grilled fish a lot of personality. If you have a larger rotisserie, you can double the recipe.

1$^{1}/_{2}$ to 2 pounds salmon
    fillets
2 tablespoons olive oil
2 teaspoons Old Bay
    seasoning

Nectarine Salsa

4 medium-size ripe
    nectarines, peeled,
    pitted, and cut into
    $^{1}/_{2}$-inch dice
$^{1}/_{2}$ cup finely chopped red
    onion
1 teaspoon salt
2 teaspoons seeded and
    finely chopped jalapeño
$^{1}/_{4}$ cup fresh lime juice
$^{1}/_{4}$ cup chopped fresh
    parsley leaves
2 tablespoons olive oil

Coat the rotisserie basket with nonstick cooking spray. Place the salmon in the grill basket.

In a small bowl, combine the olive oil and Old Bay and brush evenly over the salmon. Close the lid tightly and grill until the fish is cooked through and flakes when pierced with a knife, 20 to 25 minutes.

While the fish is cooking, in a medium-size mixing bowl, toss together the salsa ingredients, stirring to blend.

Remove the salmon from the grill basket, garnish each serving with some of the salsa (either on top, underneath, or on the side) and serve immediately.

Dillicious Salmon Burgers

Serves 6 Gorgeous salmon becomes the focal point for these burgers, which are a great way to stretch your food dollar because you only need one pound of salmon to feed six people. Serve on crusty rolls with tomato, lettuce, and Dilled Tartar Sauce (page 327).

1 pound salmon fillet, skin and any pin bones removed and cut into 1-inch cubes

$^1/_2$ cup coarsely chopped shallots

1 tablespoon chopped fresh dill or 1 teaspoon dillweed

3 shakes Tabasco sauce

1 large egg

1 teaspoon salt

$^1/_2$ teaspoon freshly ground black pepper

$^1/_2$ cup dry bread crumbs

Place the salmon in a food processor with the shallots, dill, Tabasco, egg, salt, and pepper. Pulse the machine on and off 5 to 6 times, until the salmon is chopped and the mixture is combined. Turn into a medium-size mixing bowl, add the bread crumbs, and stir until well blended. Form the mixture into 6 patties ¾ inch thick, cover with plastic wrap, and refrigerate for at least 30 minutes and up to 8 hours to firm up.

Coat the rotisserie basket with nonstick cooking spray, arrange the patties in the basket, and close the lid tightly. Load the basket onto the spit rod assembly and grill until the salmon is cooked through and the patties are golden, 10 to 16 minutes.

Remove the patties from the basket and serve immediately.

Asian Salmon Burgers

Serves 6 **These burgers are flavored with ginger, garlic, and green onions, and then crusted with sesame seeds, for a crunchy coating.**

1 tablespoon vegetable oil
1 tablespoon toasted
    sesame oil
1 teaspoon peeled and
    grated fresh ginger
1 clove garlic, minced
1 pound salmon fillet, skin
    and any pin bones
    removed and cut into
    1-inch cubes
4 green onions, white and
    light green parts, thinly
    sliced
1 tablespoon soy sauce
1 large egg white, beaten
1/2 cup panko crumbs or
    plain dry bread crumbs
    (see Smart Turn)
1/2 cup sesame seeds,
    toasted (see page 42)
Six 6-inch flour tortillas
Soy Dipping Sauce (recipe
    follows)

In a small sauté pan, heat the oils together over medium heat. Add the ginger and garlic and cook, stirring, for 2 to 3 minutes, being careful not to brown them. Remove from the heat.

Put the salmon in a food processor. Add the oil mixture and pulse the machine on and off 5 or 6 times, until the salmon is coarsely chopped. Turn the mixture into a medium-size mixing bowl and stir in the green onions, soy sauce, egg white, and panko crumbs, blending well. Shape the mixture into 6 patties ¾ inch thick, then coat evenly with the sesame seeds on both sides. Cover with plastic wrap and refrigerate for at least 2 and up to 8 hours to firm up.

Coat the rotisserie basket with nonstick cooking spray, arrange the patties in the basket, and close the lid tightly. Load the basket onto the spit rod assembly and grill until the sesame seeds are golden and the salmon is cooked through, 10 to 15 minutes.

Remove the burgers from the basket and serve immediately, wrapped in flour tortillas and drizzled with the dipping sauce.

Smart Turn

Panko are coarse bread crumbs used in Japanese cooking. You'll find them in the Asian section of your supermarket or in an Asian market.

Soy Dipping Sauce

Makes about 1 cup Salty and intensely flavored with garlic and ginger, this dipping sauce is terrific with fish or chicken.

3/4 cup soy sauce

3 tablespoons rice wine

2 teaspoons peeled and grated fresh ginger

3 cloves garlic, minced

1 tablespoon toasted sesame oil

3 green onions, white and light green parts, thinly sliced

In a small mixing bowl, combine all the ingredients, stirring until blended. This will keep, covered, in the refrigerator for up to 2 weeks.

Rolled Fillet of Sole Oreganata

Serves 6 These elegant fillets cook to a golden brown in almost no time in the rotisserie basket. Make sure that they are all about the same weight so they cook evenly. Serve on a bed of sautéed spinach with wild mushrooms.

1½ pounds fillet of sole

¼ cup olive oil

1 teaspoon salt

½ teaspoon freshly ground
   black pepper

1 cup dry bread crumbs

½ cup grated Pecorino
   Romano cheese

2 cloves garlic, minced

2 teaspoons chopped fresh
   oregano leaves

Fresh lemon slices for
   garnish

Coat the rotisserie basket with nonstick cooking spray. Place the fillets in a glass baking dish. Drizzle them with all but 1 tablespoon of the olive oil, and sprinkle with the salt and pepper, turning them to coat evenly. In a shallow dish, combine the bread crumbs, cheese, garlic, and oregano. Dip a fillet into the crumbs, coating both sides evenly. Then roll up the fillet, and arrange it in the rotisserie basket. Coat and roll up the remaining fillets in the same way.

Drizzle the fillets in the basket with the remaining 1 tablespoon of olive oil, close the lid tightly, and load the basket onto the spit rod assembly. Grill until the fish rolls are golden brown, 10 to 15 minutes.

Remove carefully from the basket and serve immediately.

Crab-Stuffed Sole

Serves 6 A recipe similar to this one was a favorite of mine from childhood, when my parents would take us to a fancy restaurant and let us order whatever we wanted. Stuffed with a savory crab mixture and grilled, this flavorful entrée is topped with a brandy cream sauce, making it a terrific dinner for company.

½ cup (1 stick) butter

2 tablespoons chopped
   fresh chives

In a small sauté pan over medium heat, melt half the butter, add the chives and 1 teaspoon of the Creole seasoning, and cook, stirring, for 1 minute. Add ½ cup of the crabmeat and toss the mixture together. Melt the remaining butter in another saucepan.

2 teaspoons Creole
    Seasoning Rub (page
    287)
$3/4$ cup lump crabmeat,
    picked over for shells
    and cartilage
$1/2$ cup crushed Ritz crackers
    (about 10 crackers)
1 tablespoon mayonnaise
2 teaspoons Worcestershire
    sauce
6 fillets of sole (about $1^1/2$
    pounds)
$1^1/2$ cups heavy cream
1 tablespoon brandy
1 teaspoon sweet paprika
Lemon wedges for garnish
    (optional)

Turn the crabmeat mixture into a medium-size mixing bowl, stir in the cracker crumbs, mayonnaise, and Worcestershire, and mix until well combined.

Sprinkle the fillets with the remaining 1 teaspoon of Creole seasoning. Spread about 1 tablespoon of stuffing over each fillet and roll up the fillet into a neat package. (Some fillets will be wide enough to fold in the sides, but others will be narrow and you won't be able to fold them in.)

Coat the rotisserie basket with nonstick cooking spray and lay the fillets in the basket in a single layer. Brush the rolls with the remaining melted butter. Close the lid tightly and load the basket onto the spit rod assembly. Grill until the fish is flaky and the outside begins to turn golden, 20 to 25 minutes.

While the sole is grilling, bring the heavy cream to a boil in a small saucepan and continue boiling until it reduces and thickens, about 4 minutes. Reduce the heat so the cream simmers and stir in the brandy, paprika, and remaining $1/4$ cup of crabmeat. Keep warm until ready to serve.

Remove the sole from the grill basket and serve in a pool of the hot brandy cream sauce. Garnish with lemon wedges, if desired, and serve immediately.

Soy- and Ginger-Glazed Swordfish

Serves 6 **This dish shows the versatility of the rotisserie: the basket is used to grill swordfish. Leftovers make a great addition to vegetable, rice, or noodle stir-fries.**

Soy-Ginger Marinade

¹/₂ cup soy sauce

¹/₄ cup rice wine

2 teaspoons peeled and
grated fresh ginger

1 clove garlic, minced

2 pounds swordfish steaks

2 tablespoons toasted
sesame oil

2 tablespoons sesame seeds
for garnish (optional)

In a small mixing bowl, combine the marinade ingredients until well blended.

Place the swordfish in a 2-gallon zipper-top plastic bag, pour in the marinade, and seal the bag. Turn over to coat the fish, and marinate in the refrigerator for at least 1 and up to 6 hours.

When ready to cook, remove the swordfish from the marinade and pat dry. Place the steaks in the rotisserie basket and close the lid tightly. Load onto the spit rod assembly and grill until cooked through, 10 to 15 minutes. (Stop the rotisserie and slash into the thickest part of the fish—it should be firm.)

Remove the fish from the basket to a serving platter, drizzle with the sesame oil, sprinkle with the sesame seeds, if desired, and serve immediately.

Romano-Crusted Swordfish

Serves 6   A great example of simple cooking, this savory swordfish grills in under 20 minutes. Serve with pasta tossed with Quick Marinara (page 318) for a taste of the Mediterranean.

1/4 cup olive oil

1/2 cup dry bread crumbs

1 cup grated Pecorino Romano cheese

1/4 cup chopped fresh Italian parsley leaves

2 pounds swordfish steaks

Pour the olive oil onto a dinner plate. On another plate, combine the bread crumbs, cheese, and parsley. Dip the fish into the oil, coating both sides, then dredge the steaks in the crumb mixture to coat evenly.

Coat the rotisserie basket with nonstick cooking spray. Arrange the coated steaks in the basket and close the lid tightly. Load the basket onto the spit rod assembly and grill until the fish is cooked through and the crumbs are golden, 16 to 18 minutes.

Remove the fish from the basket and serve immediately.

Swordfish Napoli

Serves 6 **I'm not sure that this fish is served in Naples, but its bold flavors remind me of Neapolitan cooking. A great company dish, it goes well with risotto or pasta.**

Tomato-Oregano Sauce

2 tablespoons olive oil
4 cloves garlic, minced
1 tablespoon chopped fresh
    oregano leaves
1 cup canned tomato purée
1½ teaspoons salt
½ teaspoon freshly ground
    black pepper
1 teaspoon fresh lemon juice

2 pounds swordfish steaks
¼ cup pitted Kalamata
    olives, drained and
    chopped

To make the sauce, in a small saucepan, heat the olive oil over medium heat. Add the garlic, and cook, stirring, for 2 minutes, being careful not to burn it. Add the oregano and toss it in the garlic oil for 30 seconds. Pour in the tomato purée, salt, pepper, and lemon juice and bring the mixture to a boil. Reduce the heat to medium-low and simmer for 20 minutes.

When ready to cook, coat the rotisserie basket with nonstick cooking spray. Brush the swordfish fillets with some of the sauce, arrange in the basket, and close the lid tightly. Load the basket onto the spit rod assembly and grill the fish until cooked through, 15 to 18 minutes. (Stop the rotisserie and slash into the thickest part of the fish—it should be firm.)

While the fish is cooking, return the sauce to a boil, then reduce the heat to low, and stir the olives.

When the fish is done, remove from the basket, top each portion with some of the remaining sauce, and serve immediately.

Tilapia with Herbs

Serves 6   Tilapia is a farm-raised, mild fish, which takes well to a marinade of lemon juice and fresh herbs; the rotisserie does the rest. Serve on a bed of spinach with the creamy sauce.

6 tilapia fillets (about 1½ pounds)

1 teaspoon salt

½ teaspoon freshly ground black pepper

¼ cup olive oil

3 tablespoons fresh lemon juice

¼ cup chopped fresh chives

2 tablespoons chopped fresh tarragon leaves

2 tablespoons chopped fresh Italian parsley leaves

½ cup heavy cream

Place the tilapia in a glass baking dish and season both sides with some of the salt and pepper.

In a small mixing bowl, whisk together the olive oil, lemon juice, chives, tarragon, and parsley. Pour the marinade over the fish, cover with plastic wrap, and marinate in the refrigerator for 30 minutes.

Lift the fish out of the marinade, being careful to keep the herbs on the fish, if possible. Coat the rotisserie basket with nonstick cooking spray and arrange the fillets in the basket— it is okay if they overlap a bit. Close the lid tightly and load the basket onto the spit rod assembly. Grill just until flaky, 12 to 15 minutes.

While the fish is cooking, pour the marinade into a 1-quart saucepan, bring to a boil, and continue to boil until reduced by half. Stir in the heavy cream and boil until thickened, about 5 minutes more. Keep warm over very low heat.

Carefully remove the fish from the basket and serve immediately with the hot sauce spooned over it.

Toasted nuts, such as almonds, pecans, macadamia nuts, and pine nuts, give a dish some added crunch and a slightly earthy flavor. If you have a small quantity, $1/2$ cup or less, you can toast them on top of the stove. Larger amounts should be toasted in the oven.

To toast nuts in the oven, begin by preheating it to 350 degrees. Line a baking sheet with a Silpat liner or aluminum foil and spread out the nuts in a single layer on the baking sheet. Bake until they begin to brown, 12 to 15 minutes, stirring occasionally so they brown evenly. (You will smell the fragrance of the nuts when they begin to brown.) Transfer the nuts to a plate or paper towel to cool. Don't leave them on the hot baking sheet or they will continue to cook and possibly scorch.

To toast nuts on top of the stove, spread them out in one layer in a nonstick skillet and place over low heat. Shake the skillet while the nuts are heating so that they brown evenly. You will smell them as they begin to toast; watch them carefully and when they are toasted evenly, remove them from the pan immediately and cool on a plate or paper towels.

Toasted nuts will keep for 2 to 3 days in zipper-top plastic bags at room temperature and for 3 months in the freezer.

Trout with Parsley-Almond Butter

Serves 4 **Trout are easy to cook in the rotisserie basket, and the simple parsley butter topped with almonds gives these a nice flair.**

4 trout, cleaned, gutted, and tails removed
¼ cup fresh lemon juice
¼ cup olive oil
2 teaspoons Old Bay seasoning
½ cup (1 stick) butter
½ cup chopped fresh Italian parsley leaves
¾ cup slivered almonds, toasted (see page 184)

In each fish, make 3 slashes ½ to ¾ inch deep in the skin, perpendicular to the backbone.

In a small mixing bowl, combine the lemon juice, olive oil, and Old Bay. Brush this mixture evenly over the inside and outside of the fish.

Coat the grill basket with nonstick cooking spray, arrange the fish in the basket, and close the lid tightly. Load the basket onto the spit rod assembly and grill until the fish is flaky when pierced with a knife in the thickest part of its flesh, 25 to 30 minutes.

While the fish is cooking, heat the butter in a small saucepan over medium heat until melted, then stir in the parsley.

Remove the fish from the basket, drizzle with the hot parsley butter, and sprinkle with the toasted almonds. Serve immediately.

The World's Best Seared Ahi

Serves 4 Ahi, also called yellowfin tuna, soaks in a wasabi marinade for a little extra flavor, and is then grilled on the rotisserie until medium-rare. Wasabi is a plant related to the cabbage, and has a very pungent taste. Generally used in Japanese cooking, the powder is mixed with water to form a paste. You'll find it in the Asian section of the supermarket, or in an Asian market. If you have a larger rotisserie, you can double the recipe.

2 pounds ahi steaks, 1 inch thick

Wasabi Marinade

2 teaspoons wasabi powder

$1/3$ cup soy sauce

2 tablespoons rice vinegar

2 teaspoons toasted sesame oil for garnish

2 tablespoons sesame seeds for garnish

Place the ahi in a 2-gallon zipper-top plastic bag. In a small mixing bowl, combine the marinade ingredients, stirring well. Pour over the ahi, seal the bag, and turn it over to coat the steaks. Marinate in the refrigerator for at least 1 and up to 3 hours.

When ready to cook, coat the rotisserie basket with nonstick cooking spray. Remove the ahi from the marinade, pat dry, and arrange in the basket. Close the lid tightly and load the basket onto the spit rod assembly. Grill until the desired doneness, 8 to 10 minutes for medium-rare.

Remove the ahi from the basket. Drizzle each portion with some of the sesame oil, sprinkle with the sesame seeds, and serve immediately.

Sesame-Crusted Ahi

Serves 6 Seared ahi is delicious on the rotisserie, because you can control the heat so as not to overcook the fish. This treatment is simple, but the results will make your guests think they are eating at a five-star restaurant. If ahi is unavailable, use any fresh tuna steaks.

2 tablespoons vegetable oil

3 tablespoons toasted
  sesame oil

$1/4$ cup sesame seeds

$1^1/2$ pounds ahi steaks,
  1 inch thick

4 green onions, white and
  light green parts,
  chopped, for garnish

On a flat plate, stir together the vegetable oil and 1 tablespoon of the sesame oil. Spread the sesame seeds on another flat plate. Dip the ahi into the oil mixture, then dip it into the sesame seeds, making sure to cover the tuna totally on all sides.

Place the ahi in the rotisserie basket and close the lid tightly. Load the basket onto the spit rod assembly and grill until the crust is golden but the center is still pink, about 10 minutes.

Remove the basket from the spit rod assembly and arrange the ahi on a serving platter. Drizzle with the remaining 2 tablespoons of sesame oil, garnish with the green onions, and serve.

Chesapeake Bay Crab Cakes

Makes 4 cakes   Crab cakes and other fish burgers are great in the rotisserie basket. They brown without the fuss involved in panfrying and there is no fat to deal with. These cakes are enlivened with Old Bay seasoning, which you can find in your grocer's spice section. If you have a larger rotisserie, you can double the recipe.

1 large egg

2 tablespoons mayonnaise

$1/2$ teaspoon Dijon mustard

1 tablespoon Worcestershire sauce

2 tablespoons chopped fresh parsley leaves

2 teaspoons Old Bay seasoning

$1/4$ cup saltine cracker crumbs

1 pound lump crabmeat, picked over for shells and cartilage

Dilled Tartar Sauce (page 327)

In a medium-size mixing bowl, blend together the egg, mayonnaise, mustard, Worcestershire, parsley, Old Bay, and cracker crumbs. Gently stir in the crabmeat, being careful not to break it up. Form the mixture into four 3-inch cakes, cover with plastic wrap, and refrigerate for at least 1 and up to 8 hours to firm up.

Coat the rotisserie basket with nonstick cooking spray. Arrange the cakes in the basket, close the lid tightly, and load the basket onto the spit rod assembly. Grill until golden brown, 20 to 25 minutes.

Remove the crab cakes from the basket and serve immediately with the tartar sauce.

Crawfish Jambalaya Burgers

Serves 4   Jambalaya is soul food from Louisiana, and these burgers are a great little taste of the traditional rice dish. The crawfish come from the bayous of the South; you'll find them at gourmet markets, or you can mail-order them (see Sources at the back of the book). Serve these burgers with grilled tomatoes and coleslaw. If you have a larger rotisserie, you can double the recipe.

2 tablespoons olive oil

$1/4$ cup chopped onions

$1/4$ cup seeded and chopped green bell pepper

$1/4$ cup chopped celery

1 clove garlic, minced

2 teaspoons Creole Seasoning Rub (page 287)

$1/2$ pound cooked crawfish tails

1 cup cold cooked rice

1 large egg

$1/2$ cup dry bread crumbs

Heat the olive oil in a small sauté pan over medium heat. Add the onions, green pepper, celery, garlic, and Creole rub. Cook, stirring, until the vegetables are softened, about 4 minutes.

Transfer the mixture to a medium-size mixing bowl. Fold in the crawfish tails, rice, egg, and bread crumbs and stir to blend well. Form the mixture into 4 patties about ¾ inch thick. Cover the patties with plastic wrap and refrigerate for at least 1 and up to 8 hours to firm up.

Coat the rotisserie basket with nonstick cooking spray. Arrange the burgers in the basket, and close the lid tightly. Load the basket onto the spit rod assembly and grill the burgers until they begin to turn golden, 15 to 20 minutes.

Remove the burgers from the basket and serve immediately.

Twirling Lobster Tails

Serves 4 **Lobster tails turned in the grill basket are succulent and delicious when basted with a little lemon butter flavored with cayenne and garlic. You can also cut the lobster into 1-inch pieces and alternate it on the kabob rods with shrimp or halibut cut into 1-inch chunks for a mixed seafood kabob. If you have a larger rotisserie, you can double the recipe.**

Cayenne Butter Baste

$1/2$ cup (1 stick) butter
$1/4$ cup fresh lemon juice
1 teaspoon garlic salt
Pinch of cayenne pepper

Four 8-ounce lobster tails
$1/4$ cup water
Melted butter for serving
Lemon wedges for serving

In a medium-size saucepan, heat the baste ingredients together, stirring, until the butter melts. Keep warm.

With kitchen shears, make a lengthwise cut through the top shell of each lobster tail. With a cleaver or chef's knife, cut through the tail meat, but not through the bottom shell.

Coat the rotisserie basket with nonstick cooking spray. Place the lobsters tails in the basket, brushing the meat liberally with the cayenne butter. Close the lid of the basket tightly and load the basket onto the spit rod assembly. Pour the water in the drip pan and place the cover on the pan. Grill for 20 to 25 minutes, stopping the rotisserie twice during the cooking time to baste the lobster.

Remove the lobsters from the basket and serve with additional melted butter, if desired, and lemon wedges.

Crispy Sherried Scallops

Serves 6   Scallops cook quickly and retain their nuttiness after a soak in sherry and garlic. This delicious dish is great served as an appetizer or main course.

Garlicky Sherry Marinade

¹/₄ cup cream sherry
1 teaspoon garlic salt
1 teaspoon sweet paprika

1¹/₂ pounds sea scallops
¹/₂ cup (1 stick) butter,
    melted
¹/₂ cup dry bread crumbs
2 teaspoons fresh lemon
    juice

Combine the marinade ingredients in a zipper-top plastic bag. Add the scallops, seal the bag, and turn it over to coat the scallops. Marinate in the refrigerator for at least 2 and up to 6 hours.

When ready to cook, remove the scallops from the marinade and pat dry with paper towels. Dip the scallops in the melted butter, then coat evenly all over with the bread crumbs. Thread the scallops onto the kabob rods, leaving ¹/₂ inch between each for air to circulate. Load the kabob rods onto the spit rod assembly with the spring ends on the right. Grill until the scallops are cooked through, 6 to 8 minutes.

Remove the scallops from the skewers and serve immediately, sprinkled with the lemon juice.

Seared Scallops

Serves 4 to 6   Scallops are terrific seared in the rotisserie, and they are even better dipped in a pool of one of the luscious flavored butters that follow this recipe, such as the Pesto Butter or Red Pepper Butter. You can also choose any of the sauces from the sauces chapter.

¹/₄ cup olive oil
1 teaspoon salt
¹/₂ teaspoon freshly ground black pepper
¹/₄ teaspoon sweet paprika
1 pound large sea scallops
Pesto Butter, Red Pepper Butter, and/or Cilantro Pesto Butter (recipes follow)

In a medium-size mixing bowl, combine the olive oil, salt, pepper, and paprika, stirring to blend.

Toss the scallops into the oil mixture, turning to coat them evenly, then thread them onto the kabob rods, leaving ½ inch between each for air circulation. Load the rods onto the spit rod assembly with the spring ends on the right side. Grill until the scallops are golden and cooked through, 12 to 15 minutes.

Remove the scallops from the kabob rods and serve with the sauce or butter of your choice.

Pesto Butter

Pungent with basil and garlic, this butter is lovely on fish, chicken, or vegetables. It will keep in the refrigerator for 5 days, or in the freezer for up to 2 months.

¹/₂ cup Basil Pesto (page 19) or store-bought pesto
¹/₄ cup (¹/₂ stick) butter, softened

In a small mixing bowl, cream together the pesto and butter until smooth. Refrigerate until ready to use.

Melt the pesto butter over low heat, pool on the serving plate, or spoon over grilled food.

Red Pepper Butter

Luxuriously rich and brilliantly colored, this flavored butter is delicious on any seafood. It will keep in the refrigerator for 5 days, or in the freezer for up to 2 months.

One 6-ounce jar roasted red peppers, drained and chopped

$^1/_2$ cup (1 stick) butter, softened

Place the peppers and butter in a food processor and process until smooth. Refrigerate until you are ready to use.

Melt the flavored butter over low heat and pool on the serving plate or spoon over grilled food.

Cilantro Pesto Butter

This butter has a south of the border flavor, which makes it a great accent for seafood, chicken, or vegetables. It will keep in the refrigerator for 5 days, or in the freezer for up to 2 months.

$^1/_2$ cup Cilantro Pesto (page 309)

$^1/_2$ cup (1 stick) butter, softened

In a medium-size mixing bowl, cream together the pesto and butter until smooth. Refrigerate until you are ready to use.

Melt the flavored butter over low heat and pool on the serving plate or spoon over grilled food.

Prosciutto-Wrapped Scallop and Shrimp Spiedini

Serves 4 to 6 Salty prosciutto is a great flavoring for shrimp and scallops on skewers. It not only protects the scallops from overcooking, it gives them a nice smoky taste.

1/4 pound paper-thin prosciutto slices

1/2 cup packed fresh basil leaves

1/2 pound large sea scallops

1/2 pound large shrimp, peeled and deveined

1/4 cup olive oil

2 tablespoons fresh lemon juice

1/2 teaspoon freshly ground black pepper

Lay the prosciutto on a cutting board and cut it into rectangles that are large enough to wrap around the scallops and shrimp, about 3½ x 1 inch. Center a basil leaf on a piece of prosciutto, lay a scallop on the basil leaf, and wrap the scallop in the prosciutto. Then skewer it onto a kabob rod. Next wrap a shrimp in the same fashion and skewer it. Alternate a wrapped scallop with a wrapped shrimp, leaving ½ inch between each to allow air to circulate, and continue threading the rods until both are full.

In a small bowl, combine the olive oil, lemon juice, and pepper. Brush the oil mixture over the kabobs and load the kabobs onto the spit rod assembly with the spring ends on the right. Grill until the shrimp are pink and the scallops opaque and cooked through, 15 to 17 minutes.

Remove the shrimp and scallops from the skewers and serve immediately.

Sugar Cane Shrimp

Serves 4 to 6   In the original recipe for this dish, shrimp are skewered on pieces of sugar cane. Since the kabob rods do such a nice job on the rotisserie, I changed the ingredients around a bit to end up with sweet and spicy shrimp on a skewer.

Sweet and Hot Chile Oil

2 tablespoons canola oil

2 tablespoons chile oil

2 tablespoons light corn
  syrup

1 pound large shrimp, peeled
  and deveined

2 tablespoons raw sugar
  (see Smart Turn)

4 green onions, white and
  light green parts,
  chopped

In a large mixing bowl, whisk together the canola oil, chile oil, and corn syrup. Add the shrimp and toss to coat evenly.

Load the shrimp onto the kabob rods, leaving ½ inch between each for air to circulate, and arrange on the spit rod assembly with the spring ends on the right side. Grill until the shrimp turn pink, 10 to 12 minutes.

Remove the shrimp from the kabob rods, sprinkle with the raw sugar and green onions, and serve immediately.

Smart Turn

Raw sugar has large crystals, which are terrific for caramelizing on grilled foods. If you are unable to find raw sugar, use dark brown sugar instead.

Shrimply Delicious Bayou Bites

Serves 6 These succulent shrimp are sprinkled with a little oil, then dusted with Cajun spices to give you a delicious appetizer or a main course to serve over rice.

1/4 cup olive oil

2 tablespoons fresh lemon juice

3 tablespoons Creole Seasoning Rub (page 287)

2 pounds large shrimp, peeled and deveined

1/2 cup (1 stick) butter, melted, or Artichoke Rémoulade (page 326)

In a small mixing bowl, combine the olive oil, lemon juice, and Creole seasoning, stirring until blended.

Place the shrimp in a 2-gallon zipper-top plastic bag. Pour in the marinade, seal the bag, and turn it over to coat the shrimp. Marinate in the refrigerator for at least 1 hour or overnight.

When ready to cook, remove the shrimp from the marinade, pat dry, and place in the rotisserie basket or on the kabob skewers. Load the basket or kabobs onto the spit rod assembly and grill until the shrimp are pink and cooked through, 10 to 12 minutes.

Remove from the rotisserie and serve immediately with the melted butter or rémoulade for dipping.

Buffalo Shrimp

Serves 6 to 8   Taking a little license with Buffalo wings, I am using the same technique to cook shrimp, but without the deep-frying. These shrimp are succulent and juicy and just need a salad alongside. Don't forget to serve them with Maytag Blue Cheese Dressing (page 53) for dipping. Artichoke Rémoulade (page 326) is also tasty.

2 pounds jumbo shrimp, peeled and deveined
2 tablespoons vegetable oil
³/₄ cup Louisiana hot sauce
¹/₂ cup (1 stick) butter, melted

Place the shrimp in a medium-size mixing bowl. Pour the vegetable oil and hot sauce over the shrimp and toss to blend well. Thread the shrimp onto the kabob rods, leaving ½ inch between each so the air can circulate. Load the kabob rods onto the spit rod assembly with the spring ends on the right side. Grill until pink and cooked through, 10 to 12 minutes.

Remove the shrimp from the kabob rods. Arrange attractively on a serving platter, brush with the melted butter, and serve immediately.

Smart Turn

Although these are best served hot, leftovers can be used in a salad the next day.

Honey-Mustard Shrimp

Serves 6 to 8   A little sweet, a little hot, these tasty morsels will have your taste buds clamoring for more! Great as an appetizer, or as a main course served over rice, these shrimp will become a favorite.

¼ cup honey
¼ cup Dijon mustard
2 tablespoons yellow mustard
1 tablespoon fresh lemon juice
2 pounds jumbo shrimp, peeled and deveined
1 medium-size onion, cut into wedges
2 small green bell peppers, seeded and cut into 1-inch pieces

In a small mixing bowl, stir together the honey, mustards, and lemon juice until smooth. Thread the shrimp onto the kabob rods, alternating them with the onion and peppers and leaving ½ inch between each for air circulation. Reserve ¼ cup of the glaze and brush each kabob with the remainder.

Load the kabob rods onto the spit rod assembly with the spring ends on the right side. Grill until the shrimp are pink and cooked through and the vegetables softened, 15 to 17 minutes.

Remove the shrimp and vegetables from the skewers, brush with the reserved glaze, and serve immediately.

Aloha Coconut Shrimp

Serves 6 Succulent shrimp coated with crunchy coconut make for a great appetizer or entree for a Polynesian feast. Serve them on a bed of stir-fried vegetables with Maui Sunset Sauce (page 200), Mango Salsa (page 298), or Soy Dipping Sauce (page 177).

1½ cups all-purpose flour

1 tablespoon Old Bay seasoning

2 large eggs, beaten

1 cup unsweetened shredded coconut (see Smart Turn)

½ cup panko crumbs or plain dry bread crumbs (see Smart Turn, page 176)

1½ pounds jumbo shrimp, peeled and deveined, tails left on

On a dinner plate, combine the flour and Old Bay. Place the eggs in a bowl next to the flour mixture, then place the coconut and panko crumbs on another plate, stirring to blend. Dredge the shrimp evenly in the flour, tapping off any excess. Next, dip into the eggs, then coat evenly with the coconut and panko mixture. Place on a baking sheet lined with aluminum foil, cover with plastic wrap, and refrigerate for 1 hour so the coating can firm up.

Thread the shrimp onto the kabob rods, leaving ½ inch between them for air to circulate. Load the kabobs onto the spit rod assembly with the spring ends on the right. Grill until golden brown, 15 to 17 minutes.

Remove the shrimp from the kabob rods and serve immediately with dipping sauces, if desired.

Smart Turn

Be sure to use unsweetened coconut, which you can buy in health food stores. The sugar in sweetened coconut may burn and it also will make the dish too sweet.

Maui Sunset Sauce

Makes about 4 cups   As colorful as the sun setting on the Pacific, this sweet and pungent sauce makes a delicious dip for shrimp or even plain grilled chicken.

1 cup dried apricots
1 1/2 cups water
2/3 cup sugar
1/2 cup rice vinegar or 1/3 cup white wine vinegar
1/2 cup ketchup
2 cloves garlic, minced
1/2 teaspoon peeled and finely minced fresh ginger
1/4 teaspoon chile oil

Combine all the ingredients in a 2-quart saucepan and bring to a boil. Reduce the heat to low, cover the pan, and simmer the sauce for 30 minutes, stirring occasionally.

Remove the pan from the heat and using an immersion blender, food processor, or blender, process the sauce until smooth. Serve the sauce warm or at room temperature. It will keep, tightly covered, in the refrigerator for up to 2 weeks or in the freezer for 2 months.

Apricot-Curry Shrimp

Serves 4 to 6   **Glazed with apricot preserves and a hint of curry powder, these shrimp are great as an appetizer or as a main course served over rice or vegetables. The basting mixture can be made up to a week in advance and refrigerated.**

Apricot-Curry Basting Sauce

¹/₃ cup apricot preserves
1 clove garlic, minced
2 tablespoons white wine
1 teaspoon Dijon mustard
2 teaspoons curry powder

1¹/₂ pounds large shrimp, peeled and deveined
6 green onions, chopped, for garnish
¹/₂ cup chopped salted roasted peanuts for garnish

In a small mixing bowl, stir together the basting sauce ingredients until well combined.

Place the shrimp in a zipper-top plastic bag, add ¼ cup of the basting sauce, and set aside the remaining sauce. Seal the bag and shake until all the shrimp are evenly coated with the baste. Marinate in the refrigerator for at least 2 and up to 8 hours.

When ready to cook, drain the shrimp and thread onto the kabob rods, leaving ½ inch between them for air to circulate. Load the skewers onto the spit rod assembly with the spring ends on the right. Grill until the shrimp are pink and cooked through, 10 to 12 minutes.

Remove the shrimp from the kabob rods, sprinkle each serving with some of the green onions and peanuts, and serve the reserved apricot sauce on the side for dipping.

Shrimp on the Barbie

Serves 6   These plump morsels may not be authentically Aussie, but they were our favorites during recipe testing, and since we couldn't think of a better name, this was it! The basting sauce is easy to put together and can be refrigerated for up to two weeks. It's also great on fish, kabobs, and scallops. Serve this with Rick's Blue Cheese Slaw (page 347).

**Down Under
Barbecue Sauce**

1/2 cup Worcestershire sauce

1/3 cup soy sauce

2 tablespoons firmly packed
    light brown sugar

1/3 cup ketchup

2 tablespoons fresh lemon
    juice

2 tablespoons vegetable oil

1 1/2 pounds jumbo shrimp,
    peeled and deveined,
    tails left on

In a small saucepan, combine the sauce ingredients. Bring the mixture to a boil, reduce the heat to medium-low, and simmer for 5 to 10 minutes. Remove from the heat and let cool.

Place the shrimp in a medium-size mixing bowl and toss with 1/4 cup of the sauce until well coated. Set aside the remaining sauce. Thread the shrimp onto the kabob rods, leaving 1/2 inch between them for air to circulate. Load the rods onto the spit rod assembly with the spring ends on the right. Grill until the shrimp are pink and cooked through, 10 to 12 minutes.

Remove the shrimp from the skewers and serve with the remaining sauce on the side.

Lemon-Dill Shrimp

Serves 6   Although mayonnaise may seem like a strange ingredient here, it helps to keep the shrimp moist during cooking and the flavor is terrific. The sauce can be used for rotisserie fish fillets or scallops.

Creamy Lemon Dill Sauce

1/2 cup mayonnaise

2 tablespoons fresh lemon juice

2 tablespoons chopped fresh dill or 1 tablespoon dillweed

1 teaspoon sweet paprika

Pinch of cayenne pepper

1 1/2 pounds large shrimp, peeled and deveined, tails left on

Lemon wedges for garnish

Sprigs fresh dill for garnish

In a medium-size mixing bowl, stir together the sauce ingredients. Stir in the shrimp, tossing to coat them evenly.

Drain the shrimp and thread onto the kabob rods, leaving 1/2 inch between them for air to circulate. Load the skewers onto the spit rod assembly with the spring ends on the right. Grill until the shrimp are pink and cooked through, 10 to 12 minutes.

Remove the shrimp from the kabob rods and serve immediately garnished with lemon wedges and dill sprigs.

Jamaican Jerk Shrimp

Serves 6   Spicy shrimp from the islands are just what the doctor ordered to perk up a midweek meal. Serve this dinner with rice and Mango Salsa (page 298).

1½ pounds large shrimp

Jerk Spice Paste

2 tablespoons olive oil
1 teaspoon ground allspice
½ teaspoon onion powder
Pinch of cayenne pepper
⅛ teaspoon freshly ground
    black pepper
⅛ teaspoon ground
    cinnamon
½ teaspoon dried thyme

Place the shrimp in a large mixing bowl. Add the paste ingredients and toss until the shrimp are well coated with the mixture.

Thread the shrimp onto the kabob rods, leaving ½ inch between them for air to circulate. Load onto the spit rod assembly with the spring ends on the right side. Grill until they are pink and cooked through, 10 to 12 minutes.

Remove from the kabob rods and serve immediately.

Asparagus Shrimp Kabobs

Serves 6   Colorful pink shrimp and brilliant green asparagus basted with olive oil and balsamic vinegar make this dish a delicious change of pace. Be careful not to marinate the shrimp and asparagus; just toss them lightly in the marinade, then thread them onto the skewers. The vinegar will tend to cook the shrimp and turn the asparagus a darker color if you marinate them.

20 asparagus spears, bottoms trimmed and cut into 4-inch lengths

1½ pounds extra-large shrimp, peeled and deveined

Balsamic Vinegar Marinade

½ cup extra-virgin olive oil

⅓ cup balsamic vinegar

1½ teaspoons salt

½ teaspoon freshly ground black pepper

2 cloves garlic, minced

Place the asparagus and shrimp in a 13 x 9-inch glass baking dish.

In a medium-size mixing bowl, whisk together the marinade ingredients. Pour the mixture over the shrimp and asparagus and toss to coat.

Drain the shrimp and asparagus and thread onto the kabob rods, alternating between them and leaving ½ inch in between for air to circulate. Load the kabob rods onto the split road assembly with the spring ends on the right side. Brush the skewers liberally with the marinade and grill until the shrimp have turned pink and are cooked through, 15 to 17 minutes.

Remove the asparagus and shrimp from the skewers and serve immediately.

Spicy Shrimp Burgers

Serves 4 Here ground shrimp is transformed into a spicy and crisp burger, which you can serve on crusty rolls with Artichoke Rémoulade (page 326) or Dilled Tartar Sauce (page 327). They are also delicious served over tossed field greens. Since you are grinding them, you won't need to buy the most expensive shrimp, but save yourself some time and buy them already peeled. If you have a larger rotisserie, you can double the recipe.

2 tablespoons butter

$1/2$ cup finely chopped onion

1 teaspoon Old Bay seasoning

1 cup fine dry bread crumbs

$1/4$ cup mayonnaise

2 teaspoons Worcestershire sauce

1 large egg

$1^1/2$ pounds shrimp, peeled, deveined, and finely ground in a food processor or finely chopped

In a small sauté pan over medium heat, melt the butter. Add the onion and Old Bay and cook, stirring, until softened, about 3 minutes. Transfer to a large mixing bowl and stir in the bread crumbs, mayonnaise, Worcestershire, and egg until well blended. Fold in the shrimp and stir to combine. Form the mixture into 4 to 5 patties ¾ inch thick. Cover with plastic wrap and refrigerate for at least 1 and up to 24 hours to firm up before grilling.

Coat the grill basket with nonstick cooking spray, lay the burgers in the basket, and close the lid tightly. Load the basket onto the spit rod assembly and grill until the burgers begin to turn golden and the shrimp have turned pink, 15 to 22 minutes.

Remove the burgers from the grill basket and serve immediately.

A Garden in the Rotisserie

Vegetables may have been my biggest surprise when I started testing recipes. Rotisseried asparagus was succulent, crisp, and tender. Gourmet fare such as grilled romaine with extra-virgin olive oil was amazing when sprinkled with a little balsamic vinegar and shavings of Parmigiano-Reggiano cheese. Roasted potatoes were out of this world, with a roasted outside and sweet-as-candy flesh. Grilling vegetables in the dead of winter, when there are two feet of snow on the ground, can turn your kitchen into a picnic patio, brightening up the otherwise dull culinary landscape.

For the most part, vegetables can be cooked in the rotisserie basket or on the kabob rods. Larger vegetables such as bell peppers and baking potatoes can be put right on the spit rods. I like to give the vegetables a coating of oil before cooking; this helps to seal in the natural flavor of the vegetables and keep them from drying out. If you would like, a squirt of nonstick cooking spray works just as well. Cutting vegetables into smaller pieces helps them to cook more rapidly and also ensures that more of the surface area is crispy; this is especially helpful when roasting harder vegetables, such as potatoes and other root vegetables.

A Garden in the Rotisserie

Veggie No-Brainers

When using spices, coat the veggies with some oil so that the spices will stick to them. A spray of nonstick cooking oil will work as well as olive oil.

Spicy No-Brainers

- Seasoned Salt (page 285)
- Seasoned pepper
- Lemon Pepper Rub (page 286)
- Garlic salt
- Cavender's Greek seasoning
- Creole Seasoning Rub (page 287)
- Old Bay seasoning
- Mrs. Dash (any flavor)

Saucy No-Brainers

- Bottled barbecue sauce or homemade (see Index)
- Worcestershire sauce
- Bottled Italian salad dressing
- Bottled Caesar salad dressing
- Bottled teriyaki sauce or Spicy Teriyaki Sauce (page 314) or Top Secret Teriyaki Sauce (page 315)
- Garlic oil
- Truffle oil

Garlicky Roasted Baby Artichokes

Serves 6   When baby artichokes are in season, there is nothing better to serve with a roasted chicken or a steak. Cut and prepare the artichokes early in the day and soak them in acidulated water. (Acidulated water is just water that has an acid—lemon juice or vinegar—added to it.)

4 baby artichokes

3 cups water

$1/4$ cup fresh lemon juice

$1/3$ cup olive oil

2 cloves garlic, minced

1 teaspoon fresh thyme
   leaves or $1/2$ teaspoon
   dried

1 teaspoon salt

$1/2$ teaspoon freshly ground
   black pepper

Trim any tough leaves from the bottom of the artichoke, then cut each one in half and scrape out any of the fuzzy choke near the stem end. Combine the water and 2 tablespoons of the lemon juice in a medium-size mixing bowl and add the cut artichokes to the water. At this point, you can cover with plastic wrap and refrigerate for up to 6 hours.

When ready to cook, drain the artichokes and pat dry. In a small mixing bowl, combine the olive oil, garlic, thyme, salt, and pepper. Toss the artichokes in the oil until thoroughly coated. Place the in the rotisserie basket and close the lid tightly. Load onto the spit rod assembly and roast until the artichokes are tender when the stem is pierced with a sharp knife, 25 to 30 minutes.

Remove from the basket, arrange on a platter, and drizzle with the remaining 2 tablespoons of lemon juice. Serve hot or at room temperature.

Spun Asparagus

Serves 4 to 6   This elegant side dish is better than the sum of its parts. Sprinkled with a good olive oil, salt, and pepper, it becomes succulent and tender, yet still retains its gorgeous green color.

2 tablespoons olive oil
1 teaspoon salt
$1/2$ teaspoon freshly ground black pepper
$3/4$ pound asparagus spears, bottoms trimmed and cut into 6-inch lengths

Combine the olive oil, salt, and pepper in a shallow dish. Toss the asparagus in the oil until coated evenly.

Place the asparagus in the rotisserie basket with the tips toward the middle of the basket and stuff a little crumpled aluminum foil in the corners to hold the asparagus in place. Close the lid tightly, load the basket onto the spit rod assembly, and grill until the spears still show a little resistance when pierced with a sharp knife, 5 to 7 minutes, depending upon the thickness of the stalks.

Remove the asparagus from the basket and serve immediately or at room temperature.

Lemon-Thyme Asparagus

Serves 6   This asparagus is marinated, then grilled and served as a salad with its marinade as the basis for the dressing. Garlic and thyme add spark to this dish, which is great as a part of an antipasti offering or salad niçoise.

12 ounces fresh asparagus, bottoms trimmed and cut into 6-inch lengths

1/4 cup olive oil

2 tablespoons fresh lemon juice

1 clove garlic, crushed

2 teaspoons fresh thyme leaves

1 teaspoon salt

1/2 teaspoon freshly ground black pepper

Place the asparagus in a zipper-top plastic bag. In a small mixing bowl, combine the olive oil, lemon juice, garlic, thyme, salt, and pepper. Pour the dressing over the asparagus, seal the bag, and turn over to coat the asparagus. Marinate at room temperature for 1 to 2 hours.

Remove the asparagus and drain the spears, reserving the dressing. Place the asparagus in the rotisserie basket with the tips pointing toward the center of the basket, and stuff a little crumpled aluminum foil in the corners to hold the asparagus in place. Close the lid tightly, load the basket onto the spit rod assembly, and grill until the spears still show a little resistance when pierced with a sharp knife, 5 to 7 minutes, depending upon the thickness of the stalks.

Remove from the basket, place on a serving platter, drizzle with the reserved dressing, and serve at room temperature.

Roasted Beet and Vidalia Onion Salad

Serves 6   Brightly colored beets and sweet Vidalia onions are a great combination when roasted, then dressed with extra-virgin olive oil and balsamic vinegar. Roast the vegetables in the morning, then serve them later in the day. When Vidalias are not in season, try Texas Sweets or Maui onions.

6 medium-size beets, scrubbed, peeled, and halved

4 medium-size Vidalia onions, peeled, with root end left intact, and halved

1/2 cup extra-virgin olive oil

1 1/2 teaspoons salt

1/2 teaspoon freshly ground black pepper

3 to 4 tablespoons balsamic vinegar, to your taste

Arrange the beets and onions on the kabob rods, leaving 1/2 inch between them to allow air to circulate, drizzle with a little of the olive oil, and sprinkle with some of the salt and pepper. Load the rods onto the spit rod assembly with the spring ends on the right side, and roast until the beets are tender, 25 to 35 minutes. Remove from the rods.

When the vegetables have cooled a bit but are still warm, cut the ends off the onions and slice the vegetables into 1/2-inch wedges. Drizzle with the remaining olive oil, sprinkle with the remaining salt and pepper, and toss to blend. Sprinkle the vinegar over the top and stir until well combined. Serve at room temperature.

Smart Turn

Crumble some goat cheese over the salad.

Ginger-Glazed Bok Choy

Serves 6   Baby bok choy is a terrific choice for grilling in the rotisserie basket. Here the bok choy is drizzled with a ginger and oil combination that gives it a smoky, sweet flavor.

¹/₄ cup vegetable oil
1 tablespoon peeled and
    grated fresh ginger
1 clove garlic, minced
1 teaspoon salt
Pinch of cayenne pepper
4 heads baby bok choy,
    bottoms trimmed and
    halved lengthwise

In a small mixing bowl, combine the vegetable oil, ginger, garlic, salt, and cayenne. Drizzle some of this mixture over the bok choy.

Place the bok choy in the rotisserie basket; they may overlap, but that isn't a problem. Close the lid tightly and load the basket onto the spit rod assembly. Grill until the bok choy is tender when the stem end is pierced with a sharp knife, 10 to 15 minutes.

Remove the bok choy to a serving platter and drizzle with any remaining ginger oil. Serve immediately.

Grilled Black Bean and Garlic Broccoli

Serves 6   Broccoli grills well in the rotisserie basket, and this Asian-inspired dish is a winner. You can find black bean sauce in the Asian section of your supermarket—try to buy an imported brand like Lee Kum Kee.

4 cups broccoli florets

1/4 cup fermented black
    bean sauce

2 tablespoons toasted
    sesame oil

2 cloves garlic, minced

Place the broccoli in a medium-size mixing bowl. In a small mixing bowl, whisk together the black bean sauce, sesame oil, and garlic until well blended. Pour the sauce over the broccoli and toss to coat evenly.

Remove the broccoli from the sauce with a slotted spoon and drain, reserving the sauce left in the bowl. Place the broccoli in the rotisserie basket and close the lid tightly. Load the basket onto the spit rod assembly and grill the broccoli until tender when pierced with a sharp knife, 12 to 17 minutes.

Remove the broccoli from the basket and drizzle with the leftover black bean sauce. Serve warm.

Brussels Grill

Serves 6   **Brussels sprouts are a vegetable that you either love or hate. When grilled, they retain their green color and caramelize as they roast, which gives them a wonderfully sweet flavor.**

1/4 cup olive oil

2 cloves garlic, minced

2 teaspoons salt

1/2 teaspoon freshly ground
    black pepper

1 1/2 pounds fresh Brussels
    sprouts

1 lemon, cut into wedges

In a large mixing bowl, combine the olive oil, garlic, salt, and pepper, stirring to blend. Add the sprouts and toss to coat evenly.

Thread the sprouts onto the kabob rods, leaving 1/2 inch in between them for air to circulate; save any excess oil. Load the rods onto the spit rod assembly with the spring ends on the right side. Grill until tender when pierced with a sharp knife, 25 to 35 minutes.

Carefully remove the Brussels sprouts from the kabob rods, drizzle with any remaining oil, and serve with lemon wedges. I like to squeeze the lemon over the freshly grilled sprouts.

Grilled Corn on the Cob

Serves 6   Corn on the rotisserie becomes golden and sweet, no matter whether it's fresh (my favorite) or frozen little cobs. Use the basic recipe, then make a flavored butter to serve with it (see page 217), or cut the grilled corn off the cob to use in salads, salsas, or soups. If you have a larger rotisserie, you can double the recipe.

4 ears fresh corn or 8 small frozen ears
2 tablespoons vegetable oil
1 teaspoon salt
$1/4$ teaspoon freshly ground black pepper

Arrange the corn in the rotisserie basket and close the lid tightly. Brush the corn with the vegetable oil and sprinkle with the salt and pepper. Load the basket onto the spit rod assembly and grill until the corn begins to turn golden, 15 to 20 minutes.

Remove from the basket and serve with butter.

Roasted Garlic Butter

1/2 cup (1 stick) butter, softened
4 cloves Rotisserie Roasted Garlic
(page 222), squeezed out of
the peel

Mash the butter with the garlic, then spread over the grilled corn. Leftover butter will keep, tightly wrapped in plastic, in the refrigerator for up to 1 week.

Cumin Shallot Butter

1/2 cup (1 stick) butter
2 tablespoons minced shallots
1 teaspoon ground cumin

Melt the butter in a small saucepan over medium heat, and add the shallots and cumin. Cook, stirring, until the shallots are softened, 3 to 4 minutes.

Remove from the heat and drizzle on grilled corn on the cob or over popcorn. Refrigerate the leftover butter, tightly wrapped in plastic, for up to 10 days.

Honey-Chili-Lime Butter

1/2 cup (1 stick) butter, softened
1 tablespoon honey
2 tablespoons fresh lime juice
1/2 teaspoon chili powder

In a small mixing bowl, cream the butter with the honey, lime juice, and chili powder. Spread over grilled corn on the cob. Refrigerate leftovers, covered tightly with plastic wrap, for up to 2 weeks.

Cheesy Jalapeño Butter

1/2 cup (1 stick) butter, softened
1 tablespoon green Tabasco sauce
2 tablespoons grated Pecorino
Romano cheese

In a small mixing bowl, cream together the butter, Tabasco, and cheese, and then spread on grilled corn. Refrigerate any leftover butter, tightly covered with plastic wrap, for up to 1 week.

Sun-Dried Tomato Butter

1/2 cup (1 stick) butter, softened
3 oil-packed sun-dried tomatoes,
drained and minced

In a small mixing bowl, beat together the butter and tomatoes until well blended, and spread on grilled corn. Refrigerate any leftover butter, tightly covered with plastic wrap, for up to 2 weeks.

Stuffed Baby Eggplant Cibreo

Serves 6 A small but incredibly good restaurant tucked into a side street in Florence, Cibreo serves authentic Florentine food. This baby eggplant makes for a great first course or accompaniment for grilled meats, poultry, or seafood.

4 small Japanese eggplants, about 4 inches long
1/2 cup extra-virgin olive oil
5 cloves garlic, minced
1 1/2 teaspoons salt
3/4 teaspoon freshly ground black pepper
1 cup dry bread crumbs
1/4 cup freshly grated Parmigiano-Reggiano cheese
1/4 cup capers, drained and chopped
1/4 cup chopped fresh Italian parsley leaves

Wash the eggplant and prick with the sharp point of a knife several times around each one. Rub with a bit of the olive oil, then arrange the eggplants on the spit rod assembly about 1/2 inch apart to allow air to circulate. Grill until tender, about 20 minutes. Remove from the spit rod.

When the eggplant are cool enough to handle, cut each one in half lengthwise and scoop out the insides, leaving a 1/4-inch-thick shell. Coarsely chop the eggplant flesh.

In a small sauté pan, heat 3 tablespoons of the olive oil over medium heat, add the garlic, and cook, stirring, for 1 minute. Add the chopped eggplant, season with the salt and pepper, and cook, stirring, until the eggplant begins to turn golden, 3 to 4 minutes. Remove from the heat and turn into a medium-size mixing bowl. Stir in the bread crumbs, cheese, capers, and parsley.

Stuff the eggplant shells evenly with the mixture. Pour the remaining olive oil over the serving plate, arrange the eggplant on the oil, and serve at room temperature.

Smart Turn

Japanese eggplants are smaller and more slender than traditional eggplants, and they have a slightly sweeter flavor.

Pesto-Grilled Eggplant

Serves 6 to 8   Eggplant is a great vegetable, because you can use all kinds of flavors to enhance it, whether they are Moroccan, Asian, or Italian. Here is a delicious example of what can happen when you pair an ingredient like pesto with this versatile veggie.

1 large purple eggplant, peeled and cut into 1-inch chunks

1½ teaspoons salt

½ teaspoon freshly ground black pepper

½ cup Basil Pesto (page 19) or store-bought pesto

2 teaspoons rice vinegar

Place the eggplant in a medium-size mixing bowl and sprinkle with the salt and pepper. In a small mixing bowl, whisk together the pesto and vinegar. Pour over the eggplant and toss to coat evenly.

Thread the eggplant onto the kabob rods, leaving ½ inch between them for air to circulate. Load the rods onto the spit rod assembly with the spring ends on the right side. Grill until the eggplant begins to turn golden, 20 to 25 minutes.

Remove from the skewers and serve warm or at room temperature.

Grilled Fennel with Gruyère

Serves 6   This simple side dish is a marriage of two of my favorite things—fennel and tangy Gruyère cheese. It makes a tasty side dish, and the fennel can be grilled ahead of time.

4 medium-size fennel bulbs, trimmed of feathery stalks and halved
1/4 cup olive oil
1 teaspoon salt
1/2 teaspoon freshly ground black pepper
1/2 cup grated Gruyère cheese

Place the fennel in a medium-size mixing bowl, drizzle with the olive oil, and sprinkle with the salt and pepper, stirring to coat the fennel evenly.

Place the fennel in the rotisserie basket or thread it onto the kabob rods, leaving 1/2 inch in between them for air to circulate. Load the basket or kabob rods onto the spit rod assembly and grill until the fennel is tender, 20 to 25 minutes.

Remove from the basket or rods, place on a serving platter, and sprinkle with the Gruyère. Serve immediately.

Smart Turn

If you decide to grill the fennel ahead of time, cover it with plastic and store at room temperature for 4 hours. When you are ready to serve it, sprinkle with the cheese and run under a preheated broiler until the cheese is melted, about 5 minutes.

Grilled Fennel and Orange Salad

Serves 6 **This fresh-tasting citrus-flavored salad is a great side for grilled steak or chicken. Grill the fennel earlier in the day and refrigerate until you are ready to serve.**

4 fennel bulbs, trimmed of
feathery stalks and
halved
1/2 cup vegetable oil
1 1/2 teaspoons salt
1/2 teaspoon freshly ground
black pepper
1 navel orange, peeled,
cleaned of all white pith,
and cut into 1/2-inch-
thick slices
3 tablespoons rice vinegar
2 tablespoons orange juice
1/4 cup chopped fresh
parsley leaves for
garnish

Place the fennel in a medium-size mixing bowl, drizzle with 2 tablespoons of the vegetable oil, and sprinkle with 1 teaspoon of the salt and 1/4 teaspoon of the pepper. Toss to coat the fennel evenly.

Place the fennel in the rotisserie basket and close the lid tightly. Load the basket onto the spit rod assembly and grill until the fennel is tender, 20 to 25 minutes.

Remove the fennel from the basket and let cool. On a serving plate, alternate orange slices with the fennel in an attractive pattern. In a small mixing bowl, whisk together the remaining 1/4 cup plus 2 tablespoons vegetable oil, 1/2 teaspoon salt, 1/4 teaspoon pepper, the rice vinegar, and orange juice. Pour some of the dressing over the salad and garnish with the parsley. Serve the remaining dressing on the side.

Rotisserie Roasted Garlic

Serves 6   Mellow, smoky, and amazingly good on crusty bread, roasted garlic is simple to do in the rotisserie. The great news is that you can roast several heads at a time, then store the garlic in olive oil in the refrigerator; it will keep about a month this way. Use roasted garlic to flavor other dishes, such as rotisserie chicken, vegetables, salads, and dressings.

4 heads garlic
1/4 cup extra-virgin olive oil
1 teaspoon salt
Freshly ground black pepper

Cut the tops off the garlic heads to expose the cloves. Drizzle the exposed garlic with the olive oil and sprinkle with the salt and pepper.

Load the heads into the rotisserie basket and close the lid tightly. Load the basket onto the spit rod assembly and roast until the cloves are soft, 30 to 40 minutes.

Remove from the basket and squeeze the garlic cloves out of their skins and into a small bowl. Use as much as you need, then transfer to a glass dish and cover with additional olive oil. Refrigerate for up to 1 month, but do not add additional oil to the garlic because it may cause botulism.

Grilled Leek and
Roasted Yellow Pepper Salad

Serves 6   A beautiful presentation, this colorful salad is roasted in the rotisserie, then served with a brilliant tomato vinaigrette.

6 medium-size leeks, halved lengthwise, washed thoroughly, and patted dry

1 yellow bell pepper, seeded and cut into 1-inch-wide strips

$1/2$ cup olive oil

$1^1/2$ teaspoons salt

$1/2$ teaspoon freshly ground black pepper

2 tablespoons white wine vinegar

1 clove garlic, minced

2 cherry tomatoes, chopped

2 tablespoons chopped fresh Italian parsley leaves

$1/4$ cup crumbled feta cheese

Place the leeks and pepper strips on a flat plate. Drizzle with 2 tablespoons of the olive oil and sprinkle with some of the salt and pepper. Turn the vegetables in the oil to coat, then place in the rotisserie basket. Close the lid tightly, load the basket onto the spit rod assembly, and grill until the leeks are golden and the pepper skins begin to blister, 20 to 25 minutes.

While the vegetables are grilling, in a small mixing bowl whisk together the remaining ¼ cup plus 2 tablespoons olive oil, the remaining salt and pepper, and the vinegar, garlic, tomatoes, and parsley.

Remove the vegetables from the basket and arrange on a serving platter. Pour the dressing over them and sprinkle the platter with the feta cheese. Serve immediately.

Grilled Portobellos

Serves 6   Meaty portobello mushrooms can become the stars of your next dinner when you grill them in the rotisserie. The small rotisserie will hold two large portobellos at a time, and the large one will hold four. Slices of portobellos three-quarters of an inch thick can be loaded into the basket and grilled, too, making a terrific side dish. If you have a smaller rotisserie, you might want to use portobellini. This recipe is for the smaller basket size; you can double it if you have a larger rotisserie.

2 tablespoons extra-virgin
    olive oil
1½ teaspoons salt
½ teaspoon freshly ground
    black pepper
2 portobello mushrooms,
    cleaned and stemmed

In a small mixing bowl, combine the olive oil, salt, and pepper. Brush the mixture over the mushrooms. Load them into the rotisserie basket, and close the lid tightly. Load the basket onto the spit rod assembly and grill the mushrooms until tender, 10 to 15 minutes.

Remove the mushrooms from the basket and serve immediately.

Variations

Use the grilled portobellos as a pizza "crust," and load on the toppings—pesto or traditional tomato sauce and mozzarella—and run under the broiler to melt the cheese.

Sprinkle the grilled portobellos with fresh herbs and top with crumbled goat cheese.

Sprinkle grilled portobellos with a little balsamic vinegar and shaved Parmigiano-Reggiano cheese.

Cheesy Mushroom Burgers

Serves 4   Meaty portobello mushrooms can take the place of steak in some cases, and this is one of them. Marinated in balsamic vinaigrette, then grilled and topped with fresh tomato and crumbled goat cheese, these burgers are like no other! If you have a larger rotisserie, you can double the recipe.

4 portobello mushrooms, cleaned and stemmed
1/2 cup olive oil
1/4 cup balsamic vinegar
2 cloves garlic, minced
1 teaspoon salt
1/2 teaspoon freshly ground black pepper
4 crusty rolls
4 slices ripe tomato
1/2 cup crumbled goat cheese

Put the mushrooms in a glass baking dish.

In a small mixing bowl, whisk together the olive oil, vinegar, garlic, salt, and pepper. Pour the mixture over the mushrooms and turn them over several times to coat.

Drain the mushrooms, place them in the rotisserie basket, and close the lid tightly. Load the basket onto the spit rod assembly and grill until the mushrooms are tender, 10 to 12 minutes.

Remove the mushrooms from the basket and serve on crusty rolls, topped with the sliced tomato and crumbled goat cheese.

To Wash or to Wipe, That Is the Question

Chefs have long discussed whether to wash mushrooms under cold water or just wipe them clean. I'm a washer, but I use just a little bit of water, so that the mushrooms don't absorb much. I'd rather have them really clean than eat grit in the finished dish.

Grilled Wild Mushroom Salad

Serves 6 to 8 as a side dish Earthy wild mushrooms are delicious when roasted in the rotisserie. Toss with some good extra-virgin olive oil and balsamic vinegar, and you have a salad fit for a king. I like to serve this alongside grilled steak or chicken.

2 pounds assorted fresh wild mushrooms, such as shiitake, oyster, porcini, portobellini, and chanterelle

$3/4$ cup extra-virgin olive oil

$1/4$ cup balsamic vinegar

$1^1/2$ teaspoons salt

$1/2$ teaspoon freshly ground black pepper

2 cloves garlic, minced

1 tablespoon chopped fresh thyme leaves

1 tablespoon chopped fresh sage leaves

6 cups field greens, washed and dried

Wash the mushrooms, pat dry, cut them in half or in quarters, depending on their size, and place in a large mixing bowl. In a small mixing bowl, whisk together the olive oil, vinegar, salt, pepper, garlic, thyme, and sage. Pour 3 to 4 tablespoons of the dressing over the mushrooms and toss to coat evenly.

Place the mushrooms in the rotisserie basket, close the lid tightly, and load the basket onto the spit rod assembly. Grill the mushrooms until nicely browned, about 20 minutes.

In a large salad bowl, toss the greens with ½ cup of the remaining dressing and arrange on salad plates. Top each serving with some of the mushrooms and drizzle with the remaining dressing. Serve warm.

Blue Bayou Stuffed Mushrooms

Serves 6   Stuffed mushrooms are a great dish to do in the rotisserie; you can prepare them ahead of time, then roast them just before serving. These 'shrooms are stuffed with blue cheese and spiked with a little Creole seasoning.

2 tablespoons butter

2 tablespoons chopped shallots

2 teaspoons Creole Seasoning Rub (page 287)

8 white mushrooms, about 2 inches in diameter, cleaned, stemmed, and stems chopped

1/4 cup fresh bread crumbs

2 tablespoons chopped fresh parsley leaves

1/4 cup crumbled Maytag or other good-quality blue cheese

In a small sauté pan, melt the butter over medium heat. Add the shallots and cook, stirring, until they begin to turn translucent, about 3 minutes. Add the Creole seasoning and cook another minute, stirring so the spices don't burn. Add the chopped mushroom stems and cook, stirring, until their liquid evaporates, about 4 minutes.

Remove the mixture from the pan to a medium-size mixing bowl. Add the bread crumbs, parsley, and cheese and combine well. Stuff the mushroom caps with the mixture. At this point, you may refrigerate the mushrooms, covered with plastic wrap, for up to 8 hours.

When you are ready to serve, arrange the mushrooms in the rotisserie basket, close the lid tightly, and load the basket onto the spit rod assembly. Grill until the filling is golden, 15 to 20 minutes.

Remove the mushrooms from the basket and serve immediately.

Vinny's Stuffed Mushrooms

Serves 6   Stuffed mushrooms are a snap to prepare for the rotisserie; they can be held in the refrigerator for up to two days, then roasted in the basket. In this recipe, I use medium-size portobellini, which resemble a cross between cremini and portobello. If they are not available in your area, substitute large white mushrooms.

3 tablespoons olive oil

2 shallots, chopped

10 to 12 portobellini mushrooms, cleaned, stemmed, and stems chopped

6 slices Genoa salami, about 2$^{1}/_{2}$ inches in diameter, cut into strips

$^{1}/_{3}$ cup dry bread crumbs

$^{1}/_{2}$ cup freshly grated Parmesan cheese

2 teaspoons chopped fresh oregano leaves

$^{1}/_{4}$ cup chopped oil-packed sun-dried tomatoes, drained

Heat 1 teaspoon of the olive oil in a small sauté pan over medium heat. Add the shallots, chopped mushroom stems, and salami and cook, stirring, until the shallots begin to soften, 2 to 3 minutes. Remove the pan from the heat and transfer the mixture to a medium-size mixing bowl. Add the bread crumbs, cheese, oregano, and tomatoes and stir until combined. Sprinkle 1 tablespoon of the remaining olive oil over the mixture and stir until it comes together. Stuff the mushroom caps with the mixture.

Set the mushrooms in the rotisserie basket and close the lid tightly. Drizzle with the remaining 1$^{2}/_{3}$ tablespoons olive oil. Load onto the spit rod assembly and grill until the filling is golden, 12 to 15 minutes.

Remove the mushrooms from the basket and serve immediately. Any leftovers can be reheated in the microwave or toaster oven.

Burgundian Onions

Serves 8   Sweet Vidalia onions are soaked in Burgundy wine until they turn rosy, and then roasted slowly in the rotisserie. Serve these alongside a roast or poultry for a sensational side dish.

8 medium-size Vidalia
   onions
4 cups Burgundy wine
1 teaspoon dried thyme
1/4 cup (1/2 stick) butter,
   melted
1 1/2 teaspoons salt
3/4 teaspoon freshly ground
   black pepper

Remove the peel from the onion, but do not cut off the top or root ends. Pour the wine and thyme into a 2-gallon zipper-top plastic bag and add the onions. Seal the bag, turn over to coat the onion, and marinate in the refrigerator for at least 6 hours or overnight, turning occasionally.

When ready to cook, remove the onions from the wine and thread onto the kabob rods, leaving 1/2 inch in between them for air to circulate. Brush with some of the melted butter and sprinkle with the salt and pepper. Load the rods onto the spit rod assembly with the spring ends on the right. Roast the onions until soft and golden, 45 minutes to 1 hour, turning off the machine to baste them with the remaining butter every 15 minutes or so.

Remove the onions, cut off the ends, and serve warm or at room temperature.

Roasted Balsamic Pepper Salad

Serves 6 to 8   This colorful salad is so easy to make with the help of the rotisserie. The charred peppers are paired with olive oil, balsamic vinegar, and garlic for a lovely side dish. Make sure to serve lots of crusty bread to dip into the sauce. If red and yellow peppers are expensive, substitute a few more green ones, but make sure to have at least one red and one yellow for color and flavor.

3 red bell peppers
2 yellow bell peppers
2 green bell peppers
4 cloves garlic, quartered
1¹/₂ teaspoons salt
³/₄ teaspoon freshly ground
    black pepper
¹/₂ cup olive oil
¹/₄ cup balsamic vinegar

Wash the peppers and arrange them on the kabob rods, leaving ½ inch in between them for air to circulate. Load the rods onto the spit rod assembly with the spring ends on the right. Roast until the peppers are evenly charred, 20 to 25 minutes. Turn off the rotisserie and allow them to rest for 1 hour. The steam inside the rotisserie will help to loosen their skins.

When the peppers are cool, remove the skins, stems, and seeds. Slice the peppers into 1-inch-wide strips and place in a shallow dish with the garlic. Sprinkle with the salt and pepper and pour the olive oil and vinegar over the peppers. Stir to blend. Cover loosely and leave at room temperature for at least 4 hours, stirring occasionally. Remove the garlic when you are ready to serve.

Fire-Roasted Poblanos Stuffed with Chorizo and Grilled Corn Hash

<hr>

Serves 6   This recipe has a few steps to it, but it's really worth the price of admission! A stuffing made with sweet roasted corn, spicy sausage, onion, cheese, and bread crumbs is spooned into chiles, then grilled until they are tender. It's great to serve with a grilled steak or seafood and is hearty enough to be a vegetarian main course.

6 poblano chiles

2 links chorizo sausage, cut into small dice

2 tablespoons butter

$1/4$ cup finely chopped shallots

$1/4$ cup seeded and finely chopped red bell pepper

$1^1/2$ cups grilled corn kernels (see page 216) or $1^1/2$ cups frozen corn, defrosted

1 teaspoon salt

$1/2$ teaspoon freshly ground black pepper

$1/2$ teaspoon ground cumin

$1/2$ cup fresh bread crumbs

1 cup shredded mild cheddar cheese

Wash the chiles and make a slit lengthwise down each one. Carefully remove the seeds and set the chiles aside while you make the filling.

Over medium-high heat, cook the chorizo in a medium-size skillet until it renders its fat and is cooked through, about 5 to 7 minutes. Remove the sausage from the pan, scrape into a medium-size mixing bowl, and drain off the fat. In the same skillet, melt the butter, add the shallots and red pepper, and cook, stirring, until the shallots are translucent, 4 to 5 minutes. Add the corn, salt, black pepper, and cumin and cook, stirring, until the corn softens, another 3 to 4 minutes. Transfer the mixture to the bowl containing the chorizo, sprinkle the mixture with the bread crumbs and cheese, and stir to blend.

Carefully stuff the chiles with the sausage and corn mixture and lay them in the rotisserie basket, with the slit on the side. Close the lid tightly, load onto the spit rod assembly, and grill the chiles until charred on all sides and softened, 20 to 25 minutes.

Remove the chiles from the basket and serve immediately.

Roasted Rosemary Potatoes

○—●—○

Serves 6 to 8   I'm a potato lover—I could eat them for breakfast, lunch, and dinner—and these sweet, herbed, crusty morsels are just perfect with any main course. Leftovers, if you have any, are great mixed into eggs the next day for a frittata or omelet.

1/4 cup olive oil
2 teaspoons salt
1 teaspoon freshly ground
    black pepper
2 teaspoons chopped fresh
    rosemary leaves
6 to 8 medium-size red
    potatoes, quartered
2 to 4 tablespoons balsamic
    vinegar (optional), to
    your taste

In a large mixing bowl, whisk together the olive oil, salt, pepper, and rosemary. Toss in the potatoes and stir to coat them evenly.

Thread the potatoes onto the kabob rods, leaving ½ inch between them for air to circulate. Load the rods onto the spit rod assembly with the spring ends on the right side. Roast the potatoes until golden on the outside and tender when pierced with a sharp knife, 40 to 50 minutes.

Remove the potatoes from the skewers and place in a serving bowl. Drizzle with the vinegar, if desired. Serve warm or at room temperature.

To Peel or Not to Peel

We have a dilemma at my house: one child likes his spuds peeled, while the other loves the skins. For this dish, I like to leave the skins on because they give it color and help the potatoes crisp up nicely. But if you have a family that doesn't like the skins, peel away!

Herb-Roasted New Potatoes

Serves 6   Fresh herbs and tiny new potatoes are a delicious accompaniment to grilled fish, meat, or poultry. You can vary the herbs to your taste, but the cooking method will be the same. I prefer to do this with yellow-skinned new potatoes rather than red-skinned ones because the herbs show up better against the creamy colored skins.

$^1/_3$ cup olive oil

2 teaspoons salt

$^3/_4$ teaspoon freshly ground black pepper

2 tablespoons chopped fresh thyme leaves

1 tablespoon chopped fresh sage leaves

2 teaspoons chopped fresh rosemary leaves

$1^1/_2$ to 2 pounds small new potatoes, halved

$^1/_4$ cup chopped fresh parsley leaves for garnish

In a medium-size mixing bowl, stir together the olive oil, salt, pepper, thyme, sage, and rosemary. Add the potatoes and toss to coat evenly with the oil.

Thread the potatoes onto the kabob rods, leaving ½ inch between them for air to circulate. Save any oil left in the bowl. Load the kabob rods onto the spit rod assembly with the spring ends on the right. Roast the potatoes for 30 minutes, then stop the machine and baste the potatoes with the remaining oil. Restart the machine and roast the potatoes until tender, another 25 to 30 minutes.

Remove the potatoes from the skewers, garnish with the parsley, and serve immediately.

Rotisserie Potatoes Dijon

Serves 6   These savory potato nuggets are coated with Dijon mustard, then seasoned with tarragon and garlic and roasted until they are crispy and sweet inside. Serve these with roasted meats, fish, or poultry.

$1/2$ cup Dijon mustard

2 tablespoons olive oil

2 tablespoons chopped fresh tarragon leaves

2 cloves garlic, chopped

$1^1/2$ teaspoons salt

$1/2$ teaspoon freshly ground black pepper

2 pounds red potatoes, cut into 1-inch chunks

In a large mixing bowl, combine the mustard, olive oil, tarragon, garlic, salt, and pepper. Toss the potatoes in the mixture until coated evenly.

Thread the potatoes onto the kabob rods, leaving ½ inch between them for air to circulate. Load the kabobs onto the spit rod assembly with the spring ends on the right. Roast the potatoes until tender and golden, 45 to 55 minutes.

Remove the potatoes from the rods and serve warm or at room temperature.

Variation

Rotisserie Potato Salad: For a great potato salad, roast the potatoes, then toss them with 3 tablespoons fresh lemon juice, ½ cup chopped celery, and ¼ cup chopped shallots. Serve at room temperature.

Idaho Roasters

Serves 6   Whole potatoes cook a little faster in the rotisserie than they do in a conventional oven, and the skin (my favorite part) becomes golden brown and is deliciously crisp. Use this recipe as a jumping-off point for stuffed roasted potatoes or a potato skin appetizer.

6 medium-size baking
potatoes
¹/₄ cup vegetable oil
1¹/₂ teaspoons salt

Wash the potatoes and pat dry with paper towels. Prick them several times with a sharp knife, rub with the vegetable oil, and sprinkle with the salt.

Thread the potatoes onto the kabob rods, leaving ½ inch between them for air to circulate. Load the skewers onto the spit rod assembly with the spring ends on the right side. Roast the potatoes until they feel tender when pinched with a dish towel, about 45 minutes.

Remove the potatoes from the skewers and serve immediately.

Stuffed Idaho Roasters

Serves 6   One day one of my son's friends asked Ryan what his favorite meal was at our house, and he said anything with stuffed baked potatoes. "Twice baked," "double stuffed," whatever you call them, these luxuriously rich and delicious potatoes are the perfect side for any dinner.

1 recipe Idaho Roasters (page 235)

¹/₄ cup (¹/₂ stick) butter

¹/₂ cup sour cream, plus extra for garnish

1 cup grated mild cheddar cheese

6 shakes Tabasco sauce

6 strips bacon, cooked until crisp, drained on paper towels, and crumbled

6 green onions, white and light green parts, chopped, plus extra for garnish

Preheat the oven to 400 degrees.

Cut off the tops of the cooked potatoes, and spoon the flesh into a medium-size mixing bowl, leaving ¹/₂-inch-thick shells. Beat in the butter, sour cream, cheese, Tabasco, bacon, and green onions, stirring until smooth and well combined. Restuff the potato skins with the mixture. (The potatoes can be made up to this point, covered with plastic wrap, and refrigerated for up to 24 hours. Add 5 to 7 minutes to the baking time.)

Bake the potatoes for 15 minutes, or until golden brown. Serve garnished with additional sour cream and green onions.

No-Fry Pommes Frites

— ○ ● ○ —

Serves 6   **Crispy and delicious, these fries are prepared with just two tablespoons of oil in the round basket of the George Foreman rotisserie.**

4 medium-size russet potatoes, cut into ½-inch-wide strips (peeling them is optional)

2 tablespoons olive oil

2 teaspoons salt

1 teaspoon freshly ground black pepper

Place the potatoes in a large mixing bowl, stir in the olive oil, salt, and pepper, and toss to coat evenly.

Place the potatoes in the round basket and latch the basket closed. Load the basket onto the spit road and roast until the potatoes are golden and crisp, about 45 minutes.

Remove from the basket and serve immediately.

Smart Turn

If you have a rotisserie with a flat basket, cut the potatoes into wedges. There is room for only 2 potatoes in the compact model, while 4 to 5 will fit in the larger one. Make sure to fill in the corners with crumpled aluminum foil so that none of the potatoes escape.

Roasted Dill Potato Salad

Serves 6 to 8   Roasted potatoes make a great potato salad. Try preparing this in the morning the day you plan to serve it. Good choices for potatoes would be Yukon Gold, Red Bliss, or any kind of waxy new potatoes.

1/4 cup olive oil

2 teaspoons salt

1 teaspoon freshly ground black pepper

6 to 8 medium-size potatoes, quartered

1/2 cup chopped celery

4 green onions, chopped

1 cup mayonnaise

1 tablespoon milk

1 tablespoon Dijon mustard

1 tablespoon chopped fresh dill or 1 teaspoon dillweed

1 teaspoon grated lemon zest

Place the olive oil, salt, and pepper in a large mixing bowl, add the potatoes, and toss to coat evenly.

Thread the potatoes onto the kabob rods, leaving ½ inch between them for air to circulate. Load on the spit rod assembly with the spring ends on the right side, and roast until the potatoes are golden and tender when pierced with a sharp knife, 40 to 55 minutes.

Allow the potatoes to cool to room temperature and transfer to a large serving bowl. Add the celery and green onions. In a small mixing bowl, whisk together the mayonnaise, milk, mustard, dill, and lemon zest. Pour over the potatoes, and toss to coat evenly. Refrigerate the salad at least 1 and up to 12 hours before serving.

Roasted Potato Salad Provençal

Serves 6 to 8   This salad is fragrant with garlic, Dijon mustard, and tarragon. It is best when served at room temperature.

3 pounds red potatoes, left whole if small and quartered if large

1/3 cup olive oil, plus extra for brushing

1 teaspoon salt

1/2 teaspoon freshly ground black pepper

3 tablespoons fresh lemon juice

1 clove garlic, mashed

2 teaspoons chopped fresh tarragon leaves

1 tablespoon Dijon mustard

Thread the potatoes onto the kabob rods, leaving ½ inch between them for air to circulate, then brush with olive oil. Arrange the rods on the spit rod assembly with the spring ends on the right side. Roast the potatoes until golden on the outside and tender when pierced with a sharp knife, 40 to 55 minutes.

Let the potatoes cool to room temperature, and place in a large serving bowl. Sprinkle with the salt and pepper, tossing until coated. In a small mixing bowl, whisk together the ⅓ cup olive oil, the lemon juice, garlic, tarragon, and mustard. Pour over the potatoes and toss to combine. Cover with plastic wrap and allow to sit at room temperature for at least 2 hours. You can make this 1 day in advance; remove from the refrigerator 2 hours before serving and allow to come to room temperature.

Grilled Radicchio

Serves 6   Radicchio is a beautiful vegetable, but it can be bitter. The roasting process helps to sweeten its flavor. This is great as a side dish or as part of an antipasto platter.

3 heads radicchio
1/4 cup extra-virgin olive oil
1 teaspoon salt
1/2 teaspoon freshly ground
    black pepper

Cut each radicchio into four wedges and place in the rotisserie basket. Brush the wedges with the olive oil, sprinkle with the salt and pepper, and close the lid tightly. Load the basket onto the spit rod assembly and grill until the radicchio begins to turn golden, 10 to 15 minutes.

Remove from the rotisserie and serve warm or at room temperature.

Great Caesar's Romaine

Serves 4   A delicious takeoff on the Caesar salad, the grilled romaine becomes sweet when turned on the rotisserie. Serve half a romaine per person.

4 hearts of romaine lettuce,
    halved lengthwise
2 tablespoons extra-virgin
    olive oil
1 teaspoon salt
1/2 teaspoon freshly ground
    black pepper

Put the lettuce on a plate, drizzle the olive oil evenly over the lettuce, and sprinkle with the salt and pepper.

Arrange the lettuce in the rotisserie basket, close the lid tightly, and load onto the spit rod assembly. Grill until the lettuce begins to turn golden, 4 to 6 minutes.

2 teaspoons balsamic
vinegar
2 ounces Parmigiano-
Reggiano cheese, shaved
with a swivel peeler

Remove the lettuce from the basket. Arrange 1 lettuce half on each of 4 salad plates. Sprinkle each serving with some of the vinegar, garnish with shavings of Parmigiano, and serve immediately.

Rosemary Roasted Shallot and Onion Medley

Serves 6   Onions and shallots become sweet when they are roasted slowly in the rotisserie. This is a great accompaniment to grilled steak, chicken, or seafood. It also makes a flavorful addition to a stuffing, for example Old-Fashioned Cornbread Stuffing with Rotisserie Caramelized Onions (page 354).

6 medium-size shallots
4 medium-size sweet
onions, such as Vidalia,
Texas Sweet, or Maui
$1/4$ cup olive oil
1 teaspoon salt
$1/2$ teaspoon freshly ground
black pepper
$1 1/2$ teaspoons chopped
fresh rosemary leaves
or $3/4$ teaspoon dried

Peel the shallots, leaving the root end intact, then cut them in half lengthwise and place in a large mixing bowl. Peel the onions, leaving the root end intact, and cut into quarters, adding them to the shallots in the bowl. Pour the olive oil over the shallots and onions, sprinkle with the salt, pepper, and rosemary, and toss to coat evenly.

Load the shallots and onions into the rotisserie basket and close the lid tightly. Load onto the spit rod assembly and roast until the shallots are golden brown, 35 to 45 minutes.

Remove from the basket and serve warm or at room temperature.

Grilled Summer Squash with Tarragon

○ ● ○

Serves 6   This is a simple, savory dish to serve when the zucchini is overrunning your summer garden. Try to use fresh tarragon for a right-from-the-garden taste. These skewers are also wonderful when cherry tomatoes are alternated with the zucchini. The tomatoes blister, but they taste great.

4 medium-size zucchini, cut into 1-inch chunks
3 tablespoons olive oil
2 tablespoons fresh lemon juice
1 1/2 teaspoons salt
1/2 teaspoon freshly ground black pepper
1 tablespoon chopped fresh tarragon leaves or 1 teaspoon dried

Place the zucchini in a zipper-top plastic bag. In a small mixing bowl, whisk together the olive oil, lemon juice, salt, pepper, and tarragon, then pour over the zucchini. Seal the bag and turn over to coat the zucchini. Marinate in the refrigerator for at least 2 and up to 5 hours.

When ready to cook, thread the zucchini onto kabob rods, leaving 1/2 inch between them for air to circulate, then load onto the spit rod assembly with the spring ends on the right. Grill the zucchini until they begin to turn golden brown, 15 to 20 minutes.

Remove from the skewers and serve warm or at room temperature.

Truffled Yellow Squash

Serves 6   This simple dish is magnificent; a little white truffle oil flavors yellow pattypan squash. White truffle oil is sold in fine gourmet shops and grocery stores. This richly perfumed oil is an indulgence, but a little adds an earthy, unforgettable flavor to dishes. Serves this squash with steak, chicken, or seafood.

1 pound small yellow pattypan squash, halved lengthwise

3 tablespoons white truffle oil

1½ teaspoons salt

½ teaspoon freshly ground black pepper

Place the squash in a medium-size mixing bowl, drizzle with 2 tablespoons of the truffle oil, and sprinkle with the salt and pepper. Toss to coat the squash evenly with the oil.

Place the squash in the rotisserie basket and close the lid tightly. Load the basket onto the spit rod assembly and grill until the squash is tender, 20 to 25 minutes.

Remove from the basket, drizzle with the remaining 1 tablespoon of truffle oil, and serve immediately.

Orange-Glazed Sweet Potatoes

Serves 6 to 8   The sweet potato is what I call the forgotten veggie. We seem to forget about it until Thanksgiving and Christmas, and then we cover it up with marshmallows and all manner of unkind things. These sweets roast on the rotisserie with orange slices and just a bit of ginger and brown sugar, making for a great side dish to serve with pork or poultry.

1/3 cup firmly packed dark brown sugar

2 tablespoons orange juice

2 tablespoons butter

1/2 teaspoon ground ginger

4 medium-size sweet potatoes, peeled and cut into 1-inch chunks

2 navel oranges, cut into 1/2-inch-thick slices

In a small saucepan, combine the brown sugar, orange juice, butter, and ginger and stir over medium heat until the butter melts. Remove from the stove and allow to cool slightly.

Thread the sweet potatoes and orange slices onto the kabob rods, alternating a sweet potato chunk with an orange slice and leaving 1/2 inch between them for air to circulate. Load the kabob rods onto the spit rod assembly with the spring ends on the right side, and brush with some of the brown sugar sauce. Roast until the potatoes are tender when pierced with a sharp knife, 45 to 50 minutes, stopping the machine every 15 minutes to brush the potatoes and oranges with more brown sugar sauce.

Remove the potatoes and oranges from the skewers. Serve the potatoes garnished with some of the roasted orange slices and brushed with any remaining sauce.

Fire-Roasted Tomatoes

Serves 6 to 8   Follow the instructions for the basic recipe, then try some of the variations that follow. Don't use overly ripe tomatoes for roasting, as they tend to fall apart. Serve these as an accompaniment for grilled beef, chicken, or seafood.

5 plum tomatoes, halved crosswise

1/4 cup olive oil or vegetable oil

1 teaspoon salt

1/2 teaspoon freshly ground black pepper

Place the tomatoes in a small mixing bowl. Drizzle with the olive oil, then sprinkle with the salt and pepper and stir to coat the tomatoes evenly.

Place the tomatoes in the rotisserie basket, close the lid tightly, and load onto the spit rod assembly. Grill until charred around the edges, 25 minutes.

Remove from the basket and serve warm or at room temperature.

Variations

Viva Italia Tomatoes: Follow the basic recipe above, but add the following to the olive oil: 2 cloves garlic, minced; 1 teaspoon dried basil; and 1 teaspoon dried oregano. Grill the tomatoes, remove from the basket, and sprinkle with 4 chopped fresh basil leaves.

Grilled Tomatoes Olé: Follow the basic recipe above, but add the following to the olive oil mixture: ¼ teaspoon ground ancho chile and ¼ teaspoon dried oregano. Grill the tomatoes, remove from the basket, and sprinkle with ¼ cup chopped fresh cilantro leaves.

Five-Spice Tomatoes: Although you might not associate tomatoes with Asian cooking, these are great in a salad with rice wine vinegar and rice noodles. Add 1 teaspoon Chinese five-spice powder to the olive oil and grill as directed. Garnish with ¼ cup chopped fresh cilantro leaves.

Moroccan Tomatoes: Follow the basic recipe, but add the following to the olive oil: 1 clove garlic (minced), 1 teaspoon ground cumin, 1 teaspoon sweet paprika, ½ teaspoon ground coriander, and a pinch of cayenne. Grill the tomatoes as directed and serve garnished with 2 tablespoons each chopped fresh parsley and mint leaves.

Grilled Tomato and Mozzarella Salad

Serves 6 to 8   When tomatoes are grilled, it intensifies the flavor of the fruit, thus intensifying the flavor of the finished dish. This delectable salad can be made in the dead of winter with not-so-ripe plum tomatoes (actually, even in summer you don't want to use really ripe tomatoes—they'll fall apart); all you need is your countertop rotisserie.

1/2 cup extra-virgin olive oil

2 teaspoons salt

3/4 teaspoon freshly ground black pepper

8 ripe plum tomatoes, halved crosswise

1/2 pound fresh mozzarella cheese, cut into 1/2-inch cubes

10 fresh basil leaves, chopped

In a small mixing bowl, combine the olive oil, salt, and pepper. Place the tomatoes on a plate and drizzle some of the oil mixture over them, turning to coat evenly.

Place the tomatoes in the rotisserie basket, close the lid tightly, and load the basket onto the spit rod assembly. Grill the tomatoes until charred along the edges, 10 to 15 minutes.

Let the tomatoes rest in the basket for 5 minutes, then remove and arrange them attractively on a serving platter with the mozzarella. Drizzle the remaining oil mixture over the top and sprinkle with the basil. Serve at room temperature.

Kaleidoscope Grilled Cherry Tomatoes

Serves 6 to 8   Like a mosaic, tiny yellow, orange, and red cherry tomatoes are a beautiful presentation from the rotisserie. You can serve these as an accompaniment for grilled meats, or toss them into freshly cooked pasta for a fresh new twist on a weeknight dinner.

$\frac{1}{3}$ cup olive oil

3 cloves garlic, minced

2 teaspoons chopped fresh oregano leaves

4 fresh basil leaves, chopped

$1\frac{1}{2}$ teaspoons salt

$\frac{1}{2}$ teaspoon freshly ground black pepper

4 cups assorted cherry tomatoes, stemmed

In a small mixing bowl, combine the olive oil, garlic, oregano, basil, salt, and pepper, stirring to blend. Place the tomatoes in a medium-size mixing bowl and pour in all but 2 tablespoons of the seasoned oil, tossing to coat.

Thread the tomatoes onto the kabob rods, alternating red, orange, and yellow ones and leaving $\frac{1}{2}$ inch between them for air to circulate. Load the kabob rods onto the spit rod assembly with the spring ends on the right side, and grill the tomatoes until their skins are darkened and blistered, 10 to 15 minutes.

Let the tomatoes rest for 5 minutes before removing from the rods. Place the tomatoes in a serving bowl or on a platter and drizzle with the remaining seasoned oil. Serve warm or at room temperature.

Grilled Vegetable Kabobs

Serves 6 to 8   Vegetables are simple to cook in the rotisserie, and one of my favorite ways is to load them onto the kabob rods. Because the veggies are cut into smaller chunks, a greater proportion of the vegetable is grilled and there is more of that great grill flavor. This is my favorite veggie combination, but you can use this recipe to make up your own. Just remember that some vegetables will cook

longer than others, so load those with similar cooking times onto the same skewer; you can remove them when they are cooked and continue to cook those that require more time.

Oregano-Garlic Marinade

¹/₂ cup olive oil

3 tablespoons fresh lemon juice

2 teaspoons salt

1 teaspoon freshly ground black pepper

1¹/₂ teaspoons dried oregano

2 cloves garlic, mashed

4 medium-size red onions, quartered

2 medium-size green zucchini, cut into 1-inch pieces

2 medium-size yellow zucchini, cut into 1-inch pieces

12 cremini mushrooms, stemmed

1 red bell pepper, seeded and cut into 1-inch pieces

¹/₄ pound feta cheese, crumbled, for garnish

In a small mixing bowl, combine the marinade ingredients, stirring to blend.

Place the prepared vegetables in a 2-gallon zipper-top plastic bag. Pour the marinade over the vegetables, seal the bag, and turn over to coat everything. Marinate in the refrigerator for at least 1 and up to 4 hours.

When ready to cook, remove the vegetables from the marinade and thread onto the kabob rods, alternating the vegetables for a colorful pattern and leaving ½ inch between them for air to circulate. Load the kabob rods onto the spit rod assembly with the spring ends on the right, and grill until the vegetables are golden and tender, 20 to 25 minutes.

Remove from the kabob rods and serve immediately, garnished with the crumbled feta.

Tuscan Grilled Vegetables

Serves 6 to 8   **Lemon juice and sage help to turn these vegetables into a memorable feast.**

Lemon-Sage Marinade

$1/2$ cup olive oil

$1/4$ cup fresh lemon juice

$1^1/_2$ teaspoons salt

$1/2$ teaspoon freshly ground black pepper

3 cloves garlic, mashed

Grated zest of 1 lemon

6 fresh sage leaves, thinly sliced, or 1 tablespoon dried

2 Japanese eggplants, cut into 1-inch chunks (see Smart Turn on page 218)

1 medium-size green bell pepper, seeded and cut into 1-inch squares

1 red onion, quartered, with root end left intact

16 cherry tomatoes, stemmed

$1/3$ cup pine nuts, toasted (see page 184), for garnish

In a medium-size mixing bowl, stir together the marinade ingredients.

Place the vegetables in a 2-gallon zipper-top plastic bag and pour the marinade over them. Seal the bag, turn it over to coat the vegetables, and marinate in the refrigerator for at least 1 and up to 4 hours.

When ready to cook, remove the vegetable from the marinade and thread onto the kabob rods, alternating the vegetables for a colorful pattern and leaving ½ inch between them for air to circulate. Load the kabob rods onto the spit rod assembly with the spring ends on the right, and grill until tender, 20 to 25 minutes.

Remove the vegetables from the kabob rods and serve immediately, garnished with the toasted pine nuts.

Variation

Grilled Vegetables Provençal: Substitute 1 tablespoon dried herbes de Provence for the sage and garnish with crumbled goat cheese instead of the pine nuts.

Spicy Pacific Rim Veggies

Serves 6   Soy sauce and sesame oil season these veggies, which are a great side with grilled meats, poultry, and seafood. Use shiitake, cremini, or button mushrooms.

2 medium-size zucchini, cut into 1-inch pieces

16 mushrooms, stemmed

2 medium-size onions, quartered, with the root end left intact

2 yellow zucchini or yellow crookneck squash, cut into 1-inch pieces

1 medium-size green bell pepper, seeded and cut into 1-inch pieces

Toasted Sesame Marinade

$1/2$ cup soy sauce

$1/4$ cup rice wine

2 garlic cloves, minced

1 teaspoon peeled and grated fresh ginger

$1/2$ teaspoon chile oil

1 tablespoon toasted sesame oil

2 tablespoons sesame seeds for garnish

Place the vegetables in a 2-gallon zipper-top plastic bag.

Combine the marinade ingredients in a small mixing bowl, then pour over the vegetables in the bag. Seal the bag, turn over to coat the vegetables, and marinate in the refrigerator for at least 1 but not more than 2 hours because the soy sauce will discolor the vegetables.

When ready to cook, remove the vegetable from the marinade, drain, and thread onto the kabob rods, alternating the vegetables for a colorful pattern and leaving $1/2$ inch between them for air to circulate. Load the kabob rods onto the spit rod assembly with the spring ends on the right. Grill the vegetables until tender, 20 to 25 minutes.

Remove the vegetables from the kabob rods and serve immediately, drizzled with the sesame oil and sprinkled with the sesame seeds.

Smart Turn

Any leftovers are great scrambled with eggs the next morning.

Roasted Root Vegetables

Serves 6 to 8   Flavored with rosemary and extra-virgin olive oil, these vegetables are a great side dish for a roast, or grilled steak or seafood. You can vary the herbs, using oregano, thyme, or sage instead of the rosemary.

3 medium-size red potatoes, quartered

Four 6-inch-long carrots, cut into 1-inch pieces

3 medium-size parsnips, peeled and cut into 1-inch pieces

2 medium-size beets, peeled and quartered

4 shallots, peeled

$1/4$ cup extra-virgin olive oil

$1^1/2$ teaspoons salt

$3/4$ teaspoon freshly ground black pepper

1 tablespoon chopped fresh rosemary leaves

Place the potatoes, carrots, parsnips, beets, and shallots in a large mixing bowl. Pour the olive oil over the vegetables and season with the salt, pepper, and rosemary. Toss the vegetables until evenly coated with the oil and seasonings.

Thread the vegetables onto the kabob rods, alternating them to create an attractive pattern, and leaving ½ inch between them for air to circulate. Load the kabobs onto the spit rod assembly with the spring ends on the right side, and roast until the vegetables feel tender when pierced a sharp knife, 45 minutes to 1 hour.

Remove the vegetables to a serving platter and serve immediately.

Sesame and Miso-Glazed Tofu Satay

Serves 6   Grilled tofu is a staple in Japanese cooking, and it's a great way to introduce your family to this wonderful source of protein. Because even extra-firm tofu is fragile, I recommend using the grill basket rather than the kabob rods to cook it so that you don't have to worry about it falling off the rods.

1 pound extra-firm tofu

Sesame-Miso Marinade

¹/₂ cup soy sauce
¹/₄ cup white miso powder
2 tablespoons rice wine
2 tablespoons toasted
   sesame oil
2 cloves garlic, minced
1 teaspoon peeled and
   minced fresh ginger

¹/₄ cup sesame seeds for
   garnish
4 green onions, white and
   light green parts,
   chopped, for garnish

Press the excess water out of the tofu, then cut into ¾-inch-thick slices and place in a 13 x 9-inch glass baking dish.

In a small mixing bowl, whisk together the marinade ingredients. Pour over the tofu, flip them over several times to coat, and cover with plastic wrap. Marinate in the refrigerator for 1 to 2 hours, turning occasionally.

Drain the marinade into a saucepan, bring to a boil, and simmer for 5 minutes. Pat the tofu dry with paper towels, place in the rotisserie basket, close the lid tightly, and load the basket onto the spit rod assembly. Grill the tofu until browned on the outside, 10 to 12 minutes.

Remove the tofu from the basket and brush with the hot marinade. Serve, garnished with the sesame seeds and green onions, and pass the remaining sauce.

Cajun Tofu

Serves 6   **Grilled with Creole seasonings, this tofu isn't like any you've ever had before. You can grill it, then use it in salad or serve it on the side with vegetables.**

1 pound extra firm tofu,
  drained
1/2 cup canola oil
2 tablespoons Creole
  Seasoning Rub
  (page 287)

Press the excess water out of the tofu. Cut into ¾-inch-thick slices and place in a 13 x 9-inch glass baking dish.

In a small mixing bowl, stir together the canola oil and seasoning. Brush the mixture over both sides of the tofu, cover with plastic wrap, and refrigerate until ready to cook.

Coat the rotisserie basket with nonstick cooking spray, lay the tofu in the basket, and close the lid tightly. Load the basket onto the spit rod assembly and grill the tofu until browned on the outside, 10 to 12 minutes.

Remove the tofu from the basket and serve.

Chimichurri Tofu

Serves 6   The bright taste of parsley and garlic really
packs a punch with this tofu.

1 pound extra firm tofu,
    drained
1 recipe That Spicy Green
    Sauce (page 312)

Press the excess water out of the tofu. Cut into ¾-inch-thick slices and place in a 13 x 9-inch glass baking dish.

Set aside ¼ cup of the sauce for garnish, then brush the rest over both sides of the tofu. Cover with plastic wrap and refrigerate until ready to cook.

Coat the rotisserie basket with nonstick cooking spray, lay the tofu in the basket, and close the lid tightly. Load the basket onto the spit rod assembly and grill the tofu until browned on the outside, 10 to 12 minutes.

Remove the tofu from the basket and serve, garnished with the remaining green sauce.

Twirly Roasted Apples

Serves 8 Warm and "cinnamony," these apples are good for what ails you, but they are also delectable with pork or poultry as a change-of-pace side dish.

¼ cup firmly packed light brown sugar

2 tablespoons fresh lemon juice

1 teaspoon ground cinnamon

2 teaspoons vegetable oil

6 medium-size Golden Delicious apples, peeled and cored

In a small mixing bowl, combine the brown sugar, lemon juice, cinnamon, and vegetable oil. Brush the apples with the mixture.

Thread the apples onto the kabob rods, leaving ½ inch between them for air to circulate. Load the kabob rods onto the spit rod assembly with the spring ends on the right side, and roast the apples until they feel tender when pierced with a sharp knife, 45 to 55 minutes.

Remove the apples from the kabob rods and serve warm.

Smart Turn

When choosing apples, pick softer varieties, such as Golden Delicious or Gala. Firmer apples like Granny Smith don't work very well in this recipe. (They take almost 30 minutes longer to cook, and their texture is not as pleasing.)

Fruit on the Side

Savory roasted fruits, such as apples, peaches, and pears, are perfect paired with grilled meat, poultry, and fish. You can roast the fruits ahead of time and store at room temperature until you are ready to serve them.

Golden Glazed Bananas

Serves 6   **Glazed bananas are the perfect accompaniment to jerk chicken or pork for a little taste of the tropics on the side. Use bananas that are slightly underripe (a little green on the tips) because they will hold their shape nicely while grilling.**

¹/₄ cup (¹/₂ stick) butter, melted

2 tablespoons firmly packed light brown sugar

1 tablespoon fresh lemon juice

¹/₈ teaspoon ground nutmeg

6 medium-size underripe bananas, peeled

In a 2-cup measure, combine the melted butter, brown sugar, lemon juice, and nutmeg.

Thread the bananas onto the kabob rods, leaving ½ inch between them for air to circulate, and load the kabob rods onto the spit rod assembly with the spring ends on the right. Brush the bananas evenly with the butter mixture and grill until golden brown, 12 to 15 minutes.

Allow the bananas to rest for 3 minutes, then remove from the skewers. Serve hot or at room temperature.

Gingered Peaches

Serves 6   These sweet peaches are a great side dish with poultry or pork. Very ripe peaches will fall apart in the basket, so buy them firm, but not rock hard. This is a great do-ahead dish—you can roast the peaches the day before, allow them to marinate in their juices, then warm them on the stove just before serving.

4 medium-size peaches, peeled, halved, and pitted
2 tablespoons vegetable oil
2 tablespoons firmly packed brown sugar
1 tablespoon peeled and grated fresh ginger

Put the peaches in a medium-size mixing bowl, drizzle with the vegetable oil, sprinkle with the brown sugar and ginger, and toss until coated evenly.

Place the peaches in the rotisserie basket and close the lid tightly. Save any of the juices left in the mixing bowl. Load the basket onto the spit rod assembly and grill until the peaches are tender, 25 to 35 minutes.

Remove the peaches from the basket, place in a serving bowl, and drizzle with any juice that may have accumulated in the drip pan as well as the reserved juices from the mixing bowl. Serve immediately or refrigerate for up to 8 hours. Serve warm, cold, or at room temperature.

Grilled Pineapple and Mango Kabobs

Serves 6 **Grilling fruit intensifies its flavor. These kabobs are flavored with a little jalapeño to heat up the sweetness of the fruit. Serve this with poultry or pork.**

½ medium-size fresh pineapple (about 1½ pounds)

¼ cup canola oil

1 tablespoon fresh lemon juice

1 tablespoon green Tabasco sauce

2 teaspoons dark brown sugar

2 medium-size underripe mangoes, peeled, seeded, and cut into 1-inch chunks

Cut the pineapple lengthwise in two, remove the core, and cut the flesh away from the rind. Cut the pineapple into 1-inch chunks.

In a small mixing bowl, combine the canola oil, lemon juice, Tabasco, and brown sugar, stirring to blend. Put the pineapple and mango in a large mixing bowl, pour the sauce over the fruit, and toss to coat the fruit evenly.

Thread the fruit onto the kabob rods, alternating mango and pineapple and leaving ½ inch between them for air to circulate. Load the kabob rods onto the spit rod assembly with the spring ends on the right, and grill until the fruit is tender and browned, 20 to 25 minutes.

Let the fruit rest for 5 minutes, then remove from the skewers and serve warm.

Picking a Ripe Pineapple

A pineapple is ripe when harvested, it will not ripen any further on your kitchen counter. The skin should be golden in color. Feel the fruit and make sure there are no soft spots; this could be a sign of spoilage. Smell the pineapple at the base of the leaves; if it smells like pineapple, then it's ready. If, on the other hand, it doesn't have a fragrance, chances are it won't have much flavor. Another way to test a pineapple is to pluck one of the leaves from the center; if the leaf comes out easily, the pineapple is ready to eat. I think the smell test is the best indicator, though. During the winter months, pineapples labeled Maui Gold are sold in supermarkets. These pineapples are air-shipped from the fields in which they grew and, although pricey, they are worth every penny in their pineapple sweetness.

Hot and Sweet

I know what you're thinking: this woman is mad! As strange as it may seem, the rotisserie can do some wonderful things with fruit; all you need is a little imagination, some great fruit, and a spirit of adventure!

Fruits that you will roast in the rotisserie should not be totally ripe or they will fall apart while cooking. Look for peaches, mangoes, pears, and other soft fruits that are slightly underripe. If you pinch the fruit and it gives some resistance to pressure, then that's the one you want. On the other hand, when choosing harder fruits like apples, pick a relatively soft variety. A Golden Delicious apple would be the best choice for the rotisserie, rather than a Granny Smith, which is usually rock hard. Pears should be soft as well. You can ripen them by placing them in a paper bag for a day or so. Although costly, Asian pears were the best among those we tested, but ripe red pears are also quite good. Bananas should be firm, with yellow skin, and some green near the stem end.

In order for any of the coatings to stick to the fruit, you will have to dip them first in one of the following: a vegetable oil or a fruit oil, such as lemon, orange, or lime; melted butter; citrus juice; or a liqueur.

Hot and Sweet

Fruit No-Brainers

These pantry items are just what the doctor ordered for quick grilled fruits cooked to perfection in the rotisserie.

Spicy No-Brainers

Make sure to dip the fruit into citrus juice, melted butter, or an oil before dipping into spices so they stick.

- Cinnamon sugar
- Chinese five-spice powder
- Jerk Seasoning Rub (page 290)
- Ground allspice
- Raw sugar
- Ground black pepper (trust me)

Saucy No-Brainers

- Brandy
- Kahlua
- Grand Marnier
- Dark rum
- Fruit oils, such as orange, lemon, or lime (see Sources)
- Sherry
- Port

Rotisserie Caramel Apples

Serves 6 Golden Delicious apples dipped in butter, brown sugar, and cinnamon and grilled in the rotisserie become caramelized, soft, and golden. They're the perfect accompaniment for vanilla ice cream.

1 cup firmly packed dark brown sugar
1 teaspoon ground cinnamon
1/2 cup (1 stick) butter, melted
4 large Golden Delicious apples, peeled, cored, and quartered

In a small bowl, combine the brown sugar and cinnamon.

Put the melted butter in a shallow dish and dip the apple quarters into the butter. Roll in the cinnamon sugar mixture to coat evenly.

Thread the apples onto the kabob rods, leaving ½ inch between them for air to circulate. Load the kabob rods onto the spit rod assembly with the spring ends on the right. Grill until the apples are caramelized and soft when pierced with a sharp knife, 25 to 30 minutes.

Remove the apples from the skewers and serve immediately.

Caramelized Bananas with Hot Fudge Lava

Serves 6 These delectable banana bites are coated with butter and brown sugar, then grilled on the kabob rods and covered with the world's best hot fudge sauce. Make sure to serve this with a premium vanilla ice cream.

½ cup (1 stick) butter,
   melted
1 cup firmly packed light
   brown sugar
6 small- to medium-size
   bananas, slightly
   underripe, with some
   green at the stem end
1 recipe World's Best Hot
   Fudge Sauce (recipe
   follows)
1 quart vanilla ice cream (or
   your favorite flavor)

Put the butter and sugar in separate shallow dishes. Peel the bananas and cut into 1-inch chunks. Dip in the melted butter, then roll in the brown sugar, coating them evenly.

Load the bananas onto the kabob rods, leaving ½ inch between them for air to circulate. Load the kabob rods onto the spit rod assembly with the spring ends on the right, and grill until the bananas begin to brown and the sugar begins to caramelize, 10 to 15 minutes.

Remove the bananas from the skewers. Pool some of the fudge sauce on each plate, place several banana chunks in the pool, and top with a scoop of ice cream. Serve immediately.

World's Best Hot Fudge Sauce

Makes about 3 cups   **This is also the world's easiest chocolate sauce; you can make it ahead of time and keep it in the fridge for up to two weeks.**

½ cup (1 stick) butter
4 ounces unsweetened
   chocolate
1½ cups sugar
1 cup evaporated milk

In a 2-quart saucepan over low heat, melt the butter and chocolate together. Stir in the sugar and cook, stirring, until it melts.

Gradually pour in the evaporated milk and cook until the sauce is no longer grainy and has a glossy sheen; this may take 3 to 4 minutes.

Refrigerate the sauce until you are ready to use it, then reheat over low heat on top of the stove or in the microwave.

Kahlua-Glazed Bananas Foster

Serves 6 Bananas Foster is a traditional flaming dessert served at the Brennan family restaurants in New Orleans. Everyone has her own version of this classic, and this is mine. The coffee-flavored bananas are terrific served over thinly sliced pound cake and topped with vanilla or coffee ice cream.

$^1/_2$ cup (1 stick) butter, melted

$^1/_2$ cup Kahlua

1 tablespoon ground cinnamon

1 cup firmly packed dark brown sugar

6 medium-size bananas, slightly underripe, with some green at the stem end

In a small shallow dish, combine the melted butter and Kahlua.

On a dinner plate, combine the cinnamon and brown sugar.

Peel the bananas and cut into 1-inch chunks. Dip them in the butter and Kahlua mixture, and roll in the brown sugar to coat evenly.

Thread the bananas onto the kabob rods, leaving ½ inch between them for air to circulate. Load the kabob rods onto the spit rod assembly with the spring ends on the right. Grill until the bananas begin to turn brown and the sugar begins to caramelize, 10 to 15 minutes.

While the bananas are cooking, heat the remaining butter and Kahlua.

Remove the bananas from the kabob rods and serve immediately, topped with the remaining Kahlua butter sauce.

Coco Loco Bananarama

Serves 6 Tropical coconut, rum, and bananas are a great combo to serve over ice cream or thin slices of angel food cake.

1 cup cream of coconut, such as Coco Lopez

$^1/_2$ cup dark rum, preferably Meyer's

1 cup firmly packed light brown sugar

$^1/_2$ cup sweetened flaked coconut

6 small- to medium-size bananas, slightly underripe, with some green at the stem end

In a shallow dish, blend the cream of coconut and rum together.

On a dinner plate, combine the brown sugar and coconut.

Peel the bananas and cut into 1-inch chunks. Dip them in the rum mixture and roll in the brown sugar and coconut to coat evenly.

Thread the bananas onto the kabob rods, leaving ½ inch between them for air to circulate. Load the skewers onto the spit rod assembly with the spring ends on the right, and grill until the bananas begin to turn golden and the coconut is toasted, 10 to 15 minutes.

While the bananas are cooking, heat the remaining cream of coconut and rum mixture in a small saucepan.

Remove the bananas from the skewers, drizzle with the coconut and rum mixture, and serve immediately.

Elvis Has Left the Building
Peanut Butter Banana Madness

○─●─○

Serves 6   Legend has it that the King would fly to California just to get a grilled peanut butter and banana sandwich, when all he needed was a rotisserie! This dessert requires a little bit of work, but it's really fun to make. Pound cake and peanut butter sandwiches are grilled with brown sugar-coated bananas for a taste that even the King would have loved.

1 cup (2 sticks) butter, melted
1 loaf-shaped pound cake (homemade or store-bought)
1 cup peanut butter
6 small- to medium-size bananas, slightly underripe, with some green at the stem end
1 cup firmly packed light brown sugar
1/2 cup chopped salted roasted peanuts for garnish

Pour the melted butter into a shallow dish. Cut the pound cake into 1/2-inch-thick slices and make sandwiches: Spread one side of a slice with peanut butter and top with another slice of pound cake. Brush each sandwich with melted butter on both sides and cut into quarters.

Peel the bananas and cut them into 1-inch chunks. Dip them in the melted butter, then roll in the brown sugar to coat evenly.

Thread the sandwiches and bananas onto the kabob rods, alternating them and leaving 1/2 inch between them for air to circulate. Load the kabob rods onto the spit rod with the spring ends on the right, and grill until the pound cake is golden and the bananas begin to caramelize, 10 to 15 minutes.

Carefully remove the sandwiches and bananas. Arrange on dessert plates, garnish with the chopped peanuts, and serve immediately.

Peppered Cantaloupe

Serves 6   Sweet cantaloupe is delicious on the rotisserie, and a few grinds of black pepper and some lime juice after grilling give it a spectacular flavor. You can serve this as a side dish or as an unusual dessert.

1 medium-size ripe
  cantaloupe, seeded,
  flesh removed from the
  rind, and cut into 1-inch
  chunks
2 teaspoons freshly ground
  black pepper
1/3 cup sifted confectioners'
  sugar
2 teaspoons fresh lime juice
Grated zest of 1 lime

Thread the cantaloupe pieces onto the kabob rods, leaving ½ inch between them for air to circulate. Sprinkle the cantaloupe evenly with the pepper and confectioners' sugar and load onto the spit rod assembly with the spring ends on the right. Grill until it begins to color and the sugar begins to turn golden, 12 to 17 minutes.

Remove the fruit from the skewers, sprinkle with the lime juice and zest, and serve immediately.

Grilled Drunken Figs

Serves 4 Not everyone has access to fresh figs, but this recipe was just too good to leave out. Marinate the figs in port wine, then grill them in the rotisserie basket for a delicious side dish or dessert topped with mascarpone cheese mixed with a little cinnamon and sugar.

1 cup port wine

2 tablespoons honey

12 fresh figs, halved lengthwise

1 1/2 cups mascarpone cheese

1/4 cup sugar

1/2 teaspoon ground cinnamon

1/2 cup chopped unsalted pistachios for garnish

In a 13 x 9-inch glass dish, stir together the port and honey. Put the figs in the dish and turn to coat evenly. Cover the dish with plastic wrap and refrigerate for at least 1 and up to 4 hours.

Coat the rotisserie basket with nonstick cooking spray and arrange the figs in the basket. Load the basket onto the spit rod assembly and grill until the figs begin to bubble, 10 to 15 minutes.

While the figs are cooking, in a small mixing bowl, blend together the mascarpone, sugar, and cinnamon. Refrigerate until ready to use.

Remove the figs from the rotisserie basket and arrange 3 halves on each plate, with a dollop of the sweetened mascarpone in the center of the figs. Garnish with the chopped pistachios and serve.

Rum-Glazed Mango with Macadamias

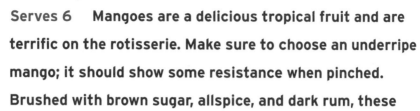

Serves 6   Mangoes are a delicious tropical fruit and are terrific on the rotisserie. Make sure to choose an underripe mango; it should show some resistance when pinched. Brushed with brown sugar, allspice, and dark rum, these mangoes are terrific over pound cake with ice cream.

1/2 cup (1 stick) butter, melted

1/2 cup dark rum

1 teaspoon ground allspice

2 tablespoons fresh lime juice

1/2 cup firmly packed dark brown sugar

2 large underripe mangoes, peeled, pitted, and cut into 1-inch chunks

1/2 cup chopped macadamia nuts, toasted (see page 184), for garnish

In a shallow dish, combine the melted butter, rum, allspice, lime juice, and brown sugar, stirring until the sugar is dissolved.

Dip the mangoes in the rum sauce and thread onto the kabob rods, leaving 1/2 inch between them for air to circulate. Load the kabob rods onto the spit rod assembly with the spring ends on the right, and grill until the mangoes are caramelized, 15 to 20 minutes.

Remove the mangoes from the skewers and serve immediately, garnished with the chopped macadamia nuts, if desired.

Jerk Mango and Pineapple Kabobs

Serves 6 The flavors of the islands come through in these kabobs, perfect for dessert. The slightly spicy and hot flavor of the jerk seasoning is a great counterpoint to the sweet fruit.

½ fresh pineapple
2 medium-size underripe mangoes, peeled, pitted, and cut into 1-inch chunks
2 teaspoons Jerk Seasoning Rub (page 290)
¼ cup chopped fresh cilantro leaves

Cut the pineapple lengthwise in two, remove the core, and cut the flesh away from the rind. Cut the pineapple into 1-inch chunks.

Thread the pineapple and mango pieces onto the kabob rods, alternating the fruit and leaving ½ inch between them for air to circulate. Sprinkle the kabobs evenly with the jerk seasoning and load the kabobs onto the spit rod assembly with the spring ends on the right. Grill until the fruit begins to caramelize, 15 to 20 minutes.

Remove the fruit from the skewers and serve immediately, garnished with the cilantro.

Selecting a Mango

The skin of a ripe mango should be gold to reddish in color, and when the fruit is pressed, it should give without resistance. You need to use a ripe mango right away because they tend to spoil quickly. Peel the mango and discard the long, flat seed in the middle. Then cut the mango into pieces and freeze in zipper-top plastic bags, if you wish. Frozen mangoes will keep for about 4 months.

Mixed Fruit Kabobs

Serves 6   This colorful fruit kabob is just the ticket to serve as a dessert or side dish with grilled meats and poultry. Not all fruit cooks at the same rate, but these do, and the result is mighty tasty.

$^1/_2$ fresh pineapple

$^1/_2$ cup (1 stick) butter, melted

$^1/_4$ cup fresh lime juice

$^1/_4$ cup firmly packed light brown sugar

$^1/_4$ teaspoon ground cinnamon

1 large underripe mango, peeled, pitted, and cut into 1-inch chunks

1 pint firm, ripe strawberries, hulled

2 kiwi fruit, peeled and cut into 1-inch chunks

$^1/_2$ cup finely chopped fresh mint leaves for garnish

Cut the pineapple lengthwise in two, remove the core, and cut the flesh away from the rind. Cut the pineapple into 1-inch chunks.

In a shallow dish, combine the melted butter, lime juice, brown sugar, and cinnamon, stirring until the sugar dissolves.

Thread the fruit onto the kabob rods, alternating them and leaving ½ inch between them for air to circulate. Brush each kabob generously with the brown sugar butter, then load the skewers onto the spit rod assembly with the spring ends on the right. Grill until the fruits begin to caramelize, 15 to 20 minutes.

Remove the kabobs from the rotisserie and brush with the remaining glaze. Serve immediately, garnished with the mint.

Ginger Five-Spice Asian Pears

Serves 6 Pungent Chinese five-spice powder and ginger pair with Asian pears for a delectable side dish or dessert. Once grilled, the pears can be filled with sorbet or ice cream. An Asian pear is a round, medium-size fruit that is crisp like an apple, but sweet and juicy like a pear. Usually found in your specialty produce section, they appear in markets around October and November.

$^1/_2$ cup (1 stick) butter, melted

$^1/_4$ cup firmly packed dark brown sugar

1 teaspoon Chinese five-spice powder

2 teaspoons ground ginger

4 Asian pears (substitute slightly underripe red pears, if not available), peeled, cored, and quartered

In a small shallow dish, combine the melted butter, brown sugar, five-spice powder, and ginger.

Dip the pears into the butter mixture, then thread them onto the kabob rods, leaving ½ inch between them for air to circulate. Load the kabob rods onto the spit rod assembly with the spring ends on the right, and grill until the pears are golden brown and feel soft when tested with a sharp knife, 35 to 40 minutes.

Remove the pears from the skewers and serve immediately.

Ginger-Roasted Asian Pears
with Warm Brandy Sauce

Serves 6 **These pears can be served as a side dish with poultry or pork or for dessert with Warm Brandy Sauce.**

¹/₂ cup (1 stick) butter, melted

¹/₃ cup firmly packed dark brown sugar

1 teaspoon ground ginger

2 tablespoons brandy

4 Asian pears (use slightly underripe red pears, if unavailable), peeled, cored, and quartered

Warm Brandy Sauce (optional, recipe follows)

In a shallow dish, stir together the melted butter, brown sugar, ginger, and brandy.

Dip the pear quarters into the butter and thread onto the kabob rods, leaving ½ inch between them for air to circulate. Load the skewers onto the spit rod assembly with the spring ends on the right. Roast until the pears are golden brown on the outside and feel soft when tested with a sharp knife, 35 to 40 minutes.

Remove the pears from the skewers and serve immediately with the brandy sauce drizzled on top, if desired.

Warm Brandy Sauce

Makes about 2 cups **This is deliciously warm and comforting sauce for ice cream, fruit, or cake. You can make it into a buttered rum sauce by substituting dark rum for the brandy.**

¹/₄ cup (¹/₂ stick) butter

1 cup firmly packed light brown sugar

1 cup whipping cream

2 tablespoons brandy

Melt the butter in a saucepan over medium heat, then add the sugar and stir until it dissolves. Stir in the whipping cream and bring to a boil. Reduce the heat to low and stir in the brandy.

Serve warm or cover tightly and refrigerate for up to 1 week. Reheat over low heat or in the microwave at 50 percent power before serving.

Fire-Roasted Pineapple with Macadamia Caramel Sauce

Serves 6   Pineapple is delicious grilled in the rotisserie. I sometimes grill pineapple to present on the side with grilled meats, but it makes a dynamite dessert served with ice cream and this caramel sauce.

1 fresh pineapple (about 3 pounds)

1/2 cup (1 stick) butter, melted

1/4 cup dark rum

1/2 teaspoon ground cinnamon

1 cup firmly packed light brown sugar

1 pint vanilla ice cream

Macadamia Caramel Sauce (recipe follows)

Cut the pineapple into quarters, remove the core, and cut the flesh away from the rind. Cut into 1-inch chunks.

In a shallow dish, combine the melted butter, rum, cinnamon, and brown sugar and stir until the sugar is dissolved.

Dip the pineapple in the buttered rum mixture and thread onto the kabob rods, leaving 1/2 inch between them for air to circulate. Load the skewers onto the spit rod assembly with the spring ends on the right, and grill until the pineapple is golden brown, 15 to 20 minutes.

Remove the pineapple from the skewers and serve with ice cream and macadamia caramel sauce drizzled on top.

Macadamia Caramel Sauce

Makes about 2 1/2 cups   This rich caramel sauce is great over ice cream, chocolate cake, grilled bananas, or straight from the saucepan.

1/4 cup (1/2 stick) butter

1/2 cup chopped unsalted macadamia nuts

1 cup firmly packed light brown sugar

In a 2-quart saucepan, melt the butter over medium heat, then add the nuts and toast them for 2 to 3 minutes. Stir in the brown sugar and continue stirring until it has dissolved. Pour in the cream and stir constantly until the sauce comes to a boil. Add the rum, if desired.

1 cup whipping cream
1 teaspoon dark rum
(optional)

Remove from the heat and serve immediately or cover tightly and refrigerate for up to 1 week. Reheat over low heat or at 50 percent power in the microwave.

Grilled Brown Sugar Strawberries

Serves 6 **Strawberries are delicious grilled and these are extra special—dipped in balsamic vinegar, then brown sugar, for a real twist. Serve garnished with mint, or with pound cake and unsweetened whipped cream.**

$^1/_2$ cup balsamic vinegar
1 cup firmly packed brown sugar
2 pints firm, ripe strawberries, hulled
$^1/_4$ cup chopped fresh mint leaves for garnish

Pour the vinegar into a shallow dish and put the brown sugar in another.

Dip each strawberry into the vinegar, then roll in the brown sugar to coat evenly.

Thread the berries onto the kabob rods, leaving $^1/_2$ inch between them for air to circulate. Load the kabob rods onto the spit rod assembly with the spring ends on the right, and grill until the berries begin to caramelize and the sugar is bubbling on the berries, 12 to 17 minutes.

Remove the strawberries from the skewers, garnish with the mint, and serve immediately.

Straw-Annas

Serves 6   My mom's favorite dessert was an ice-cream confection called a Straw-Anna from a Boston area ice-cream shop. It was a strawberry and banana sundae, so when I started grilling fruits, this combination occurred to me.

½ cup (1 stick) butter, melted
1 cup firmly packed light brown sugar
3 medium-size bananas, slightly underripe, with some green at the stem end, peeled and cut into 1-inch rounds
1 pint firm, ripe strawberries, hulled
1 pint vanilla ice cream
½ cup chopped unsalted pistachios for garnish

Pour the melted butter in a shallow dish and put the brown sugar in another.

Dip the fruit into the melted butter, then roll in the brown sugar to coat evenly.

Thread the fruit onto the kabob rods, alternating the bananas with the strawberries and leaving ½ inch between them for air to circulate. Load the skewers onto the spit rod assembly with the spring ends on the right, and grill until the bananas are golden, 10 to 15 minutes.

Remove the fruit from the skewers and serve immediately with vanilla ice cream, garnished with the pistachios.

Strawberry S'mores

Serves 6   Traditional s'mores are made with marshmallow and chocolate, but when we decided to grill the marshmallows with strawberries instead, we came up with a winner.

¼ cup (½ stick) butter, melted

½ cup firmly packed light brown sugar

2 pints firm, ripe strawberries, hulled

16 large marshmallows

32 graham crackers or sixteen ½-inch-thick slices pound cake, halved

Pour the butter into a shallow dish and put the brown sugar in another one.

Dip the strawberries in the melted butter, then roll in the brown sugar to coat evenly.

Coat the kabob rods with nonstick cooking spray. Load the strawberries and marshmallows onto the skewers, alternating them and leaving ½ inch between them for air to circulate. Load the kabob rods onto the spit rod assembly with the spring ends on the right, and grill until the marshmallows are golden, 10 to 15 minutes.

Carefully remove the strawberries and marshmallows from the skewers. To assemble, arrange 1 marshmallow on a graham cracker square, top with 2 strawberries, and then 1 more graham cracker square, and serve.

Bittersweet S'mores

Serves 6 **That old campfire favorite can be recreated in your rotisserie by grilling marshmallows, then sandwiching them between graham crackers and bittersweet chocolate. Lindt or Tobler are great choices for the chocolate; if your grocer does not carry them, try Ghirardelli.**

16 large marshmallows

32 graham cracker squares

12 ounces bittersweet
  chocolate, broken into
  16 pieces

Coat the kabob rods with nonstick cooking spray and load the marshmallows onto the skewers, leaving ½ inch between them for air to circulate. Load the skewers onto the spit rod assembly with the spring ends on the right, and grill until the marshmallows are golden, 10 to 15 minutes.

While the marshmallows are grilling, set out 16 graham crackers and cover each with 1 piece of the bittersweet chocolate.

When the marshmallows are done, place one on each graham cracker, cover with the remaining graham crackers, and serve immediately.

Nutella S'mores

Serves 6 Nutella is a European chocolate and hazelnut spread that is almost addictive. At continental hotels, it usually comes on your breakfast tray with rolls for breakfast. It is also wonderful in this takeoff on the traditional s'more.

1/2 cup Nutella
1 loaf-shaped pound cake, homemade or store-bought, cut into 1/2-inch-thick slices
1/4 cup (1/2 stick) butter, melted
16 large marshmallows

Spread Nutella on one side of a slice of pound cake, then top with another slice to make a sandwich. Brush the sandwiches with melted butter on both sides and cut into quarters.

Coat the kabob rods with nonstick cooking spray and load the sandwiches and marshmallows onto the skewers, alternating them and allowing the marshmallow to touch the sandwiches. Load the skewers onto the spit rod assembly with the spring ends on the right. Grill until the pound cake is golden and the marshmallows begin to turn color, 10 to 15 minutes.

Carefully remove the s'mores from the skewers. To serve, place a sandwich on a plate, top with a marshmallow, and place another sandwich over the marshmallow. Drizzle with additional Nutella, if desired.

A Whole Lot of Saucin' Going On

Dry rubs are part and parcel of what makes delicious rotisserie and grilled food. They are made from dried herbs and spices, then rubbed into the meats before they are grilled, giving them a crispy outside crust and nicely flavored meat. Rubs are great for spur-of-the-moment grilling. It's a good idea to mix up a batch or two and keep them at the ready in the pantry.

Marinades are another way to flavor meats. They usually contain an acid of some sort, such as vinegar, lemon juice, or wine, combined with oils and spices. Marinades do not really tenderize meats; rather, the acid breaks down and cooks the protein, as in seviche, a raw seafood cocktail that is actually "cooked" in lime juice. Although I'm usually of the school "if a little is good, *a lot* is great," that is not the case with marinades. Marinating for extended periods is not a good idea; the meats can actually get mushy and spongy from soaking in some marinades, so follow the recipe directions for the best results. Seafood doesn't really need to be marinated; the marinades are used to infuse a little flavor into already tender fish or shellfish.

Fuel injections are liquid solutions that are, not surprisingly, injected into meats for flavor. Most rotisseries come with an injector, which looks like a syringe. You can also purchase one in your local gourmet store. These liquids are a matter of taste, and I recommend that you start experimenting with a chicken, which is rather inexpensive.

Once your rotisserie meal is done, it is nice to have a special salsa or sauce to serve on the side—a refreshing mango salsa to accompany rotisserie fish, chicken, or pork; a dynamite red wine and thyme sauce for rotisserie beef; or a teriyaki sauce to serve with chicken, beef, or seafood. You'll be happy to have these extra touches to make your already delicious meal extraordinary.

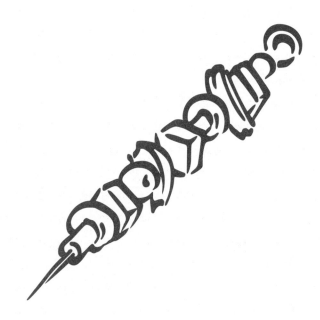

A Whole Lot of Saucin' Going On

Au Jus

Makes 3 cups   This recipe is designed for the drippings from any type of roast, including chicken, beef, lamb, or pork. By adding some stock you can make a thin sauce to pour over the meat slices.

Drippings from the pan
3 cups stock (chicken, beef, lamb, or pork, or a combination of chicken and beef)
Salt and freshly ground black pepper to taste

Skim the fat from the drippings, and pour the drippings into a 2-quart saucepan.

Add the stock and bring to a boil. Simmer the sauce for 10 minutes, and taste and correct the seasoning by adding more salt and pepper, if needed.

Smart Turn

You can add wine and some herbs, according to your taste.

Wavy Gravy

Makes about 2½ cups   With the drippings in the pan, a little flour, and some stock you can have a gravy on the table while the roast is resting.

3 tablespoons pan drippings
3 tablespoons all-purpose flour

Heat the drippings in a 2½-quart saucepan and add the flour, whisking until well blended.

2 cups stock (chicken, beef,
lamb, or pork, or a
combination of lamb
and pork)
Salt and freshly ground
black pepper to taste

Cook the flour mixture over medium heat until white bubbles form on the top of the mixture, about 3 minutes.

Whisk in the stock, and bring the gravy to a boil. Reduce the heat and simmer for 5 to 7 minutes. Taste and add salt or pepper, if needed, and keep warm until ready to serve. The gravy will keep, covered, in the refrigerator for 3 to 4 days, or in the freezer for up to 1 month.

Seasoned Salt

Makes 1¼ cups   Seasoned salt is an all-purpose rub for anything you'd like to cook on the rotisserie. On nights when your creativity quotient is low, this is a great rub to use for a homey, comforting meal. This makes a large quantity, so store it in an airtight container.

³/₄ cup sea salt
¹/₄ cup garlic salt
1¹/₂ teaspoons freshly
ground black pepper
1 teaspoon dried oregano
2 teaspoons sweet paprika
2 teaspoons celery salt
¹/₂ teaspoon dry mustard

In a small mixing bowl, stir together all the ingredients until blended. Store in an airtight container for up to 6 months.

All-American Barbecue Rub

Makes about ¾ cup   Massage this sweet and savory rub into poultry, beef, and pork for delicious roasts, ribs, chops, and steaks. The seasonings can be used in marinades as well. Try blending 2 tablespoons of rub with ½ cup olive oil and ¼ cup white wine vinegar for an all-American marinade for steaks, chicken, or pork.

¼ cup kosher salt
¼ cup sweet paprika
½ teaspoon cayenne pepper
⅓ cup firmly packed light
   brown sugar
1 tablespoon granulated
   garlic
1 tablespoon granulated
   onion
2 teaspoons celery salt

Combine all the ingredients in a small mixing bowl, stirring to blend. Store in an airtight container for up to 6 months.

Lemon Pepper Rub

Makes 2 cups   Lemon pepper adds zest and spice to chicken, fish, beef, and lamb. Rub the spices onto beef and lamb, then refrigerate for 24 hours before grilling. Chicken and fish can be rubbed just before cooking.

1/3 cup dried lemon peel

1 cup freshly ground black pepper

3 tablespoons coriander seeds

1/4 cup dried thyme

1/4 cup onion powder

Combine all the ingredients in a small mixing bowl, and stir to blend. Store in an airtight container for up to 6 months.

Creole Seasoning Rub

Makes about 3/4 cup   **Hot and spicy, Creole seasoning will light up any entrée you want to make in the rotisserie.**

3 tablespoons salt

1 1/2 tablespoons sweet paprika

1 tablespoon onion powder

1 tablespoon cayenne pepper

1/2 teaspoon white pepper

2 teaspoons dried thyme

1/2 teaspoon freshly ground black pepper

1 teaspoon dried oregano

Combine all the ingredients in a small mixing bowl and stir to blend. Store in an airtight container for up to 6 months.

Confetti Pepper Rub

Makes about 2 cups   Green, white, black, and red pepper team up to give you a rub for beef or lamb that will knock your socks off. Grind the peppers in a pepper mill or an electric coffee grinder that you use for blending spices, or place the peppercorns in a zipper-top plastic bag and crush them with a rolling pin, wine bottle, or hammer. Green peppercorns are sold freeze-dried in the spice section of your supermarket.

$1/2$ cup white peppercorns
$1/2$ cup green peppercorns
$3/4$ cup black peppercorns
$1/4$ cup red pepper flakes

Combine all the ingredients in a small mixing bowl, stirring to blend. Store in an airtight container for up to 3 months.

When ready to use, grind as much of the mixture as you need.

All-Purpose Rotisserie Rub

Makes $2/3$ cup   Like the All-American Barbecue Rub (page 286), this is the seasoning for those nights when you just want to set it and forget it. It's great on chicken, fish, beef, lamb, and pork, and you may want to keep some close by the stove to flavor veggies as well.

2 tablespoons sugar

1 tablespoon garlic salt

1 tablespoon onion salt

1 teaspoon celery salt

1/4 teaspoon cayenne pepper

1/3 cup sweet paprika

1 tablespoon freshly ground
black pepper

Combine all the ingredients in a small mixing bowl, and stir to blend. Store in an airtight container for up to 6 months

Herbes de Provence Rub

Makes about 1 1/3 cups **These aromatic herbs are typical of the Mediterranean region of France. You can use them as a rub or seasoning for chicken, beef, fish, lamb, and vegetables.**

2 tablespoons dried oregano

2 tablespoons dried
rosemary

1/2 cup dried thyme

1/4 cup dried basil

3 tablespoons salt

2 teaspoons freshly ground
black pepper

Combine all the ingredients in a small mixing bowl, stirring to blend. Store in an airtight container for up to 6 months.

Jerk Seasoning Rub

Makes ½ cup **Flavors of the islands combine in this fragrant rub, which is great for chicken, pork, and seafood.**

1 teaspoon ground nutmeg

1 teaspoon ground cinnamon

2 teaspoons dried thyme

2 teaspoons ground allspice

2 teaspoons freshly ground
   black pepper

2 teaspoons cayenne pepper
   (less, if you don't like the
   heat)

2 tablespoons onion salt

2 teaspoons sugar

2 teaspoons garlic salt

Combine all the ingredients in a small mixing bowl and stir to blend. Store in an airtight container for up to 6 months.

Grecian Formula Rub

Makes 1 cup   The sunny flavors of the Mediterranean permeate this rub, which is wonderful on lamb, beef, chicken, and fish.

2 teaspoons dried lemon
  peel
2 teaspoons garlic salt
1 tablespoon dried parsley
2 tablespoons dried
  rosemary
2 tablespoons dried thyme
2 teaspoons freshly ground
  black pepper

Combine all the ingredients in a small mixing bowl and stir to blend. Store in an airtight container for up to 6 months.

Fiesta Rub

Makes about 1⅛ cups   Chili powder, cumin, and oregano team up for a spicy rub to use on chicken, pork, beef, and potatoes.

½ cup chili powder
¼ cup ground cumin
2 tablespoons garlic salt
2 tablespoons onion salt
3 tablespoons dried oregano

Combine all the ingredients in a small mixing bowl and stir to blend. Store in an airtight container for up to 6 months.

Ranch House Rub

Makes ¼ cup   This yummy herb rub is similar to the ranch style dressing mix you can purchase in the supermarket. It's excellent rubbed on chicken or seafood.

2 tablespoons dried parsley
1½ teaspoons dried oregano
1½ teaspoons dried tarragon
2 teaspoons garlic salt
2 teaspoons lemon pepper
2 teaspoons dried chives

Combine all the ingredients in a small mixing bowl and stir to blend. Store in an airtight container for up to 6 months.

Citrus-Ancho Chile Marinade

Makes about 2 cups   This sunny and spicy marinade is great with shrimp, chicken, or fish. If you want to increase the heat, add additional ground chile. Ancho chiles are sweet, smoky, and have quite a kick.

⅔ cup olive oil
⅓ cup fresh lime juice
½ cup fresh orange juice
2 tablespoons ground ancho chile
2 cloves garlic, minced
¼ cup chopped red onion

In a small glass mixing bowl, combine all the ingredients, stirring to blend. Refrigerate, tightly covered, for up to 5 days.

Bloody Mary Marinade

Makes about 4 cups **Everyone loves the taste of a Bloody Mary, that prebrunch eye-opening drink. This marinade, based on the drink, is great for marinating beef, lamb, and chicken.**

2 cups Bloody Mary mix or
　　spicy tomato juice
¹/₄ cup olive oil
2 tablespoons
　　Worcestershire sauce
¹/₄ cup vodka
2 ribs celery, finely chopped
¹/₄ cup chopped shallots
Pinch of cayenne

In a medium-size glass mixing bowl, combine all the ingredients, stirring to blend. Refrigerate, tightly covered, for up to 5 days.

All-Purpose Sherry Marinade

Makes about 1½ cups   This is a versatile basic marinade that I keep in my fridge just in case I need it. It's great for poultry, beef, and lamb, and the soy sauce gives it the added benefit of brining for a more tender dinner.

½ cup dry sherry
⅓ cup red wine vinegar
¼ cup soy sauce
¼ cup Worcestershire sauce
1 teaspoon dried oregano
½ teaspoon dried rosemary, crumbled
1 teaspoon dried basil
2 teaspoons garlic salt

Combine all the ingredients in a small glass mixing bowl and whisk together until blended.

Cajun Fuel Injection

Makes about 1⅔ cups   Spicy, but not too hot, this solution will help to flavor otherwise bland chicken, turkey, or pork. For poultry, inject the breast and thigh areas for the best results; it's not necessary to inject the entire bird. This can also be used as a marinade.

2 tablespoons Creole
    Seasoning Rub
    (page 287)
1/2 cup apple juice
2 tablespoons honey
2 teaspoons Creole mustard
    (Zatarain's is widely
    available)
1/2 cup chicken broth
2 tablespoons
    Worcestershire sauce

Combine all the ingredients in a blender and process until the spices are dissolved, 2 to 3 minutes. Store the injection in the refrigerator for up to 3 days, tightly covered.

Fuel Injections

These liquid solutions of spices are injected into poultry, pork, beef, and lamb. Most gourmet gadget stores sell injectors, and your rotisserie may even come with one. The purpose of injecting the meat is to flavor it all the way through. When a whole chicken or turkey is injected, the breast meat takes on an almost marbled effect when it is done properly. If you decide to do injecting, I recommend that you try a chicken first, then move on to turkey and other meats. You may find that you don't like the pungent flavor of the injection, and it's better to discover that on a not so expensive chicken, rather than a fifty-dollar beef tenderloin.

Larger items, such as pork shoulder and a whole turkey, can be refrigerated for up to 24 hours after they are injected, but smaller chicken, pork, and beef roasts will not need that amount of time; I find that 4 to 6 hours is sufficient to allow the solution to flavor the meat. Since the solution needs to be very thin, mix the injections in a blender, to purée all the spices.

Below are some no-brainer injections that you can buy in the grocery store.

- Worcestershire, both dark and white
- Zatarain's Crab and Shrimp Boil
- Bottled Caesar or Italian dressing
- Bottled teriyaki sauce, thinned with water or canola oil
- Stonewall Kitchen's basting sauces, thinned if necessary with water or canola oil

Orange-Chile Injection

Makes about 1½ cups   This citrus-flavored, spicy injection is great for turkey, chicken, beef, and lamb. I would inject the meat just before cooking, because this injection is pretty potent and if it's left to marinate the meat, you'll end up with one pretty hot tamale.

½ cup frozen orange juice
    concentrate, defrosted
2 tablespoons garlic salt
2 tablespoons ground ancho
    chile
2 teaspoons grated orange
    zest
2 tablespoons canola oil
1 teaspoon dried oregano
¼ cup soy sauce
2 tablespoons honey

Combine all the ingredients in a blender and process for 2 to 3 minutes to dissolve the seasonings. Refrigerate this, tightly covered, for up to 3 days.

Salsa Fresca

Makes 2 cups   Salsa fresca is the ketchup of the South-west—there are more recipes for it than there are cooks in that region. You will find it on most restaurant tables there, whether it's the local burger joint or a favorite breakfast haunt. This recipe is simple, straightforward, and about a six on the heat meter. If you prefer yours hotter, by all means, kick up the heat with additional chiles, or cayenne, or Tabasco. Salsa fresca will keep about a week in the refrigerator, and the longer it stands, the hotter it gets.

4 medium-size vine-ripened tomatoes, seeded and chopped, or 4 cups canned whole plum tomatoes, drained and chopped

1/3 cup finely chopped red onion

2 cloves garlic, minced

2 jalapeños, seeded and finely chopped

1/4 cup chopped fresh cilantro leaves

2 teaspoons chopped fresh oregano leaves

1 1/2 teaspoons salt

1/2 teaspoon freshly ground black pepper

1/8 teaspoon cayenne pepper

2 tablespoons fresh lime juice

In a medium-size glass mixing bowl, stir together all the ingredients.

Cover the bowl with plastic wrap and refrigerate for at least 4 hours to let the flavors develop. Stir the salsa before serving.

Variations

If you would like a smooth salsa, purée the ingredients in a food processor or with an immersion blender.

Winter Salsa: When the tomatoes in the store aren't looking or tasting their best, use 4 cups canned whole plum tomatoes, chopped and drained.

Mango Salsa

Makes about 2 cups   A fruit salsa makes a sweet and spicy side to serve with grilled fish, chicken, or pork. If fresh mangoes are not in season, buy frozen, defrost them, and drain the juice.

2 cups peeled, seeded, and
  chopped ripe mango
1 clove garlic, minced
1 teaspoon salt
Pinch of cayenne pepper
2 tablespoons chopped
  fresh cilantro leaves
2 tablespoons chopped
  fresh parsley leaves
1/3 cup finely chopped green
  onions, white and light
  green parts
1/3 cup sugar
1/4 cup rice vinegar
2 tablespoons fresh lime
  juice

In a medium-size glass mixing bowl, stir together all the ingredients until blended.

Cover the bowl tightly with plastic wrap and refrigerate for at least 4 hours to let the flavors develop. Stir the salsa before serving, to blend the flavors.

Basil-Tomato Salsa

Makes about 3 cups   Basil and tomatoes are a match made in heaven, and this tasty salsa combines the best of summer, perfect served alongside chicken, fish, and meats. Make sure to use vine-ripened tomatoes for the best results.

4 medium-size vine-ripened
   tomatoes, seeded and
   chopped
1 cup packed fresh basil
   leaves, chopped
1$^1/_2$ teaspoons salt
$^1/_2$ teaspoon freshly ground
   black pepper
3 tablespoons olive oil

In a medium-size glass mixing bowl, stir together all the ingredients until well blended.

Cover the bowl with plastic wrap and refrigerate for at least 2 and up to 3 days to develop the flavors. Stir the salsa before serving.

Bruschetta Salsa

Makes about 2 cups   Bruschetta are little toasts that are topped with a savory mixture; sometimes it is a mixture of tomatoes, garlic, herbs, and olive oil; other times it's wild mushroom ragout, or the cook's whim. This salsa was inspired by tomato and basil bruschetta; I've added little bits of fresh mozzarella to it for a unique texture. Serve this with chicken, beef, lamb, or fish.

4 medium-size vine-ripened tomatoes, seeded and chopped
2 cloves garlic, minced
1 cup packed fresh basil leaves, thinly sliced
1½ teaspoons salt
½ teaspoon freshly ground black pepper
¼ cup extra-virgin olive oil
¼ pound fresh mozzarella cheese, cut into ½-inch dice

In a medium-size glass mixing bowl, blend together all the ingredients.

Cover the bowl with plastic wrap and allow to sit at room temperature before serving. (If you plan to serve this later, it can be refrigerated for up to 24 hours, but make sure to remove it from the refrigerator at least 1 hour before serving because the oil will solidify when it's refrigerated.)

Chipotle-Corn Salsa

Makes 2 cups   Chipotle peppers have a smoky flavor, and they turn this salsa into a spicy little number. This is about a six on the heat meter; if you would like yours hotter, then add another chipotle, minced. Adding corn gives the salsa a confetti-like appearance.

3 medium-size vine-ripened
  tomatoes, seeded and
  chopped
1 canned chipotle chile in
  adobo sauce, drained
  and minced
2 tablespoons fresh lime
  juice
1/3 cup chopped red onion
2 cloves garlic, chopped
1 cup corn kernels, either
  fresh cut from the cob or
  frozen (and defrosted)
1 1/2 teaspoons salt
1/2 teaspoon freshly ground
  black pepper
1 teaspoon sugar

In a medium-size glass mixing bowl, stir together all the ingredients until well combined.

Cover the bowl with plastic wrap and refrigerate for at least 2 hours and up to 4 days to develop the flavors.

Cucumber-Mint Salsa

Makes about 2 cups   Pale green in color, cool, and minty, this salsa is beautiful as a bed for a rack of lamb or served alongside it. The salsa should be made the day you wish to serve it because the cucumbers lose some of their crunch after 24 hours.

1 English cucumber, cut into
$\frac{1}{2}$-inch dice

2 green onions, white and
light green parts,
chopped

$\frac{1}{2}$ cup finely chopped fresh
mint leaves

1 tablespoon rice vinegar

2 tablespoons canola oil

1 teaspoon sugar

$\frac{1}{4}$ teaspoon ground cumin

$\frac{1}{2}$ teaspoon salt

Pinch of cayenne pepper

In a medium-size glass bowl, stir together all the ingredients until well blended.

Cover the bowl with plastic wrap and refrigerate for at least 2 hours to develop the flavors. Toss again and serve cold.

Avocado-Corn Salsa

Makes about 1½ cups   **This colorful salsa makes an elegant presentation over fish fillets, chicken, or beef. You can make this a few hours ahead of time and refrigerate it, but I would advise using it the day that you make it, as the lime juice will tend to "cook" the avocado, and make it mushy after a day in the refrigerator.**

1 large ripe Haas avocado,
   peeled, pitted, and diced
½ cup corn kernels, freshly
   cut from the cob or
   frozen (and defrosted)
4 green onions, white and
   light green parts,
   chopped
1 tablespoon seeded and
   minced jalapeño
2 tablespoons fresh lime
   juice
1½ teaspoons salt
½ teaspoon freshly ground
   black pepper
2 tablespoons chopped
   fresh cilantro leaves

In a small glass mixing bowl, combine all the ingredients, stirring to blend. Serve immediately or cover and store in refrigerator until ready to serve.

Cantaloupe-Red Pepper Salsa

Makes 2 cups   This beautiful salsa is sweet and savory, with a kick from Tabasco. Serve it with fish, chicken, or pork for a winning side dish.

2 cups seeded cantaloupe cut into $1/2$-inch dice (from about $1/2$ medium-size melon)

$1/2$ cup seeded and finely diced red bell pepper

$1/4$ cup finely diced red onion

3 tablespoons fresh lime juice

4 shakes Tabasco sauce

$1 1/2$ teaspoons salt

$1/2$ teaspoon freshly ground black pepper

$1/4$ cup chopped fresh mint leaves

In a medium-size glass mixing bowl, combine all the ingredients, stirring to blend.

Cover the bowl with plastic wrap and refrigerate for at least 1 and up to 24 hours before serving to develop the flavors.

Ann's Black Bean Salsa

Makes 3 cups My sister-in-law Ann loves to make this salsa. She serves it with tortilla chips, but you could just as easily serve it as a colorful accompaniment for any beef, chicken, or pork dish that you have done in the rotisserie.

1 medium-size vine-ripened tomato, seeded and chopped

$1/2$ cup peeled, pitted, and chopped ripe avocado

$1/4$ cup chopped red onion

$1/4$ cup seeded and chopped Anaheim chile

1 clove garlic, minced

One $15^1/2$-ounce can black beans, drained and rinsed

$1/4$ cup fresh lime juice

$1/2$ cup canola oil

1 teaspoon salt

$1/2$ teaspoon freshly ground black pepper

In a large glass mixing bowl, stir together all the ingredients until blended.

Cover the bowl with plastic wrap and refrigerate for at least 2 hours and up to 5 days. Drain the salsa before serving.

Green Grape Relish

Makes about 3½ cups   Here is a refreshing sauce to serve alongside fish or chicken. The sweetness of the grapes is accented by the full-bodied flavor of the balsamic vinegar.

3 cups seedless green
   grapes, halved
¼ cup finely chopped
   shallots
¼ cup chopped fresh Italian
   parsley leaves
1 teaspoon salt
½ teaspoon freshly ground
   black pepper
2 tablespoons olive oil
⅓ cup balsamic vinegar

In a medium-size glass mixing bowl, combine all the ingredients, stirring to blend.

Cover the bowl with plastic wrap and refrigerate for at least 2 and up to 6 hours to develop the flavors. Stir the relish before serving.

Just Peachy Cranberry Relish

Makes 5 cups   This is a favorite dish that I teach my students to make at Thanksgiving time. It is sweet and savory, with onions and peaches added to the tart cranberries. Serve it cold with poultry or pork.

One 15 1/2-ounce can peach
halves packed in syrup,
drained, and syrup
reserved

1 cup chopped onions

1 1/2 cups sugar

One 12-ounce bag fresh
cranberries, rinsed and
picked over for stems

1 teaspoon ground cinnamon

1/2 teaspoon ground ginger

1 cup pecan halves

In a 3-quart saucepan, combine the reserved peach syrup, onions, sugar, cranberries, cinnamon, and ginger. Bring the mixture to a boil and continue boiling until the cranberries begin to split and pop, about 10 minutes.

Meanwhile, coarsely chop the peaches and add them to the cranberries, along with the pecans. After the cranberries have popped, cook the relish for another 5 minutes. Remove from the stove and allow to cool to room temperature. Store, tightly sealed in jars, in the refrigerator for up to 1 month.

Apple-Mint Chutney

Makes about 1 1/2 cups   **When I was a kid, every time we had lamb, my mom would search the back of the cupboard for the mint jelly, which reminded me of slime, the way it just oozed out of the jar onto the plate. This chutney has all the flavor of the mint, but none of the ooze that turned me off so many years ago.**

1 tablespoon canola oil

1 cup chopped red onions

1 cup peeled and cored
   Granny Smith apple
   cut into 1/2-inch dice

1/2 cup golden raisins

1/8 teaspoon ground
   coriander

Pinch of cayenne pepper

1/2 teaspoon salt

1/2 cup sugar

1/2 cup rice vinegar

1 cup chopped fresh mint
   leaves

In a 2-quart saucepan, heat the canola oil over medium heat, then add the onions and apple and cook, stirring, until the apple begins to soften, about 4 minutes. Add the raisins, coriander, cayenne, salt, sugar, and vinegar. Bring the mixture to a boil, reduce the heat to a simmer, and cook for 5 minutes.

Remove the chutney from the stove and stir in the mint. Allow the mixture to cool, then refrigerate for at least 4 hours and up to 1 week to develop the flavors. Serve cold.

Tropical Pesto

Makes about 1 1/4 cups   This recipe is a terrific dip for Aloha Coconut Shrimp (page 199), but it's also a nice sauce to serve on the side with grilled fish, chicken, or pork. You can buy unsweetened shredded coconut in health food stores.

1/2 cup packed fresh cilantro
   leaves

4 green onions, white and
   light green parts, cut
   into several pieces

1 tablespoon fresh lime juice

Place the cilantro, green onions, lime juice, ginger, garlic, salt, nuts, and coconut in a blender and process until smooth, about 30 seconds. With the machine running, gradually add 1/4 cup of the canola oil and process until the mixture is emulsified.

1 tablespoon peeled and
    grated fresh ginger
1 clove garlic, peeled
1/2 teaspoon salt
2 tablespoons chopped
    macadamia nuts
1/4 cup unsweetened
    shredded coconut (see
    Smart Turn, page 199)
1/4 cup plus 1 to 2
    tablespoons canola oil

Remove the pesto from the blender and store in a glass jar. Float the remaining oil on top of the pesto, cover tightly, and store for up to 5 days in the refrigerator. When you are ready to use the pesto, stir the floating oil into it and serve cold.

Cilantro Pesto

Makes about 1 cup The pungent cilantro and garlic in this pesto make it a real change of pace from traditional basil pesto. Tasty served with chicken, fish, and potatoes, and you can freeze it for up to 2 months.

2 cups packed fresh cilantro
    leaves
6 cloves garlic, peeled
1/2 cup packed fresh parsley
    leaves
1/4 cup blanched almonds
1 teaspoon salt
1/2 teaspoon freshly ground
    black pepper
6 shakes Tabasco sauce
1/4 cup plus 2 tablespoons
    olive oil

In a food processor or a blender, put the cilantro, garlic, parsley, almonds, salt, pepper, and Tabasco. Process the mixture until smooth, about 30 seconds. Scrape down the sides and, with the machine running, gradually pour in 1/4 cup of the olive oil. Process until the oil is incorporated and emulsified.

Remove the pesto from the work bowl, transfer to an airtight container, and pour the remaining 2 tablespoons of olive oil on top. Refrigerate for up to 5 days or freeze for up to 2 months.

Tapenade

Makes about 2 cups   A French condiment, tapenade is savory and spicy with olives, capers, anchovies, and garlic. It's a terrific accompaniment for chicken, fish, or vegetables. It also makes a great snack to serve with goat cheese and crackers.

2 cups pitted Kalamata
  olives, drained
$1/4$ cup capers, drained
2 teaspoons anchovy paste
2 cloves garlic, peeled
1 teaspoon fresh thyme
  leaves
2 tablespoons chopped
  fresh parsley leaves
3 tablespoons red wine
  vinegar
1 tablespoon fresh lemon
  juice
$1/3$ cup olive oil

Place the olives, capers, anchovy paste, and garlic in a food processor. Pulse the mixture on and off 4 or 5 times, until coarsely chopped.

Turn the mixture into a bowl, add the remaining ingredients, and toss to blend. Cover the bowl with plastic wrap and refrigerate for at least 2 hours to and up to 5 days to blend the flavors.

Fire-Roasted Caponata

Makes about 4 cups   Smoky rotisserie-roasted eggplant pairs here with garlic, capers, tomato, and olives to make a great relish to serve alongside beef, lamb, chicken, or seafood. It can also be used as part of an antipasto tray or served like bruschetta, on toast rounds.

1 large eggplant
$^1/_4$ cup olive oil
2 cloves garlic, minced
$^1/_2$ cup chopped onion
One 15$^1/_2$-ounce can
   chopped tomatoes, with
   their juice
$^1/_4$ cup capers, drained
$^1/_2$ cup pitted green olives,
   drained and coarsely
   chopped
$^1/_4$ cup balsamic vinegar
1$^1/_2$ teaspoons salt
$^1/_2$ teaspoon freshly ground
   black pepper
2 tablespoons chopped
   fresh basil leaves or
   2 teaspoons dried

Cut off the top of the eggplant and make several slits in the skin with the tip of a sharp knife. Load the eggplant onto the spit rod assembly and brush with some of the olive oil. Roast the eggplant until it is tender when pierced with a knife, 40 to 50 minutes. Remove the eggplant from the spit rod assembly. When it is cool enough to handle, cut it in half, scoop the flesh onto a cutting board, and coarsely chop it.

In a 12-inch skillet, heat the remaining olive oil over medium heat and cook the eggplant, garlic, and onion, stirring, until the onion is softened but not browned, about 5 minutes. Add the tomatoes and cook, stirring, until the juices from the tomatoes have evaporated, another 5 minutes.

Transfer the mixture to a medium-size glass mixing bowl and stir in the capers, olives, vinegar, salt, pepper, and basil, mixing until well combined.

Cover the bowl with plastic wrap and refrigerate for at least 4 hours and up to 1 week to allow the flavors to develop.

That Spicy Green Sauce

Makes about 2 cups   **Chimichurri is an Argentine sauce that is used to season grilled meats, but I like to serve it on the side with chicken, beef, lamb, and seafood, too. It's a little hot and spicy, and you'll love the clean taste of the fresh parsley, which counteracts the spiciness.**

1½ cups chopped fresh
    Italian parsley leaves
6 cloves garlic, minced
1 tablespoon chopped fresh
    oregano leaves
½ teaspoon crushed red
    pepper
1 teaspoon salt
½ teaspoon freshly ground
    black pepper
⅓ cup red wine vinegar
¾ cup olive oil

In a medium-size glass mixing bowl, stir together all the ingredients until well combined. Refrigerate, covered with plastic wrap, for at least 4 hours and up 2 days. Stir the sauce before serving.

Smart Turn

You can also use this as a marinade; I recommend marinating chicken for 1 to 2 hours, and beef or lamb for up to 4 hours.

Open Sesame Sauce

Makes about 2 cups   Ribs basted with this Asian-inspired ginger-sesame sauce emerge from the rotisserie with a beautiful mahogany glaze.

1 cup soy sauce

2 cloves garlic, minced

2 teaspoons peeled and grated fresh ginger

$1/2$ cup firmly packed light brown sugar

$1/4$ cup rice wine or rice vinegar

2 tablespoons canola or peanut oil

1 tablespoon toasted sesame oil

$1/4$ cup chopped green onions, white and light green parts

3 tablespoons sesame seeds

In a 2-quart saucepan, stir together the soy sauce, garlic, ginger, brown sugar, rice wine, the oils, and 2 tablespoons of the green onions. Bring the mixture to a boil, reduce the heat to medium-low, and simmer for 20 to 30 minutes, stirring occasionally.

Remove the sauce from the heat and add the remaining 2 tablespoons of green onions and the sesame seeds. Use immediately or refrigerate the sauce, covered, until you are ready to use it, up to 7 days.

Spicy Teriyaki Sauce

Makes about 2 cups This delicious sauce is great as a marinade for chicken, fish, pork, or beef, and it also makes a great dipping sauce on the side. This version gets a little kick from garlic chile oil, which can be found in the Asian section of your supermarket, or check Sources on page 361.

2 tablespoons canola oil

2 teaspoons peeled and grated fresh ginger

1 1/2 teaspoons garlic chile oil

1 1/2 cups soy sauce

1/4 cup firmly packed brown sugar

2 tablespoons rice wine or rice vinegar

2 tablespoons toasted sesame oil

In a small saucepan, heat the canola oil over medium heat, then add the ginger and cook, stirring, for 2 minutes. Add the chile oil, soy sauce, brown sugar, and rice wine and bring the mixture to a boil. Reduce the heat to a simmer and cook until the sauce has thickened, about 15 minutes.

Remove the sauce from the heat and stir the sesame oil. Cool the sauce, cover with plastic wrap, and store in the refrigerator for up to 1 week.

Top Secret Teriyaki Sauce

Makes about 3 cups   **This teriyaki sauce is served at several steak houses here in California. It is thicker than most other sauces, and really should be used as a basting and dipping sauce, rather than a marinade.**

2 tablespoons sesame seeds

1 cup soy sauce

$^{1}/_{2}$ cup sugar

1 tablespoon Tabasco

$^{1}/_{2}$ teaspoon freshly ground
    black pepper

6 cloves garlic, minced

2 teaspoons peeled and
    grated fresh ginger

2 tablespoons sesame oil

2 tablespoons light brown
    sugar

1 cup water

$^{1}/_{4}$ cup pineapple juice

3 tablespoons cornstarch
    dissolved in 3
    tablespoons water

In a 2½-quart saucepan, combine the sesame seeds, soy sauce, sugar, Tabasco, black pepper, garlic, ginger, sesame oil, brown sugar, water, and pineapple juice and bring to a boil.

Reduce the heat and add the cornstarch and water mixture, stirring until the sauce is thickened. Remove from the heat and use immediately or store in the refrigerator, covered with plastic wrap, for up to 10 days.

Beefy Merlot Sauce

Makes about 3½ cups   **This bold sauce is the perfect accompaniment for a roast beef or grilled steak. Fragrant with fresh thyme and red wine, the sauce can be prepared ahead of time and refrigerated or frozen for future use.**

2 tablespoons butter
½ cup chopped shallots
6 sprigs fresh thyme or
    1 tablespoon dried
1 cup Merlot
Two 10¾-ounce cans
    condensed beef broth

In a 2½-quart saucepan, melt the butter over medium heat. Add the shallots and thyme and cook, stirring, until the shallots begin to soften, 3 to 4 minutes. Pour in the Merlot and bring the mixture to a boil. Reduce the heat to medium-low and simmer until the wine reduces by a quarter, about 20 minutes.

Add the broth and continue to simmer for another 30 minutes; the sauce should have the consistency of a medium-thick white sauce and coat the back of a spoon. Remove the thyme sprigs from the sauce and serve. The sauce will keep, covered, in the refrigerator for up to 5 days and can be frozen for up to 6 weeks.

Sun-Dried Tomato and Pesto Cream Sauce

Makes 3 cups   **This pink sauce flavored with sun-dried tomatoes and garlicky pesto is dynamite on chicken or seafood.**

2 cups heavy cream
1/4 cup Basil Pesto (page 19) or store-bought pesto
1/2 cup oil-packed sun-dried tomatoes, drained and thinly sliced
1 teaspoon salt
1/2 teaspoon freshly ground black pepper

In a 2½-quart saucepan, heat the cream over medium heat until tiny bubbles form around the edge of the saucepan. Add the pesto, tomatoes, salt, and pepper, stirring to combine. Bring the sauce to serving temperature and use immediately. If you would like to refrigerate the sauce, cool it to room temperature, transfer to a container, cover, and refrigerate for up to 5 days. Reheat over low heat before serving.

Cucumber-Yogurt Sauce

Makes 3 cups   **This spicy, cooling sauce is great to serve with rotisserie chicken or lamb.**

2 cups nonfat plain yogurt
3 cloves garlic, minced
1 cup diced cucumber
1/2 teaspoon freshly ground black pepper
2 tablespoons chopped fresh dill

In a small mixing bowl, stir together all the ingredients until well combined.

Cover the bowl with plastic wrap and refrigerate for at least 2 hours and up to 4 days to develop the flavors. Stir to reblend before serving.

Quick Marinara

Makes about 6 cups   Everyone needs a couple of tricks in an apron pocket for getting dinner on the table fast, and this quick little sauce can be the basis for many great meals, whether you serve it with chicken, fish, or beef, or over pasta. Having a few containers of this sauce in your freezer can mean the difference between dinner and calling the pizza delivery man.

2 tablespoons olive oil
1 large onion, chopped
2 cloves garlic, minced
Three 14$^1/_2$-ounce cans
   crushed tomatoes
1$^1/_2$ teaspoons dried basil
1 teaspoon sugar
1$^1/_2$ teaspoons salt
$^1/_2$ teaspoon freshly ground
   black pepper

In a 5-quart stockpot, heat the olive oil over medium heat, add the onion and garlic, and cook, stirring, until the onion is softened, 3 to 4 minutes. Add the remaining ingredients and bring the sauce to a boil. Reduce the heat to low and simmer for 45 minutes.

Taste the sauce and correct the seasoning if necessary. Cool the sauce and store in zipper-top plastic bags in the refrigerator for up to 4 days or in the freezer for up to 2 months.

Horseradish Sauce

Makes 1 generous cup   Horseradish sauce is a wonderful accompaniment for prime rib and other beef dishes. This sauce goes together while the roast is resting.

1 cup sour cream

1 tablespoon prepared
   horseradish

1/2 teaspoon sweet paprika

In a small mixing bowl, combine all the ingredients, stirring to blend.

Use immediately or store in the refrigerator, covered with plastic wrap, for up to 5 days.

Hoisin Barbecue Sauce

Makes about 2 cups **Hoisin is the ketchup of China, and you will find it in the Asian section of the supermarket. Buy an imported brand such as Lee Kum Kee. This sauce is delicious with pork ribs, pork tenderloin, and chicken. Since there is some sugar in the sauce, make sure to do most of the basting in the last 20 minutes of cooking so that the sauce doesn't burn.**

1/2 cup hoisin sauce

1/2 cup soy sauce

2 tablespoons rice wine or
   rice vinegar

2 cloves garlic, minced

2 teaspoons peeled and
   grated fresh ginger

2 tablespoons firmly packed
   light brown sugar

1/4 cup canola oil

In a small saucepan, combine all the ingredients and heat until the mixture comes to a boil. Reduce the heat to low and simmer the sauce for 10 minutes. Remove from the heat and let cool. The sauce can be refrigerated, covered with plastic wrap, for up to 10 days.

Once you have touched raw meat with a marinade, baste, or sauce, make sure to boil the remainder vigorously to kill any bacteria that might have contaminated the sauce if you plan to serve it on the side with your meal.

KC Barbecue Sauce

Makes about 2½ cups **Similar to many of the sweet barbecue sauces on the market, this one is simple and delicious.**

2 tablespoons vegetable oil
1 large onion, chopped
1 clove garlic, minced
One 8-ounce can tomato
    purée
½ cup ketchup
2 tablespoons
    Worcestershire sauce
2 tablespoons mustard
2 tablespoons honey
¼ cup firmly packed light
    brown sugar
Several shakes Tabasco
    sauce, to your taste

In a 3-quart saucepan, heat the vegetable oil over medium heat, add the onion, and cook, stirring, until translucent, 3 to 4 minutes. Add the garlic and cook, stirring, another 1 to 2 minutes, until the onion begins to turn golden. Add the remaining ingredients and stir until the mixture comes to a boil.

Reduce the heat to low and simmer the sauce, uncovered, for about 30 minutes. Remove the sauce from the heat and use immediately or refrigerate, covered, for up to 2 weeks or freeze for up to 2 months.

Smokin' Joe's Barbecue Rib Sauce

Makes about 1³⁄₄ cups   This rib sauce is smoky without the sweet taste of brown sugar; it gets a spicy kick from vinegar and Tabasco. This sauce is also great on pork chops and roasts.

2 tablespoons canola oil
¹⁄₂ cup chopped onion
4 cloves garlic, minced
1 cup cider vinegar
¹⁄₄ cup molasses
¹⁄₂ cup bottled chili sauce
1 tablespoon Tabasco or
   other hot sauce
1 tablespoon Worcestershire
   sauce
1 teaspoon Liquid Smoke

In a 2-quart saucepan, heat the canola oil over medium heat. Add the onion and garlic, and cook, stirring, until the onion is softened, about 3 minutes. Reduce the heat to medium-low, add the remaining ingredients, and bring the mixture to a simmer. Continue to simmer the sauce over low heat until thickened, about 30 minutes. Use immediately or refrigerate, covered, until you are ready to use it, up to 4 days. Reheat to serving temperature and brush on the ribs.

Barbecue Sauce—The Importance of Being Timely

Barbecue sauce lends a lot of flavor to food grilling on the rotisserie, but it should only be applied during the last 30 minutes of cooking time so that the sugar in the sauce doesn't have time to scorch. If your food will cook through in only 20 minutes or so, brush on the sauce, then rebrush it during the last 5 to 7 minutes of the cooking time. It's also important to brush the food with the sauce after it comes off the rotisserie, to refresh and intensify the flavor, but bring it to a vigorous boil before that final baste, or set some aside for that purpose.

Southwestern Fiesta Rib Sauce

Makes about 2 cups **This spicy red sauce is terrific for a south of the border celebration, and you can also use it for basting chops or roasts.**

2 tablespoons canola oil

$1/2$ cup chopped onion

2 cloves garlic, minced

$1/2$ teaspoon ground cumin

1 teaspoon dried oregano

2 canned chipotle chiles in adobo sauce, drained and finely chopped

One 8-ounce can tomato purée

2 tablespoons tequila

1 tablespoon honey

2 tablespoons fresh lime juice

$1/4$ cup chopped fresh cilantro leaves

In a 2-quart saucepan, heat the canola oil over medium heat. Stir in the onion, garlic, cumin, and oregano, and cook, stirring, until the onion is softened, 3 to 4 minutes. Stir in the chipotles. Stir in the tomato purée, tequila, honey, lime juice, and 1 tablespoon of the cilantro. Bring the sauce to a simmer, reduce the heat to medium-low, and continue to simmer for 30 minutes, stirring occasionally. Use immediately, stirring in the remaining 3 tablespoons of cilantro before basting. Or refrigerate, covered with plastic wrap, until you are ready to use, up to 4 days.

Lynn's Really Good Pork Barbecue Sauce

Makes about 1¾ cups   My friend Lynn gave me this recipe, which she uses on pork tenderloins, but I love it on ribs. Sweet, and tangy, it's great on baby backs or country-style ribs.

1 tablespoon butter
3 cloves garlic, minced
½ cup bottled chili sauce
¼ cup ketchup
½ cup sherry
3 tablespoons soy sauce
¼ cup honey

In a small saucepan, melt the butter over medium heat. Add the garlic and cook, stirring, until it begins to soften, about 3 minutes, being careful not to let it brown. Add the remaining ingredients and stir to blend. Bring to a simmer, reduce the heat to medium-low, and continue simmering for 30 minutes, stirring occasionally. Use immediately or refrigerate, covered with plastic wrap, for up to 4 days.

Old-Fashioned Barbecue Sauce

Makes about 4 cups   This is the barbecue sauce that Dad used to paint on the chicken before the charcoal burned off all the skin. Smoky and sweet, it brings back memories of picnics and barbecues from a simpler time. Use this on pork or chicken; it's terrific on beef or pork ribs, too.

2 tablespoons canola oil

1/2 cup chopped onion

2 cloves garlic, minced

Four 8-ounce cans tomato
    sauce

1 tablespoon Worcestershire
    sauce

2 teaspoons Dijon mustard

1/4 cup firmly packed light
    brown sugar

2 tablespoons soy sauce

Heat the canola oil in a 2½-quart saucepan over medium heat, add the onion and garlic, and cook, stirring, until the onion is softened, about 3 minutes. Add the remaining ingredients and bring the sauce to a boil. Reduce the heat to medium-low and simmer for 30 minutes.

Remove the sauce from the heat and let cool to room temperature. If you are not using the sauce immediately, refrigerate, covered, for up to 1 week or freeze for up to 1 month.

All-American Barbecue Sauce

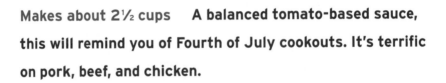

Makes about 2½ cups   A balanced tomato-based sauce, this will remind you of Fourth of July cookouts. It's terrific on pork, beef, and chicken.

2 tablespoons butter

1/2 cup chopped onion

2 cloves garlic, minced

Two 8-ounce cans tomato
    sauce

1/2 cup ketchup

1 tablespoon Worcestershire
    sauce

1/4 cup firmly packed light
    brown sugar

2 tablespoons soy sauce

1 teaspoon yellow mustard

Melt the butter in a medium-size saucepan over medium heat. Add the onion and garlic, and cook, stirring, until the onion is translucent, 4 to 5 minutes. Add the remaining ingredients, stir, and bring to a boil. Reduce the heat to medium-low and simmer the sauce for 15 to 20 minutes. It will keep, covered, in the refrigerator for up to 2 weeks or in the freezer for up to 2 months.

Tennessee Mopping Sauce

Makes about 1½ cups   Barbecue is serious business in Tennessee, with everyone guarding their secret recipes. I'm not sure that this one is authentic, but it does contain bourbon, which is the drink of choice in that state. Mops are generally brushed on with a little tool that looks like a mop, but you can also use a brush to baste the meat. You will need to stop and start the rotisserie to mop the meat, but the results are worth the trouble because the meat becomes more moist and flavorful with each baste. This sauce is great on pork and chicken.

2 teaspoons salt
1 teaspoon freshly ground
    black pepper
¼ cup vegetable oil
1 tablespoon Worcestershire
    sauce
2 teaspoons sweet paprika
½ teaspoon cayenne pepper
1 teaspoon dry mustard
½ cup bourbon
1 teaspoon garlic powder
½ cup beef broth

In a small saucepan over medium heat, combine all the ingredients. Stir the mixture to dissolve the spices. If not using immediately, you can refrigerate the sauce, tightly covered, for up to 5 days or freeze for up to 6 weeks.

When you are ready to mop, heat the sauce to barely a simmer and brush on the meat while it cooks.

Southwestern Mayonnaise

Makes about 2 cups   This spicy mayonnaise makes a great coating for fish in the rotisserie, or serve it as a dipping sauce on the side. It's also delicious mixed with tuna.

1½ cups mayonnaise
1 canned chipotle chile in adobo sauce, drained and finely chopped
2 tablespoons chopped fresh cilantro leaves
2 tablespoons fresh lime juice
2 tablespoons finely chopped red onion
½ teaspoon ground cumin

In a medium-size mixing bowl, stir together all the ingredients until well combined. The mayonnaise will keep in the refrigerator, covered with plastic wrap, for up to 5 days.

Artichoke Rémoulade

Makes about 2 cups   I've taken the traditional New Orleans sauce and added a few twists to it. A delicious change from tartar sauce, it's a wonderful partner for seafood or chicken. You'll need some Creole mustard: Zatarain's is sold nationwide.

1½ cups mayonnaise

¼ cup Creole mustard or coarse-grained mustard

1 clove garlic, peeled

1 teaspoon sweet paprika

¼ teaspoon cayenne pepper

½ cup chopped green onions, white and light green parts

One 4-ounce jar marinated artichoke hearts, drained

Place all the ingredients in a food processor. Pulse on and off 4 to 6 times, scraping down the sides several times, until the sauce looks fairly smooth, and is dotted with small nuggets of artichoke.

Transfer the sauce to bowl, cover with plastic wrap, and refrigerate for at least 2 hours and up to 10 days to develop the flavors.

Dilled Tartar Sauce

Makes 1½ cups **Tartar sauce is usually served alongside fried seafood, but this sauce, fragrant with dill and lemon zest, can be paired with any seafood from your rotisserie.**

1¼ cups mayonnaise

6 green olives stuffed with pimientos

2 tablespoons capers, drained

1 small dill pickle, quartered

1 medium-size shallot, quartered

2 teaspoons grated lemon zest

1 tablespoon chopped fresh dill

½ teaspoon freshly ground black pepper

Combine all the ingredients in a food processor. Pulse on and off 5 to 7 times, until there are no longer large pieces of pickle, shallot, or olive. The sauce will keep, covered with plastic wrap, in the refrigerator for up to 5 days.

Quick Béarnaise Mayonnaise

Makes 2 cups   **The perfect accompaniment to beef, lamb, chicken, veggies, or fish, this creamy sauce, flavored with tarragon and shallot, is great to have on hand to perk up a rotisserie creation or leftovers.**

¹/₄ cup white wine vinegar
1 medium-size shallot, finely
   chopped
2 tablespoons chopped
   fresh tarragon leaves or
   1 tablespoon dried
¹/₂ teaspoon freshly ground
   black pepper
1¹/₄ cups mayonnaise

Place the vinegar, shallot, 1 tablespoon of the tarragon, and the pepper in a small nonreactive saucepan and bring to a boil. Reduce the heat to low and simmer until reduced to 2 tablespoons. Let the vinegar mixture cool.

In a small mixing bowl, whisk together the mayonnaise and cooled vinegar until smooth. Stir in the remaining 1 table-spoon of tarragon, cover with plastic wrap, and refrigerate for at least 1 hour and up to 1 week to develop the flavors. Stir before serving.

Mustard-Dill Sauce

Makes 2 cups   Made with zesty Dijon mustard and fragrant dill, this creamy sauce is just perfect for fish fillets, shrimp, or chicken. It's also a wonderful sandwich spread for chicken, turkey, or seafood sandwiches.

1^1/$_4$ cups mayonnaise

^{1}/$_2$ cup Dijon mustard

^{1}/$_2$ cup sour cream

2 teaspoons fresh lemon
   juice

^{1}/$_2$ teaspoon freshly ground
   black pepper

2 tablespoons chopped
   fresh dill

1 tablespoon chopped fresh
   chives

In a small mixing bowl, whisk together all the ingredients until well blended. The sauce will keep, covered with plastic wrap, in the refrigerator for up to 1 week. Stir before serving.

Hollandaise is the queen of sauces for vegetables, chicken, or fish, and it's simple to make in the blender or food processor. There are so many variations on this theme that I've decided to give you a lot from which to choose. My students always ask me how to keep the sauce warm; I put the finished sauce in a thermal container, or keep it warm by placing the bowl over simmering water on the stove top. A thermal container will keep the sauce warm for about 1 hour.

Basic Blender Hollandaise

Makes 1 cup   Quick as a wink you can have this sinfully sublime sauce to cover vegetables, chicken, seafood, or egg dishes, including, of course, eggs Benedict. Make sure that the butter is hot when you pour it into the blender, so that it will cook the eggs.

3 large egg yolks
1 tablespoon fresh lemon
     juice
$1/2$ teaspoon salt
$1/4$ teaspoon freshly ground
     black pepper
1 cup (2 sticks) butter,
     melted and kept hot

Place the eggs, lemon juice, salt, and pepper in a blender or food processor.

With the machine running, pour the hot butter slowly through the feed tube and process until the sauce thickens. Serve immediately or keep the sauce warm for up to 1 hour in a thermal container.

Orange Hollandaise

Makes about 1 cup A wonderful variation on the theme, this sunny hollandaise is made with orange juice and zest and is especially good with seafood.

3 large egg yolks
1 tablespoon fresh orange
 juice
1 tablespoon grated orange
 zest
1/2 teaspoon salt
Pinch of cayenne pepper
1 cup (2 sticks) butter,
 melted and kept hot

In a blender or food processor, combine the egg yolks, orange juice and zest, salt, and cayenne.

With the machine running, slowly pour the hot butter through the feed tube and process until the sauce thickens. Serve immediately or keep warm for up to 1 hour in a thermal container.

Dilled Hollandaise

Makes about 1 cup This sauce is one of my favorites spooned over salmon, but I also use it for other seafood and vegetables. It is best made with fresh dill, but in a pinch you can use half as much dried.

3 large egg yolks

1 tablespoon fresh lemon
juice

2 tablespoons chopped
fresh dill

1/2 teaspoon salt

1/4 teaspoon freshly ground
black pepper

1 cup (2 sticks) butter,
melted and kept hot

In a blender or food processor, process the egg yolks, lemon juice, dill, salt, and pepper together until well combined.

With the machine running, slowly pour in the hot butter through the feed tube and process until the sauces thickens. Serve immediately or keep warm for up to 1 hour in a thermal container.

Cucumber Hollandaise

Makes 2 cups   This sauce is best served right after it's made because it does have a tendency to separate. It's delicious over seafood or poultry.

3 large egg yolks

2 tablespoons fresh lemon
juice

1/2 teaspoon dry mustard

2 tablespoons finely
chopped fresh parsley
leaves

1 tablespoon finely chopped
fresh chives

1/2 cup chopped cucumber

3/4 cup (11/2 sticks) butter,
melted and kept hot

In a blender or food processor, process the egg yolks, lemon juice, mustard, parsley, chives, and cucumber until smooth.

With the machine running, slowly pour in the hot butter through the feed tube and process until the sauce thickens. Serve immediately or keep warm for up to 1 hour in a thermal container.

Classic Béarnaise

Makes 1¼ cups **Fragrant with tarragon, this classic sauce is delicious on vegetables or served with chicken, beef, lamb, or seafood.**

3 tablespoons white wine
1 tablespoon white wine
  vinegar
1 medium-size shallot, finely
  chopped
1 tablespoon chopped fresh
  tarragon leaves, plus
  extra for garnish
¼ teaspoon salt
Pinch of freshly ground
  black pepper
3 large egg yolks
½ cup (1 stick) butter,
  melted and kept hot

In a small nonreactive saucepan, combine the wine, vinegar, shallot, tarragon, salt, and pepper and bring to a boil. Reduce the heat to medium, and simmer until the mixture has reduced to 2 tablespoons.

In a blender or food processor, process the egg yolks with the reduced tarragon mixture.

With the machine running, slowly pour in the hot butter through the feed tube and process until the mixture thickens. Serve immediately or keep warm for up to 1 hour in a thermal container.

Béarnaise Sauce

No one is really sure who this delectable sauce was named for, although legend has it that it was first served in 1863 at the Pavillion Henry IV, a restaurant not far from Paris. Since the restaurant was named for King Henry IV, who was known as "the great Béarnaise," having been born in the village of Bearn, most culinarians subscribe to this theory. However, the first recipe for béarnaise appeared in a cookbook called *La Cuisinière des Villes et des Campagnes*, published in 1808. In any case, the person who invented this sauce has made me a happy camper every time I have served it with steak, grilled fish, chicken, or vegetables.

A compound butter is butter mixed with herbs and spices, then served over vegetables or grilled meats, fish, or poultry. It is easily frozen for later use, and having a stash of these in your freezer can mean the difference between a good meal and an inspired one. Try stirring a pat of one of these flavored butters into mashed potatoes or topping a baked potato with one. Compound butter can be frozen for up to 6 months, wrapped tightly in plastic wrap.

Avocado Butter

Makes 1½ cups   This butter is sinfully rich and delicious when served with grilled seafood or chicken (just put a pat of it on top). It will keep in the refrigerator for a day.

½ cup (1 stick) butter, softened
1 large, ripe avocado, peeled, seeded, and chopped
2 tablespoons fresh lime juice
1 tablespoon chopped fresh cilantro leaves, plus extra for garnish
½ teaspoon garlic salt
¼ teaspoon Tabasco Chipotle Pepper Sauce

In a medium-size mixing bowl, mash together the butter and avocado. Add the remaining ingredients, stirring to blend. Store the butter, covered with plastic wrap, in the refrigerator for up to 24 hours.

Garlic-Herb Butter

Makes 1 cup This compound butter is one of the great tricks of the trade for busy home cooks. Once the butter is made, it can be frozen for months, then taken out and used on vegetables, beef, or chicken.

1 cup (2 sticks) butter, softened
2 cloves garlic, minced
1 tablespoon chopped fresh basil leaves
1 teaspoon chopped fresh oregano leaves
Pinch of cayenne pepper
1/2 cup chopped fresh parsley leaves

In a medium-size mixing bowl, beat the butter until smooth, then stir in the garlic, basil, oregano, and cayenne.

Sprinkle the parsley evenly over a piece of plastic wrap and turn out the butter onto the parsley. Using the plastic wrap, form the butter into a log about 1 inch in diameter, making sure that the parsley covers the log. Wrap the butter in the plastic wrap and store in the refrigerator for up to 5 days or freeze for up to 3 months.

And a Few
on the Side

Every rotisserie main course needs a little something on the side to make it special. These side dishes are the kind you will be happy to serve your family because not only are they simple, they are also really tasty. Whether it's Rick's Blue Cheese Slaw (page 347) or Garlic Smashed Potatoes (page 342), one of these side dishes on the table will help turn a weeknight dinner into a five-star meal.

And a Few on the Side

Refried Bean Bake

Serves 6 to 8   Filled with chiles and sour cream and topped with melting cheese, this is terrific with grilled steak, chicken, or pork.

2 tablespoons canola oil
1 large onion, chopped
$^1/_4$ cup finely minced jalapeños
Three 15$^1/_2$-ounce cans refried beans
1$^1/_2$ cups sour cream
1 teaspoon ground cumin
$^1/_4$ teaspoon ground ancho chile (optional; if you don't like it hot, omit it)
1 cup grated Monterey Jack cheese
1 cup grated mild cheddar cheese
$^1/_4$ cup chopped fresh cilantro leaves for garnish

Preheat the oven to 350 degrees. Coat a 13 x 9-inch baking dish with nonstick cooking spray.

In a 10-inch sauté pan, heat the canola oil over medium heat, then add the onion and jalapeños and cook, stirring, until the onion softens, 3 to 4 minutes.

Turn the mixture into a large mixing bowl. Add the beans, 1 cup of the sour cream, the cumin, and ground chile and stir until well blended. Spread the bean mixture over the bottom of the prepared dish and cover evenly with both grated cheeses. At this point, the casserole can be refrigerated, tightly covered with plastic wrap, for up to 24 hours. Allow it come to room temperature before baking.

Bake the casserole until the cheese is bubbling, 30 to 40 minutes. Remove the casserole from the oven, garnish with the cilantro, and serve the remaining ½ cup of sour cream on the side.

Cowboy Baked Beans

Serves 6 to 8   These hearty baked beans are made with ground beef and bacon and are cooked in a rich tomato sauce. If you like, you can make these three days ahead of time, then reheat in a slow cooker.

6 strips bacon, cut into
    $^{1}/_{2}$-inch dice
1 large onion, chopped
$^{1}/_{2}$ pound lean ground beef
Two 15$^{1}/_{2}$-ounce cans plain
    baked beans
$^{1}/_{2}$ cup ketchup
1 tablespoon yellow mustard
1 tablespoon Worcestershire
    sauce
$^{1}/_{2}$ cup firmly packed light
    brown sugar

In a 5-quart Dutch oven, fry the bacon over medium heat until crisp. Drain all but 1 tablespoon of the bacon fat from the pan.

Add the onion and cook, stirring, until it softens and begins to turn golden, about 5 minutes. Add the ground beef and cook, breaking it apart, until it loses its pink color. Drain off any excess fat or water that may have accumulated in the pan. Add the beans, ketchup, mustard, Worcestershire, and brown sugar. Bring the beans to a simmer, and cook over low heat for 45 minutes to 1 hour.

Smart Turn

If you would like to make the beans in a slow cooker, cook the bacon, onion, and beef, remove any excess fat or water, and spoon them into the slow cooker. Add the remaining ingredients, and cook on medium for 6 to 8 hours.

Caramelized Shallot and White Corn Mashed Potatoes

Serves 6   These mashed potatoes aren't like Mom used to make. Sweet caramelized shallots and corn make them the perfect side for roasted meats and poultry.

2 1/2 pounds Yukon Gold or russet potatoes, cut into 1-inch chunks
3 tablespoons butter
1/2 cup chopped shallots
1/4 cup heavy cream
1 cup white corn kernels, freshly cut from the cob or frozen and defrosted
Salt and freshly ground black pepper

Place the potatoes in a 3-quart saucepan with water to cover. Bring to a boil, reduce the heat to medium, and simmer the potatoes until tender when pierced with a sharp knife, 15 to 20 minutes.

While the potatoes are cooking, melt 2 tablespoons of the butter in a small sauté pan, add the shallots, and cook, stirring, until golden, 8 to 10 minutes. Set aside.

Drain the potatoes in a colander and return them to the pan. Mash the potatoes with the shallots, the remaining 1 tablespoon of butter, and the heavy cream. Stir in the corn and season with salt and pepper. Serve hot.

Garlic Smashed Potatoes

Serves 6   In case you haven't noticed, lumpy mashed potatoes are trendy now, served in the finest establishments instead of the creamy whipped variety. These potatoes are spiced up with garlic, and we've left the skins on the potatoes for some color, too. Serve these with rotisserie prime rib, steak, or lamb.

2¹/₂ pounds red potatoes, Yukon Gold, or new white potatoes, cut into 1-inch chunks

4 cloves garlic, peeled

2 teaspoons salt

¹/₄ cup (¹/₂ stick) butter

¹/₄ to ¹/₃ cup heavy cream, to your taste

¹/₂ teaspoon freshly ground black pepper

Place the potatoes, garlic, and salt in a 3-quart saucepan and add water to cover. Bring the potatoes to a boil, reduce the heat to medium, and simmer until tender when pierced with the tip of a knife, 15 to 20 minutes.

Drain the potatoes and garlic, return them to the pan, and shake the pan to dry out the potatoes. Add the butter, heavy cream, and pepper and mash the potatoes and garlic, leaving some lumps. Serve immediately.

Creamy Scalloped Potatoes

Serves 8   These potatoes cooked in cream and covered with a golden crust of Gruyère cheese are just what you need to serve alongside a rotisserie entrée. You can vary the cheese and use blue, cheddar, or smoked Gouda if you prefer.

2 ½ pounds medium-size red potatoes, sliced ¼ inch thick
1 medium-size onion, sliced ¼ inch thick and separated into rings
1 ½ teaspoons salt
½ teaspoon freshly ground black pepper
2 ½ cups half-and-half or light cream
2 cups grated Gruyère cheese

Preheat the oven to 400 degrees. Coat a 13 x 9-inch baking dish with nonstick cooking spray.

Spread out the potatoes evenly on the bottom of the casserole dish and layer the onions on top. Blend the salt and pepper into the cream and pour over the potatoes. Sprinkle the cheese evenly over the top of the potatoes and bake until the cheese is bubbling and the potatoes are tender, 30 to 45 minutes. Remove the dish from the oven and serve immediately.

Variations on the Theme

Sauté the onions in 1 tablespoon of butter until they are caramelized, 15 to 20 minutes. Layer on top of the potatoes in the casserole dish, and proceed with the recipe as directed.

Add 1 cup crumbled blue cheese to the cream mixture and omit the Gruyère.

Fry 6 strips bacon until crisp, crumble over the top of the potatoes and onions in the casserole dish, and sprinkle with grated white cheddar cheese in place of the Gruyère. Serve with a dollop of sour cream and a sprinkle of chopped green onions.

Asian Slaw

Serves 6   This simple cabbage salad is a favorite at
potluck dinners, and the possible variations on this theme
are infinite. Flavored with ginger and mandarin oranges,
the slaw makes a great side dish for poultry, pork, beef, and
seafood. Or, you can make this a main course salad by adding
grilled chicken or shrimp.

8 cups cored and thinly
  sliced green cabbage
  (about 1½ small heads)
4 green onions, white and
  light green parts,
  chopped
2 medium-size carrots,
  grated
1 cup canned mandarin
  orange segments,
  drained
¼ cup soy sauce
½ cup rice vinegar
¾ cup canola oil
1 teaspoon minced garlic
1 teaspoon peeled and
  grated fresh ginger
⅓ cup sugar
2 tablespoons toasted
  sesame oil
2 tablespoons sesame seeds
  for garnish

In a large salad bowl, combine the cabbage, green onions,
carrot, and oranges.

In a small mixing bowl, whisk together the soy sauce,
vinegar, canola oil, garlic, ginger, sugar, and sesame oil.
Pour the dressing over the cabbage and toss to combine well.
Refrigerate until ready to serve, up to 4 hours.

When ready to serve, garnish the salad with sesame seeds.

Smart Turn

For extra-quick slaw, prepackaged coleslaw is available in
the produce section of the grocery store. Or use your food
processor to make quick work of slicing the cabbage.

Mom's Pretty in Pink Slaw

Serves 6   Raspberry vinegar gives this slaw an attractive pink color as well as a tangy flavor. The slaw can be made up to eight hours in advance; after that, it will wilt a bit.

6 cups cored and thinly sliced green cabbage (about 1 small head)

1 cup cored and thinly sliced red cabbage

2 carrots, grated

1 cup mayonnaise

2 tablespoons raspberry vinegar

2 tablespoons sugar

1 to 2 tablespoons milk, as needed

3 tablespoons poppy seeds

In a large salad bowl, toss together the cabbage and carrots.

In a small mixing bowl, whisk together the mayonnaise, vinegar, sugar, and enough of the milk to achieve a creamy consistency. Pour the dressing over the cabbage and toss to coat evenly. Refrigerate for at least 2 and up to 8 hours to develop the flavors before serving.

Just before serving, stir in the poppy seeds.

Mango-Onion Slaw

Serves 6   A smooth and spicy mango dressing tops cabbage and Maui onions. This cooling slaw is just the ticket to serve with spicy meats and poultry. It's really good on rotisserie burgers, too.

6 cups cored and thinly sliced green cabbage (about 1 small head)

1 large Maui or other sweet yellow onion, thinly sliced and separated into rings

1 cup mango purée (see Smart Turn, page 58)

1/2 cup canola oil

1/4 cup rice vinegar

4 shakes Tabasco sauce

2 tablespoons sugar

1/4 cup chopped fresh cilantro leaves

1/2 cup finely chopped macadamia nuts, toasted (see page 184), for garnish

Place the cabbage and onion in a large salad bowl and toss together.

In a medium-size mixing bowl, whisk together the mango purée, canola oil, vinegar, Tabasco, sugar, and cilantro. Pour half of the dressing over the slaw and toss to coat evenly. Add additional dressing if needed. At this point, the slaw can be refrigerated for up to 2 hours.

When ready to serve, toss the salad again, add additional dressing if necessary, and garnish with the macadamia nuts.

Rick's Blue Cheese Slaw

Serves 6   **My friend Rick Rodgers, the author of many wonderful cookbooks, introduced me to blue cheese slaw when he wrote about it in his book** *Barbecue 101*. **I've fiddled with his recipe and I'm grateful for his inspiration.**

3/4 cup mayonnaise

2 tablespoons red wine vinegar

1 teaspoon Worcestershire sauce

1 tablespoon sugar

1/4 pound Maytag blue cheese or your favorite brand, crumbled

Salt and freshly ground black pepper

2 carrots, coarsely grated

6 cups cored and thinly sliced green cabbage (about 1 small head)

2 thin slices red onion, cut into thin strips

1/2 cup chopped pecans, toasted (see page 184), for garnish

In a small mixing bowl, whisk together the mayonnaise, vinegar, Worcestershire, sugar, and blue cheese until blended. Taste and adjust the salt and pepper. Cover and refrigerate for up to 3 days.

When you are ready to assemble the slaw, put the carrots, cabbage, and onion in a large salad bowl. Toss with the dressing and refrigerate, covered tightly with plastic wrap, for up to 2 hours.

Toss again before serving and garnish with the pecans.

Crunchy Cabbage Salad with Cashews

Serves 6 to 8   Similar to Asian Slaw (page 344), this colorful salad has ramen noodles, a touch of chile oil, and cilantro to give it a new spin.

6 cups cored and shredded green cabbage (about 1 medium-size head)

4 green onions, white and light green parts, chopped

1/2 cup canola oil

1 tablespoon toasted sesame oil

1 teaspoon chile oil

1 package chicken-flavored ramen noodles

3 tablespoons sugar

2 tablespoons rice vinegar

1/2 cup chopped fresh cilantro leaves

1/2 cup coarsely chopped cashews for garnish

In a large mixing bowl, toss together the cabbage and green onions.

In a small bowl, whisk together the oils. Remove the flavor packet from the ramen noodles and stir it into the oils. Whisk in the sugar and vinegar until blended.

Toss the cabbage with the dressing, cover, and refrigerate for at least 1 and up to 8 hours to develop the flavor.

Before serving, crush the ramen noodles and sprinkle them over the cabbage. Toss the salad with the noodles and cilantro, then garnish with the cashews.

Basic Risotto

Serves 6 **Risotto is a creamy rice dish from Italy, and it's terrific with anything off the rotisserie. You can also stir in leftovers from the rotisserie, such as grilled asparagus, seafood, baby artichokes, mushrooms, or shallots. Arborio rice is a medium-grain rice, which you can find in the rice section of your supermarket.**

3 cups chicken broth
1 teaspoon saffron threads
½ cup (1 stick) butter
2 tablespoons olive oil
½ cup chopped yellow onion
2 cups Arborio rice
¼ cup white wine
¾ cup freshly grated
   Parmigiano-Reggiano
   cheese

Pour the chicken broth into a small saucepan, bring to a boil, and remove from the heat. Dissolve the saffron in the broth and set aside.

In a 3-quart saucepan, heat 6 tablespoons of the butter and the olive oil together. When the foam subsides, add the onion and cook, stirring, until softened, about 5 minutes. Add the rice and cook, stirring constantly, until the grains are opaque, about 3 minutes.

Add the wine and allow it to boil for 2 minutes. Then add enough of the broth to barely cover the rice. Stir the risotto and continue to cook over high heat until the broth has been absorbed, about 5 minutes. Continue in this way, adding more broth as needed. After 15 minutes, the rice should be tender and creamy, yet still a little firm to the bite. Add the remaining 2 tablespoons butter and ½ cup cheese, stirring to blend.

Serve the risotto garnished with the remaining ¼ cup cheese.

Perfect Sticky Rice

Serves 6   A side of plain, short-grain sticky rice can be just the thing for a spicy grilled dinner. If you have leftover rice, refrigerate it and use it to make Kitchen Sink Fried Rice (page 351).

1¹/₂ cups short-grain rice, such as Calrose
3 cups water
1 teaspoon salt

Place the rice, water, and salt in a 2½-quart saucepan. Cover and bring to a boil. Reduce the heat to medium-low and simmer until the water is absorbed and the rice is tender, 16 to 18 minutes.

Remove from the heat and allow it to sit for 3 minutes before serving.

Kitchen Sink Fried Rice

Serves 6   A great way to use leftover rice and any bits of meat and vegetables, this side makes a colorful presentation. Make sure the rice is cold, otherwise, it will clump together when it's fried.

2 tablespoons vegetable oil

2 large eggs, beaten

1/4 cup soy sauce

2 tablespoons rice wine

2 teaspoons toasted sesame oil

1/3 cup chopped green onions, white and light green parts

2 cloves garlic, minced

2 teaspoons peeled and grated fresh ginger

1 cup diced leftover cooked chicken, pork, beef, or seafood (1/2-inch dice)

1/4 pound snow peas, strings removed

1 small carrot, cut into matchsticks (about 1/2 cup)

4 cups cold cooked rice

Heat a wok or sauté pan over high heat, and add 1 tablespoon of the vegetable oil. When it is close to smoking, add the beaten eggs and scramble them until they are dry. Remove from the wok.

In a small bowl, combine the soy sauce, rice wine, sesame oil, and green onions and set aside.

Heat the remaining 1 tablespoon of vegetable oil in the wok until almost smoking, then add the garlic and ginger and stir-fry for 1 to 2 minutes. Add the meat and toss in the flavored oil. Add the snow peas and carrots and toss to coat. Add the rice and eggs and cook until the rice is heated and mixed with the vegetables and meat.

Pour in the reserved soy sauce mixture and cook, stirring, to combine the ingredients and heat them through. Serve immediately.

Southwestern Rice

Serves 6   Spiked with cumin and Anaheim chile pepper, this rice dish is a great side with south of the border foods.

2 tablespoons canola oil

1 cup chopped onions

1/4 cup seeded and finely chopped Anaheim chiles

1 teaspoon ground cumin

1 cup canned chopped tomatoes, with their juices

1 1/2 cups converted rice, such as Uncle Ben's

3 1/2 cups chicken broth

In a 3-quart saucepan, heat the canola oil over medium heat. Add the onions, chiles, and cumin and cook, stirring, until the onions begin to soften. Add the tomatoes and cook until the liquid in the pan begins to evaporate. Stir in the rice and cook until the grains are coated, about 2 minutes.

Pour in the broth and bring the mixture to a boil. Reduce the heat to medium-low, and simmer, covered, until the rice is tender and the broth has been absorbed, 17 to 20 minutes.

Zucchini Parmesan Rice

Serves 6 to 8 **This is a terrific side dish to make when you have an overabundance of zucchini in your garden. Grate the zucchini in your food processor, then freeze it in 2-cup zipper-top plastic bags. Then, whenever you want to make this savory side, you'll just need to add the rice and cheese.**

2 tablespoons olive oil

1 cup chopped onion

2 cloves garlic, minced

4 cups grated zucchini
(about 5 medium-size)

1 teaspoon salt

1/2 teaspoon freshly ground
black pepper

2 1/2 cups milk

3/4 cup white rice

1 1/2 cups freshly grated
Parmesan cheese

Preheat the oven to 375 degrees. Coat a 13 x 9-inch casserole dish with nonstick cooking spray.

In a large sauté pan, heat the olive oil over medium heat. Add the onion and garlic, and cook, stirring, until the onion begins to turn translucent, about 3 minutes. Add the zucchini and season with the salt and pepper. Cook, stirring, until the liquid from the zucchini has evaporated, another 5 minutes. Pour the milk into the skillet and bring to a boil.

Transfer the zucchini mixture to the prepared baking dish and stir in the rice. Sprinkle the top with the cheese and bake until the cheese is bubbling and the rice is tender, 35 to 40 minutes. Remove from the oven and serve.

Smart Turn

The cooked casserole will keep in the freezer for about 1 month. Defrost in the refrigerator overnight and reheat, covered with aluminum foil, in a preheated 350 degree oven until heated through and bubbling, about 20 minutes.

Old-Fashioned Cornbread Stuffing with Rotisserie Caramelized Onions

Serves 6   If you have leftover onions from the rotisserie, this stuffing is a delicious way to use it and is perfect with poultry or pork.

2 tablespoons butter

1 cup chopped leftover Rosemary Roasted Shallot and Onion Medley (page 241)

1/2 cup chopped celery

6 cups crumbled cornbread or packaged dry cornbread crumbs

1 1/2 teaspoons dried thyme

1/2 cup chopped dried apricots

2 cups hot chicken broth

2 tablespoons butter, melted

Preheat the oven to 350 degrees. Coat a 13 x 9-inch casserole dish with nonstick cooking spray and set aside.

In a small sauté pan, melt the butter over medium heat, add the leftover onions and shallots and the celery and cook, stirring, until the celery softens, about 3 minutes. Transfer to a large mixing bowl. Add the cornbread, thyme, and apricots, then pour 1 cup of the broth over the mixture and stir to blend. If you like a wet stuffing, add more of the remaining broth; if you like a drier stuffing, 1 cup might be enough.

Spoon the stuffing into the prepared pan, drizzle with the melted butter, and bake until the stuffing is golden brown, 30 to 40 minutes.

Sweet Corn, Spinach, and Bacon Sauté

Serves 6   Sweet corn and smoky bacon combine with vibrant spinach for a tasty side dish to serve with roasted meats, chicken, or seafood.

4 strips bacon, cut into
   ½-inch dice
½ cup chopped onion
3 cups corn kernels, freshly
   cut from the cob or
   frozen (and defrosted)
One 10-ounce package fresh
   baby spinach
Salt and freshly ground
   black pepper to taste

In a 12-inch sauté pan, fry the bacon over medium heat until crisp. Drain all but 1 tablespoon of the fat from the pan.

Add the onion to the skillet and cook, stirring, until it begins to turn golden but not brown, about 5 minutes. Stir in the corn and toss with the onion. Add the spinach and stir together with the corn. Cover the pan for 2 minutes to let the spinach wilt.

Remove the cover, taste the dish for seasoning, and add salt and pepper to your taste. Serve immediately.

Swiss Beans

Serves 6 **These wickedly rich beans are a great side for grilled beef, lamb, or chicken. Tangy and creamy, they will be the star of your next barbecue.**

$^{1}/_{4}$ cup ($^{1}/_{2}$ stick) butter

$^{1}/_{4}$ cup all-purpose flour

1 teaspoon salt

$^{1}/_{2}$ teaspoon freshly ground black pepper

2 teaspoons sugar

2 cups sour cream

$^{1}/_{2}$ pound yellow wax beans, ends trimmed, blanched for 2 minutes in boiling water, and drained

$^{1}/_{2}$ pound green beans, ends trimmed, blanched for 2 minutes in boiling water, and drained

2 cups grated Swiss cheese

2 tablespoons butter, melted

$^{1}/_{2}$ cup dry bread crumbs

Preheat the oven to 400 degrees. Coat a 13 x 9-inch baking dish with nonstick cooking spray.

Melt the butter in a 3-quart saucepan over medium heat and stir in the flour, salt, pepper, and sugar. Stir in the sour cream, and continue cooking, stirring constantly, until the mixture has thickened. Fold in the cooked beans and toss to coat.

Pour the beans into the prepared casserole and sprinkle evenly with the cheese. Combine the melted butter and bread crumbs in a small dish and sprinkle the casserole with the buttered bread crumbs. (At this point, the casserole may be refrigerated overnight.)

Bake the casserole until bubbling, 20 to 25 minutes.

Hot Ginger Pickled Cucumbers

Serves 6   Sweet and hot, these cucumbers are a cooling side dish to serve with grilled meats. They also make a nice garnish for burgers as well.

2 English cucumbers, peeled
 and cut into ¹/₈-inch-
 thick slices
1 carrot, grated
2 thin slices red onion
²/₃ cup rice vinegar
¹/₃ cup sugar
2 teaspoons peeled and
 grated fresh ginger
Pinch of red pepper flakes

Place the cucumbers, carrot, and onion in a large glass bowl.

In a small mixing bowl, whisk together the vinegar, sugar, ginger, and red pepper flakes until the sugar has dissolved. Pour the vinegar mixture over the cucumbers and stir to blend. Cover the bowl tightly with plastic wrap and refrigerate for at least 1 and up to 6 hours.

Drain the vegetables and serve.

Layered Vegetable Salad with Creamy Dill Parmesan Dressing

Serves 8   This make-ahead salad is perfect to serve with grilled meats and chicken. If you have a large glass salad bowl, it makes a beautiful presentation because you can see each layer of vegetables.

One 10-ounce package baby spinach

1 large red bell pepper, seeded and cut crosswise into 1/2-inch-thick rings

1 English cucumber, cut into 1/2-inch-thick slices (leave the skin on for color)

1/2 red onion, cut into 1/2-inch-thick slices and rings separated (about 1/2 cup)

One 10-ounce bag red leaf lettuce, romaine, or field greens, leaves separated

4 carrots, grated

One 6-ounce jar marinated artichokes, drained and quartered, and marinade reserved

2 cups mayonnaise

1/2 cup freshly grated Parmesan cheese

1/4 cup milk

1 teaspoon lemon pepper seasoning

3 tablespoons dillweed

2 cups herbed croutons for garnish

In a large salad bowl, layer the spinach, bell pepper, cucumber, red onion, leaf lettuce, carrots, and artichokes.

In a medium-size mixing bowl, whisk together the mayonnaise, 1/4 cup of the reserved artichoke marinade, the cheese, milk, lemon pepper, and dillweed until smooth. Carefully spoon the dressing on top of the salad, smoothing it with a rubber spatula. Cover the salad tightly with plastic wrap and refrigerate for at least 4 and up to 8 hours to let the flavors develop.

When ready to serve, garnish the top of the salad with the croutons, and toss the salad.

Cold Sesame Noodle Salad

Serves 6 Creamy peanut butter and sesame oil flavor this luscious salad. Try to get fresh soba noodles in the supermarket. Otherwise, you can use cold leftover spaghetti.

$^1/_2$ pound soba noodles or spaghetti

3 tablespoons toasted sesame oil

4 green onions, green part only, chopped

2 carrots, cut into matchsticks (about $^1/_2$ cup)

$^1/_2$ cup soy sauce

$^1/_4$ cup creamy peanut butter

$^1/_4$ cup rice vinegar

2 tablespoons honey

1 tablespoon canola oil

$^1/_2$ cup chopped fresh cilantro leaves for garnish

$^1/_3$ cup sesame seeds for garnish

$^1/_4$ cup salted roasted peanuts, chopped, for garnish

Cook the soba noodles in a large pot of boiling water until *al dente* ("firm to the bite"). Drain and toss with 1 tablespoon of the sesame oil in a large bowl, and add the green onions and carrots.

In a food processor or blender, process together the soy sauce, peanut butter, vinegar, the remaining 2 tablespoons sesame oil, the honey, and canola oil until smooth. Pour half of the dressing over the noodles and toss to blend until evenly coated. Add more dressing as needed.

Garnish the salad with the cilantro, sesame seeds, and peanuts and serve.

Sources

Below are some good mail-order sources for ingredients that you may not be able to find locally. I have also listed the major manufacturers of rotisserie ovens. Contact any of them to help you find the nearest merchant.

Rotisseries

DELONGHI
Consumer Services
Park 80 West, Plaza One, 4th Floor
Saddle Brook, NJ 07663
(800) 322-3848
www.delonghi-countertop.com

FARBERWARE
Farberware Products
c/o Lifetime Hoan Corp.
Customer Service
One Merrick Avenue
Westbury, NY 11590
(800) 233-9054
www.salton-maxim.com

GEORGE FOREMAN LEAN MEAN FAT REDUCING ROASTING MACHINE
Salton-Maxim, Inc.
Consumer Relations
1801 North Stadium Blvd.
Columbia, MO 65202
(800) 233-9054
www.salton-maxim.com

RONCO SHOWTIME ROTISSERIE AND BBQ
Popeil Inventions, Inc.
P. O. Box 2418
Chatsworth, CA 91391
(800) 486-1806
www.showtimeRotisserie.com

SUNBEAM CAROUSEL AND OSTER
ROTISSERIES
Sunbeam Corporation
P. O. Box 948389
Maitland, FL 32794-8389
(800) 458-8407
www.sunbeam.com

Tools and Ingredients

BOYAJIAN, INC.
349 Lenox Street
Norwood, MA 02062
(800) 419-4677
www.boyajianinc.com
*Flavored oils, smoked salmon, vinegars,
caviar, and Asian oils*

GRILL LOVER'S CATALOGUE
P. O. Box 1300
Columbus, GA 31902
(800) 241-8991
www.grilllovers.com
*A nifty electric rotisserie for your grill, kabob
rods, baskets, and lots of other great stuff
for the outdoor grill*

MO HOTTA-MO BETTA
P. O. Box 1026
Savannah, GA 31402-1026
(800) 462-3220
www.mohotta.com
Chiles, hot sauces, and salsas

MRS. DASH
Alberto Culver USA
2525 Armitage Avenue
Melrose Park, IL 60160
(708) 450-3163
www.mrsdash.com
Herb and spice blends

NEW ORLEANS FISH HOUSE
921 South Dupre Street
New Orleans, LA 70125
(504) 821-9700
www.nofh.com
Crawfish, crab, and seafood

VANN'S SPICES
6105 Oakleaf Avenue
Baltimore, MD 21215
(800)583-1693
www.vannsspices.com
Spices and rubs

SUR LA TABLE
1765 Sixth Avenue South
Seattle, WA 98134-1608
(800) 243-0852
www.surlatable.com
*Tools, oils, vinegars, and anything else your
culinary heart desires*

Question, Comments, Chat

DIANE PHILLIPS
www.dianephillips.com

Index

Turkey Club, 64
Wonton, 158
Zorba's Gyros, 114
Burgundian Onions, 229
Burgundy Marinade, 101
Butter Baste, Cayenne, 190
Butters, flavored
about, 334
Avocado, 334
Cheesy Jalapeño, 217
Cilantro Pesto, 193
Cumin Shallot, 217
Garlic-Herb, 335
Honey-Chili-Lime, 217
Jalapeño-Cilantro, 167
Lemon-Dill, 165
Mustard-Chive, 173
Pesto, 192
Red Pepper, 193
Roasted Garlic, 217
Sun-Dried Tomato, 217

C

Cabbage
Asian Slaw, 344
Ginger-Glazed Bok Choy, 214
Mango-Onion Slaw, 346
Mom's Pretty in Pink Slaw, 345
Rick's Blue Cheese Slaw, 347
Salad, Crunchy, with Cashews, 348
Cajun Fuel Injection, 294–95
Cajun Tofu, 253
Cajun Turbo Dogs, 151–52
Cantaloupe, Peppered, 267
Cantaloupe–Red Pepper Salsa, 304
Caponata, Fire-Roasted, 311
Caramel Apples, Rotisserie, 262
Caramel Sauce, Macadamia, 274–75
Caramelized Bananas with Hot Fudge Lava, 262–63
Caribbean Pork Chops with Tropical Salsa, 140–41
Carrots
Asian Slaw, 344
Cold Sesame Noodle Salad, 359

Layered Vegetable Salad with Creamy Dill Parmesan Dressing, 358
Mom's Pretty in Pink Slaw, 345
Rick's Blue Cheese Slaw, 347
Roasted Root Vegetables, 251
Cayenne Butter Baste, 190
Cheese
Basic Risotto, 349
Blue, Slaw, Rick's, 347
Blue Bayou Stuffed Mushrooms, 227
Boursin-Stuffed Chicken Breasts, 48–49
Bruschetta Salsa, 300
Cheesy Jalapeño Butter, 217
Cheesy Mushroom Burgers, 225
Creamy Scalloped Potatoes, 343
Fire-Roasted Poblanos Stuffed with Chorizo and Grilled Corn Hash, 231
Great Caesar's Burgers, 110–11
Great Caesar's Romaine, 240–41
Greek Burgers, 112
Grilled Drunken Figs, 268
Grilled Fennel with Gruyère, 220
Grilled Tomato and Mozzarella Salad, 246
Hot Doggers, 153
Layered Vegetable Salad with Creamy Dill Parmesan Dressing, 358
Mamma Mia's Burgers, 111
Maytag Blue, Dressing, 53
Refried Bean Bake, 339
Rolled Fillet of Sole Oreganata, 177–78
Romano-Crusted Swordfish, 181
Stuffed Idaho Roasters, 236
Swiss Beans, 356
Vinny's Stuffed Mushrooms, 228
Wild Blue Mushroom–Stuffed Filet Mignon, 88–89

Zucchini Parmesan Rice, 353
Chesapeake Bay Crab Cakes, 188
Chicken
All-American Rotisserie, 12
Athenian, with Red Wine and Garlic, 28
Balsamico, 21
Breasts, Boursin-Stuffed, 48–49
Breasts Stuffed with Prosciutto and Basil, 49–50
Burgers, Pesto, 63
Cilantro-Lime, 24
cooking times, 10
Fresh Herb and Citrus Roasted, 27
Ginger-Orange Rotisserie, 13–14
Gingery Sesame-Garlic, 14–15
Honey-Mustard, 50–51
If You Can't Stand the Heat, 20
It Isn't Easy Being Green Basil Pesto, 18
Kabobs, Calypso Jerk, 58
Kabobs, Curried, 61
Kabobs, Miso-Glazed Shiitake, 59
Kabobs Provençal, 60
Lemon, Marcella's, 23
Lemon-Rosemary Rotisserie, 11
Moroccan, 22
"No-Brainer" cooking ideas, 9
Porcini Roasted, 31
Rosemary-Dijon, 29
Rotisserie Buffalo Wings with Maytag Blue Cheese Dressing, 52–53
Satay, Hot Coconut, 55
Spicy Thai, 26
Sun-Dried Tomato Pesto, 16
Tandoori, 25
Tenders, Grilled Pineapple-Cilantro, 57
Tuscan, 51–52
whole roasted, tips for, 10
Wings, Spicy Teriyaki-Glazed, 54

Plums, Drunken, Glazed Pork
Loin Stuffed with, 125–26
Poblanos, Fire-Roasted, Stuffed
with Chorizo and Grilled
Corn Hash, 231
Porcini-Marsala Marinade, 31
Pork. *See also* Ham; Sausages
Brine, Basic, 119
burgers, cooking, 154
Burgers, Honey Dijon, 157
Burgers, Pacific Rim, 110
Burgers, Pineapple Teriyaki, 156
Burgers, Rasta Barbecue, 154
Burgers, Wonton, 158
Chops, Caribbean, with
Tropical Salsa, 140–41
chops, cooking, 139
Chops, Honey-Lime Basted,
145
Chops, Old-Fashioned Stuffed,
142–44
Chops, Plum Crazy, 139–40
cooking tips for, 115–16
kabobs, preparing, 148
Kabobs, Santa Fe, 146
Loin, Fourth of July Fireworks,
122
Loin, Glazed, Stuffed with
Drunken Plums, 125–26
Loin Roast, Apricot-Mustard,
123
"No-Brainers" cooking ideas,
118
Rib Boil, 136
ribs, cooking, 136
Ribs, Country-Style, 138
Ribs, Rotisserie Baby Back, 137
Roast, Aloha, 127
Roast, Peach and Ginger, 120
Roast, Sugar and Spice, 121
Roast, Tuscan Herbed, 124
Satay, Indonesian, 148–49
Spicy Meatball Meat Loaf, 108
Spiedini, Nona's, 147
Tenderloin, Asian, 128
Tenderloin, Cranberry-Pecan,
129
Tenderloin, Red Roasted,
Shanghai Style, 130–31

testing for doneness, 126
Twirling Picnic, 131–32
Potato(es)
Creamy Scalloped, 343
Dijon, Rotisserie, 234
Garlic Smashed, 342
Idaho Roasters, 235
Mashed, Caramelized Shallot
and White Corn, 341
New, Herb-Roasted, 233
No-Fry Pommes Frites, 237
peeling, 232
Roasted, Salad Provençal, 239
Roasted Dill, Salad, 238
Roasted Root Vegetables, 251
Roasted Rosemary, 232
Stuffed Idaho Roasters, 236
Sweet, Orange-Glazed, 243–44
Poultry. *See also* Chicken; Duck;
Game Hens; Goose; Quail;
Turkey
burgers, cooking times, 10
cooking times, 10
kabobs, cooking times, 10
kabobs, threading, 56
preparing for rotisserie, 15
raw, handling, 15
testing for doneness, 10, 48
whole roasted, tips for, 10
Prosciutto
-Wrapped Scallop and Shrimp
Spiedini, 194
and Basil, Chicken Breasts
Stuffed with, 49–50
and Basil-Wrapped Filet
Mignon, 86–87
Provençal Marinade, 60

Q

Quail
Basic Brine for, 30
cooking times, 10
Honey-Thyme Rotisserie, 35–36

R

Radicchio, Grilled, 240
Ranch House Rub, 292

Red Currant Basting Sauce, 46
Relish
Fire-Roasted Caponata, 311
Green Grape, 306
Just Peachy Cranberry, 306–7
Tapenade, 310
Rémoulade, Artichoke, 326–27
Rice
Basic Risotto, 349
Crawfish Jambalaya Burgers,
189
Fried, Kitchen Sink, 351
Southwestern, 352
Sticky, Perfect, 350
Zucchini Parmesan, 353
Risotto, Basic, 349
Romaine, Great Caesar's,
240–41
Romano-Crusted Swordfish, 181
Rosemary
-Dijon Marinade, 29
-Garlic Marinade, 52
-Lemon Marinade, 11
-Pancetta Paste, Garlicky, 21
and Garlic, Veal Chops with,
94
Grecian Formula Rub, 291
Herb-Roasted New Potatoes,
233
Herbes de Provence Rub, 289
Mediterranean Marinade, 81
Nona's Leg of Lamb Roast, 82
Nona's Pork *Spiedini*, 147
Potatoes, Roasted, 232
Roasted Root Vegetables, 251
Roasted Shallot and Onion
Medley, 241
Sage, Parsley, and Thyme
Turkey Breast, 41
Tuscan Herb Paste, 124
Tuscan Marinade, 100
rotisserie ovens
buying considerations, 1–2
cleaning tips, 5–6
cooking foods in, 5
kabob rods, 4
outside grill rotisseries, 2
rotisserie basket, 4
spit rod assembly, 3